Participative Design

for

Participative Democracy

Edited by Merrelyn Emery

Revised and Updated, 1993

D1274914

Centre for Continuing Education
The Australian National University

First published, November 1989
Revised and updated, February 1993

Merrelyn Emery
Centre for Continuing Education
Australian National University
G.P.O. Box 4, Canberra ACT 2601

Computer typeset using Xerox Ventura Publisher®, Version 1.1, with MicroLogic® typeface 'Imperial' (Baskerville); 10/13 pt. Cover design by Lee Hardy.

February 1993

ISBN 073 151 484 X

Acknowledgements

This book reflects many years of close collaboration between the authors, and I would like to thank Alan and Fred for the mateship and exciting times we have shared during this period.

I also thank Cathy Craig for typing the book, and Lee Hardy for the typesetting.

Merrelyn Emery
February, 1993

TABLE OF CONTENTS

Introduction to the 1993 Edition   *Merrelyn Emery*   1

General Introduction   7

     Three landmarks leading to participative design   11

     The fourth landmark: participative design   13

     A comprehensive open systems approach   18

     In summary: the path ahead

Part I

The Context

Section Introduction   28

The Agenda for the Next Wave   *Fred Emery*   30

Educational Paradigms: An Epistemological Revolution   *F. Emery*   40

     The emergence of a new paradigm of learning   49

     Extraction vs abstraction   56

     Confronting the challenge   63

     Some educational implications   65

     Summary table   83

Part II

Participative Design at the Organizational Level

Section Introduction   86

The Light on the Hill: 'Skill formation' or 'democratization of work'   *F. Emery*   89

Participative Design: Work and   *Fred and Merrelyn Emery*   100
Community Life

     Section A: the content   100
     The design principles   102
     A democratic modified form   107
     Section B: the participative design workshop   110
     Preparation and planning   116
     Other issues   119

Further Learnings about Participative Design   *M. Emery*   123

     Workshops with mirror groups   124
     A larger mirror group unit   125
     Workshops without mirror groups   127
     Replications   127
     Vertical integration   128
     Workshops strictly for education   129
     Importance of 'deep slice'   130
     Other pitfalls   132
     Individual vs group work   133
     Sanction, safeguards and support   134
     The implication for minorities   135

The Difference Between STS and PD   *M. Emery*   141

     The history of STS in the USA   142
     Critical differences between STS and PD   142
     The adaptive dimension   146

The Concept of TLC: Trainer, Leader, Coach   *M. Emery*   148

Human Resource Management   *F. Emery*   153

The Management of Self-Managing Groups   *F. Emery*   156

Management by Objectives   *F. Emery*   162

Matching Effectivities to Affordances in Job Design   *F. Emery*   167

Laissez-Faire vs Democratic Groups   *F. Emery*   172

Getting to Grips with the Great 'Small Group' Conspiracy   *M. Emery*   176

Part III

Democracy Throughout the System

Section Introduction   180

Towards Real Democracy   *F. Emery*   182

Adaptive Systems for our Future Governance   *F. Emery*   185

    Alternatives to management   189
    Alternative to company board   190
    Towards matrix organizations   192
    Towards a village development service   197

Industry Councils: Comments on the Jackson Report *F. Emery*   200

    Staffing of the councils   200
    Initiatives and reporting   203
    Resources   204
    Modus operandi   205

The Jury System and Participative Democracy   *F. Emery*   207

    Two-up, one-down   209
    Precedents   209
    Misrepresentativeness   210

Part IV

In Education

Section Introduction   214

An Inadequate Dichotomy   *F. Emery*   222

Training Search Conference Managers   *M. Emery*   226

    Another wave of confusion   228
    The introductory workshop   231
    Content   233
    The experience with integrated concepts   241

Design principles 244

The strategy of the indirect approach 250

Other concepts that should be fitted in 252

Diffusion 254

At the end 254

The role of the SC in the total process 255

The process of implementation 256

An Alternative General Studies Curriculum *Alan Davies* 258

First session 259

Second session 260

Third session 261

Fourth session 263

Fifth session 264

Evaluation, results and conclusions 265

Participation and Self Management in Course, *Alan Davies* 271
Workshop and Conference Design

Underlying assumptions 273

Courses and workshops 277

In-course evaluation and adjustments 288

Conferences 291

Concepts 299

Tools and handouts 305

Index 314

Name Index 319

Introduction to the 1993 Edition

Merrelyn Emery

WHY A NEW EDITION within five years? The simple answer is the extraordinary rate of change in the field. Hidden behind this simple answer are new problems which have arisen directly from previous successes and some clear signals from the field as to where further clarity of concepts and methods is required. The changes between the 1989 edition and today's are an attempt to meet those problems and needs.

In 1989 I began the introduction to this volume by describing a new and major wave of activity to democratize organizations for more learning, multiskilling and productivity. That wave continues to grow, both in Australia and internationally.

One of the stimuli to further action on both the Australian and international fronts since 1989 was the Workplace Australia conference held in Melbourne, February 1991. With over 750 participants from many countries and designed to practice participation as well as to preach it, it was a first in many ways.

The overall event fell into three parts: workplace visits and discussions, twenty Search Conferences running in parallel, and a market place covering many different aspects of work reform. The site visits showed to the world some of Australia's achievements in this area. The twenty Search Conferences constituted the largest Multisearch ever tried, a rich case study. It generated a coherent vision of the desirable workplace (Thomson and Nash, 1991, pp 149-150). The market place allowed individuals and teams to participate from their own starting points, from sharing detailed experience of success, failure or progress with different approaches to just gathering impressions of what it all meant and how to get started.

With such a radical and idealistic design, there were shortcomings in all areas, as well as in the total event. The task of evaluation has begun (Thomson and Nash, 1991; Emery M, 1993), but there is much anecdotal evidence to suggest that Workplace Australia was a significant 'learning event', inspiring to action.

It should be noted that these discussions are far from being confined to social scientists or consultants. Workplace Australia was remarkable in that academics and consultants formed a minority of participants. Now more than ever before, change is in the hands and minds of enterprises and unions, workers, and managers.

There are also new national parties entering the field. Turkey is a case in point, beginning later, but aiming to learn from earlier experiences and avoid some of the dead ends explored previously. At the symposium on National Participation and Consensus (sponsored by the Turkish Tusiad in April 1992), eight national models were presented and discussed.

Of these reports from countries which included such leaders in the field as Scandinavia, it was noteworthy that Australia was the only country that could document real progress. Diffusion towards democratization and revitalization have accelerated since the first Accord (1983), despite the longest economic downturn in two hundred years (Emery F, 1992). Change in Scandinavia appears to have foundered since the action research phase was replaced by the LOM program. LOM ostensibly aimed for diffusion by 'democratic dialogue' based on the theories of Habermas, rather than on open systems or sociotechnical systems (Naschold et al. 1992).

Towards the 'Learning Organization'

One of the most positive aspects of the new wave is the trend towards explicit recognition that the enterprise or workplace of the future is a 'learning organization'. *A learning organization is one structured in such a way that its members can learn and continue to learn within it. The organizational structure itself is an environment for continuing education.*

It represents a fundamental transition from a bureaucratic, scientific management or economic rationalist view of people as instruments or cogs in the machine to the most genuinely human- centred appreciation of people engaged in productive activity. It goes straight to the core of being human, and that is our ability to consciously learn. It re-centres the debate about the purpose of this whole wave of change.

No previous theory has really homed-in so precisely on this unique gift of conscious learning, and the circumstances within which it is best developed to the benefit of all. Certainly, the Human Relations school acknowledged our nature as group animals and the Job Enrichment school got close with attempting to match the individual need for challenge and variety with individual job requirements. But it is only within the open systems framework with its supporting concepts of the organizational design principles and purposeful systems that a comprehensive practical theory has evolved to enable individuals and organizations to use the most effective methods to pursue the best possible development for both individuals and organizations.

To this point I have documented the good news. Unfortunately, rapid diffusion brings its own problems.

There are cases where action has outrun diffusion of existing knowledge. For example, some organizations have now invested heavily in participatively producing guidelines, consisting variously of statements of values, principles, philosophy, etc., stressing their commitment to adaptive relationships with their environments and to 'continuous learning and improvement'. Many have made significant change within those guidelines. Some have achieved design principle 2 structures based on self-managing groups at the operational levels without any clear understanding of how to manage these. This problem is relatively easy to fix and it is particularly for these organizations that some of the new papers about design principle 2 management in Part II have been included.

Focusing on the Design Principles

More serious is another class of problem which expresses itself in different ways. It can be variously described as a disregard for, or failure to perceive concepts, an ever-present tendency towards fashions or names in good currency, or a tendency to assume that a specific is a general.

Some examples are discussed below, but the only effective answer to these symptoms of galloping action is to take the debates back to first principles, in this case the two basic principles for organization design. There is a direct analogy with mathematics—if you understand the principles, you can solve problems without having to remember the formulae. If you understand the organization design principles, you can not only make systemic change without introducing dreadful inconsistencies and confusions, but you can also easily evaluate competing methods for introduction and see through trendy, superficial and confusion-generating fashions.

The Design Principles can be summarized as:

Design Principle 1, the redundancy of parts, results in an organization built on the one person one shift unit, where responsibility for co-ordination, control and outcome is located one level above where the work is being done.

Design Principle 2, the redundancy of functions, results in an organization built on self-managing groups who hold responsibility for their own work, their own co-ordination and control.

These principles are discussed in more detail in Part II. The following examples document lack of understanding of them.

Example 1. Recently the concept of 'equifinality' has become a very trendy buzz word. Equifinality is the term taken from Bertalanffy to express the fact that in living systems, as distinct from inanimate systems, "the final state may be reached from different initial conditions and in different ways" (Bertalanffy, 1950; Emery F, 1981 p.89).

Equifinality is now being used to say that, regardless of what is done in a change process, 'you will get there in the end'. Leaving aside for the moment the question of where 'there' is, this sentiment is rapidly subjected to another logical slide to say in effect that all methods are equal.

We have here a multiple confusion. Equifinality has been distorted far from its original technical meaning to justify a range of clearly different processes towards an undefined end.

It has also become clear that recent widespread adoption of the term 'work reform' is no accident (cf QWL). It expresses the fact that ideas about the desirable goal (getting there) are, in many quarters, very vague. This is also reflected in the fact that while Australia is changing rapidly, the success rate at the enterprise level is a very hit-and-miss affair. Without any idea of the design principles, this is understandable.

Unless some greater conceptual clarity is injected not only into debate but also into methods of introduction and implementation, Australia is going to waste a lot of time, energy and money. More than this, the failures and inefficiencies of muddling around are going to cast doubt once again on structural, organizational change and its relation to increased productivity. Despite the current momentum towards change, the advocates of bureaucracy will have a field day finding fertile ground for the view that dominant hierarchies cannot really be replaced.

Example 2. Participative Design or the PD workshop has been generalized from a specific method employing a specific set of concepts and tools to a class of behaviours for change which is in some way participative. Van Eijnatten (1992) in a comprehensive overview of Sociotechnical Systems Design (STSD) has interpreted PD to include a range of "off-site/do it yourself workshops", union-management negotiation, "new kinds of co-operation", "the participative approach". He quotes personal communications about "careful application" of PD, but continues to confuse it with Search Conferences and a range of other participative methods (all quotes from pp 47-48). All of these are described as the Participative Design track of 'modern STSD' (p.38).

To the end of re-introducing some clarity about the differentiation of methods, the original paper on the PD workshop has been substantially enlarged, with significantly more specific guidance for application. It has also been clearly differentiated from the original method of STS as practised in the experimental phase of the new paradigm (see Introduction to 1989 edition).

Example 3. We have in Part IV 'Training Search Conference Managers', an example of how easily concepts in general—and the organizational design principles in particular—are lost if they are not known or recognized.

In an interpretation of the 'mixed mode' (mixing the design principles in one event), Weisbord lost the concept of design principle. Through this loss he opened the floodgates to conceptual confusion and a pseudo debate about Searching and training. The result of this loss is that the Search Conference as a pure design principle 2 event, with its special defining characteristics, could become lost in the fog of 'participation'.

Experimentation has long characterized this field, but there is a difference between careful and documented experimentation and a laissez-faire attitude towards concepts, methods and names.

There are *two* ironies here. First, the notion of Search Conference was the stimulus to Weisbord's book *Discovering Common Ground* (1992). Second, the confusion generated by Weisbord's loss of the concept of design principle only emphasises the need for training Search Conference managers, a need which Weisbord appears to dispute.

So now we have confusion piled on confusion. Van Eijnatten confuses the PD workshop as a method of *structural change* with the Search Conference. Weisbord loses the Search Conference as a design principle 2 method of *participative planning* in a grab bag of participative events.

When people lack conscious knowledge of the design principles, it is easy to see how they come to confuse participation with democratization, 'participative management' with structural change.

These examples illustrate the major need for a revision of the 1989 version. There needed to be a much more concentrated focus on the organizational design principles as the central, most basic and guiding concepts of organizational and cultural change.

I hope that this flaw in the 1989 version has now been overcome. The paper 'Participative Design' now includes a more specific and precise discussion of the design principles and their translation into organizational structures and methods.

For additional clarity I have also included the little papers 'The Concept of TLC—Trainer, Leader and Coach' and 'The Differences between STS and Participative Design'. They address issues which are of vital concern in the current push towards change, but neither could be fully understood without awareness that workplace 'reform' is about changing the organizational design principle. Clearly, those who are advocating a change in role for the supervisor from 'cop to coach' do not have this awareness. Apart from the fact that STS is an inefficient, expensive method, it is also inappropriate for diffusion because it fails to educate about the design principles.

Other Differences

The major changes documented above are to be found in Parts II and IV. There are no substantive changes to Part I and Part III. The future context as spelt out in Part I remains an ideal, at the moment timeless. While there is minor experimentation with the ideas in Part III, they remain as a major area awaiting concentrated experimental attention.

In addition to the greater focus on the design principles in Part IV, I have also included mention of the flow-on effects from workplace democratization to the education system and the resistance to changes in this system. Both of these areas are in their early infancy in Australia, but may alert others to what they may expect when a change of design principle begins to take effect at the national level.

References

von Bertalanffy L, 1950. 'The Theory of Open Systems in Physics and Biology', in *Systems Thinking* Vol.1, 1981. Emery F E (ed).

Emery M, 'Workplace Australia: Lessons for the Planning and Design of Multisearches', *Journal of Applied Behavioural Science*, Vol.28, No.4. In Press.

Naschold F and commentators, 1992. *Evaluation Report*, commissioned by the Board of the LOM Programme, Science Centre, Berlin (WZB), translated by Andrew Watt.

Thompson P and Nash K, 1991. *Designing the Future: Workplace Reform in Australia*. Workplace Australia, Melbourne.

Van Eijnatten, F, 1992. 'The Paradigm that Changed the Workplace', *Annals of STSD*. Draft. Industrial Engineering and Management Science, Eindhoven University of Technology, The Netherlands.

Weisbord M R, 1992. *Discovering Common Ground*. Berrett-Koehler. San Francisco.

Introduction

Merrelyn Emery, 1989

A NEW AND MAJOR WAVE of activity to democratize is now evident in Australia. It ranges across the Office Structures Review in the Public Service, various second tier wage/productivity agreements signed by major institutions to a continuing sequence of smaller scale changes in both private and public sectors. In short, those who forecast the end of democratization when there was a slackening of interest and a sense of demoralization about the problems involved in the first waves, underestimated the *power of a good idea*. The immediate sources of the new wave are many but these are less important than the fact that this good idea is now much more in tune with a large proportion of people's aspirations and values.

Amongst other things, the successive waves of democratization in Australia reveal that good ideas have influences and consequences apart from a direct and immediate effect on widespread organizational change or national policy. It will never be possible to dissect out what proportions or bits of this current wave are due to changes in the value base of the external social field or to the educational effects of the previous waves, but surely they have influenced and in a very real sense, made each other. Previous waves have influenced values and higher expectations of the quality of life in virtually all spheres, paid employment, domestic relations and others. Regardless of short term setbacks, failures and disillusionment, ideas were implanted for incubation and good ideas, good for people, are difficult to put down.

Given all this, there are still no guarantees that this wave will produce the critical mass of understanding and motivation that is required to bring about a genuinely democratic culture. Hence this volume. It is simply one more step in such an effort. The judgement of the authors herein is that it is timely to bring together in one volume some of the most important ideas and practices informing the changes we see about us.

But there were always problems lurking around in the minds of many which some made explicit. How after even a very successful introduction of participative democracy at say the operational level of a work organization can we extend it to all levels and particularly to the crucial mechanisms and processes which must link self managing groups across and up and down the remaining hierarchy? Does it only apply to work organizations or can it be adapted to organizations with other purposes and to our various levels and types of government? How can it best be incorporated into the education system so that learning of and about participative democracy can begin before we enter organizations as adults? In short, how can it be extended into a culture wide system?

While most energy has been put into democratizing work places, this has by no means been the only area in which it has been tried and also, there are clear indications of the way ahead in making participative democracy work effectively in the area of government.

Now that we are in a new wave it is important that people have access to these ideas, their origins and evolutions as well as best guesses as to their implications for the future. In addition, there are many misunderstandings of the processes and goals of participative democracy. Whatever their origins and some are discussed here, progress will not be made on the broad canvas until they are opened to widespread debate and trial.

Our goals therefore are to:

° put in one easily accessible volume the most effective and up-to-date methods for introducing democratic forms at all levels of society;

° enable more learning about the concept of democracy so that our path through to a more participative and, therefore, genuinely democratic society can be as free of pot-holes and rocks as possible;

° head off any regressive trends towards greater autocracy by the previous two.

Part I consists of two papers by Fred Emery. They are totally different in kind but each has a specific purpose in forming the context for the reader. 'The agenda for the next wave' sets the scene as perceived by a social scientist at the forefront of international social science. It is an edited transcript of a keynote address he delivered to a small but select gathering of international social scientists and apprentices in the action research tradition, in Canada in 1985. I believe the sense of this paper will be immediately obvious to any reader. It outlines the choices we have before us as we confront our multiple problems and what we must attempt to do if we are not only to save, but also to enhance our democratic heritage.

It opens the way for the papers in Part II which centre around the concepts and practices of organizational democratization and their function to create learning and environments which generate continuing learning. Unless this vicious cycle replaces the really vicious cycle of de-skilling, apathy, dissociation and their consequences such as gratuitous violence, we will inevitably return to a more undemocratic society. This latter cycle both feeds on and produces contempt, distrust, oppression, cruelty and general inhumanity—not a pretty scenario for us.

The second paper in Part I presents not an overview but a detailed analysis of where we have gone wrong in the most fundamental assumptions we have made about ourselves; how our perceptual system works and how we have translated it into what we call the 'education system'; that which often bears little relation to the learning we wish to produce.

This volume is about the nexus between learning and democracy, learning about democracy through concepts and practice and learning how to set up democratic structures which are intrinsically learningful. It is not about teaching except as part of an integrated learning process. This, to be successful cannot be divorced from the broadest context in which the learning is required and the purposes it is serving. Useful learning, particularly for adults who are trying to understand and behave responsibly in an environment characterized by rapidly growing uncertainty, must utilize every available ability to perceive, correlate and act adaptively. While education has traditionally been conceived as putting things into people's heads, there is now a desperate need for people to understand what their heads (and the rest of them incidentally) are into—what is going on out there, what do we make of it and how do we work with others, and the environment generally, to bring it under our adaptive control?

Knowing the environment and its complexities, including its many diverse ideas is an essential component. When given opportunities to elucidate our environment and share collective and individual ideals and hopes, we find a great commonality, but these opportunities are few and far between and the human ideals rarely surface otherwise. Life is too busy, too dissociated and too full of short term problems for us to sit down together and think about what is going around us. Every change is treated as a problem to be solved and put behind us as quickly as possible. Context and thought through adaptive strategies fall by the wayside. This is the pattern documented in the 'next agenda' paper and specifically addressed in terms of philosophies and beliefs of learning in 'Educational Paradigms'.

If we do not know how to look at our extended environment it is certainly predictable that we will not understand the growing uncertainties of our age and the changing allegiances of our kids, for example. Conflict will grow past the point where we can control it. There are many now who trust their own perceptions above the so called traditional wisdoms stuffed into them by parents, teachers and other authorities alike. They have a point. *Human beings are not machines in a mechanical universe* (as is implicitly claimed by the first educational paradigm).

Theoretically, there is a clear alternative. It consists of integrating ecological perception with a design principle which acknowledges and builds upon a multifunctional and creative human nature. Part II discusses and demonstrates these at the organizational level. Part III presents the thinking and practical work which has been done on diversifying this into other areas and levels. It makes clear the fact that democratization is not simply something for a multinational or a small group; a discrete organization. It is as applicable to a community, industry or nation, any body or grouping which needs to plan, devise a policy and work effectively towards it.

The two main methods we have designed and progressively developed, the Participative Design Workshop and the Search Conference are different but overlapping forms. Both were conceived within and derived from the same set of concepts and principles; those which comprise *Open Systems Thinking* (Emery F, 1969, 1981). The Participative Design Workshop's specific purpose is to achieve structural organizational change and participant's learning of how to achieve it. The Search Conference is designed as an alternative to elitist and optimizing planning and specifically includes appraisal of the extended social field and its changes.

By virtue of this element and its inherently democratic processes and discourse, it is highly effective for almost any form of planning, policy making or future oriented activity. It is this broad applicability of the Search Conference which has demonstrated that participative democracy need not be confined to discrete organizations or more narrowly to work organizations. Any group coming together around a common purpose can practice in the participative democratic mode and as Alan Davies has shown, it can be equally well adapted to the planning and conduct of an educational course or conference, which is anyway, only a temporary organization or community.

Democratic principles and mechanisms are also as feasible vertically as they are horizontally. There are no good reasons why we should not have organizations in every sector comprised of non dominant hierarchies of functions (objectives) where participative democracy is comprehensively practised, replacing the various current autocratic and representative structures. Our traditional belief that a hierarchy, one above another, must mean that the superordinate has the right to order and the subordinate to obey, is increasingly proving unworkable and is, therefore, obsolete. All that is required now is the foresight and will to bring more of the alternative precedents into being, to show that it is possible and practical.

There are two companion volumes. A comprehensive treatment of the context, theory and practice of Search Conferences can be found in *Searching* (1982). Rather than attempt to replicate much of that here, I have included only a short paper on the brief introductory workshop for those interested in becoming Search Conference managers. This spells out some of the basic assumptions and concepts but those who want to know more are referred to *Searching*. The second, *Towards Real Democracy* (Emery F, 1989) is a rich elaboration of democratic concepts at the larger system level. It will answer many of the remaining questions about the structures and processes required for a coherent democratic culture. The rest of this book will serve its purpose if it alerts some to the possibilities which already exist and the need to get started.

Time and effort will certainly be required to fulfil this next agenda. And in many ways we are only at a beginning. But there was a previous beginning and that also has a history.

Three Landmarks Leading to Participative Design

This publication has a direct ancestry spanning 18 years from the first socio-technical design performed by the workers themselves (participative design) in 1971 with the Royal Australian Air Force. A second stream of the history which shares the ideals and purposes of the first began with the first Search Conference (participative planning and policy making) designed by Fred Emery and Eric Trist in 1958 (Emery M, 1982).

These streams converged in the early seventies into a coherent strategy and tool kit for restoring dignity in organizational and community settings by re-involving people in the decision making that affects their lives. The emphasis is clearly that of effective participation and the goal is a participative democracy.

The history of the move towards the redesign of organizational structures is, of course, longer. The **first landmark** was the group climate or leadership experiments in 1938-9 (Lippit and White, 1939). These laboratory experiments established that there were only three structural genotypes; autocracy (now technically termed bureaucracy) democracy and laissez-faire (essentially a non-structure). In addition, they established that these structures have profound and predictable effects on the people who live and work within them, regardless of the personalities involved.

In the autocratic (bureaucratic) structure there was a marked increase in quarrelling, hostility, scapegoating, damage to equipment and a reduced creativity, initiative, commitment to, and time spent on, the task. Laissez-faire with its absence of leadership, rules and procedures produced a similar pattern but also included feelings of being lost and inadequate which were relieved by ridiculing the weaker and less competent. Democracy produced greater vitality, creativity, cooperation, commitment to, and time spent on, the task. These differences continue to be reaffirmed as in the note on 'Laissez-faire vs Democratic Groups' (Part II).

In fact laissez-faire continues to be a major concern and mention of it pops up in various places in both Parts II and III. It has contaminated many variations on the methods described in here because so many people cannot see or do not wish to believe that it is not democratic. Which only goes to show how far there is to go before we have a democratic culture where there is widespread understanding of this philosophy and way of life. *unfreeze, freeze, refreeze*

During this early period, the term Action Research was coined to describe the method of testing and developing theories by creating and changing practical, action based settings. The philosophy was 'there is nothing so practical as a good theory' and its operational form was expressed as 'you don't know how a thing works until you change it'.

The excitement of these results created a wave of attempts to introduce democratic forms in the real world of work and the **second major landmark** was erected in the English coalfields (Trist and Bamforth, 1951). British miners had traditionally worked the face in cohesive multi-skilled teams but industrialization designed to increase productivity brought with it the one-man, one- skill job, destroying the old team structure. Rather than the dramatic economic benefits expected from the introduction of 'scientific management', there was an increase in absenteeism and accidents amongst other phenomena.

The social scientists were called in and discovered a pattern of four interrelated 'defence mechanisms' against the new work patterns. Named Informal Organization (forming cliques), Individualism (competition, playing politics), Scapegoating (passing the buck) and Withdrawal (absenteeism, 'psychosomatic' illness), they corresponded exactly to the effects of bureaucratic structure found in 1939, thereby demonstrating that the relation of structure and effect held regardless of artificial or real setting. Needless to say, the only cure was to design and implement a variation of the old team structure geared to the new technologies. Socio-technical analysis was born.

Again, this work excited considerable attention and was followed by intensive conceptual as well as practical exploration (Emery F, 1959). It created the groundwork for the **third landmark**, the Norwegian Industrial Democracy project (Emery and Thorsrud, 1969; Emery and Thorsrud, 1975/76).

Norway entered industrialization late and although there was resistance to its introduction, a war torn economy demanded a national effort. Thorsrud, a resistance hero and social scientist saw the application of the coal study findings as a way through and called in the Tavistock Institute socio-technical team. An historic tripartite national agreement was signed to test, through action research, democracy in four of Norway's key industries. Years of effort were poured into the analyses and redesigns and it was pronounced a success—the first demonstration of planned socio- technical change at the national level.

There were two major consequences of the Norwegian success. Firstly, Norway became the destination of an immense 'tourist trade'. Anybody who was interested or thinking of democratizing their workplace felt a compulsion to see the new systems in action and this created a rash of new problems for the organizations involved. Indeed, to this very day, we have platoons of Australians trooping off to Scandinavia to study the effects of democratization which, as I discuss below, is a silly and expensive demonstration of the cultural cringe.

The second consequence is now known as 'paradoxical inhibition,' a concept derived from Pavlov's classical experiments on conditioning dogs. It means that the areas or people closest to the changes feel most threatened and develop a resistance to them while others at a safer distance adopt the changes. It is now recognized that this is one of the consequences of treating structural change as an 'experiment' and focussing attention on it and the 'guinea pig' people involved. In the Norwegian case, there were certainly other influential factors such as the more advanced industrialization of Sweden but for Norway, it meant a slow diffusion while democratization jumped the fence into Sweden and galloped far beyond.

The Fourth Landmark: Participative Design

Recognition of paradoxical inhibition was a contributing factor to the advent of Participative Design which is the **fourth landmark** in this potted history. The main factor, however, was the return of Fred Emery to

Australia in 1969. Some enterprises and unions in Australia has heard of the Norwegian ID program or the work in the UK and were ready to give it a go. Fred was not only the established leader of democratization, he was also the only person in Australia who knew how to do it. He had more work than he could handle. Remember that at this stage, all the work had been done by those trained and experienced in socio-technical analysis and design and it was an extraordinarily time consuming and intensive task. It was a job for the experts!

Fred swung into gear with a two pronged attack. One, to train up a competent team to democratize Australia and two, to find a way to speed up the process. It was the second that proved the breakthrough. A major part of an old style socio-technical analysis entailed the social scientists clambering all over the plant or office, detailing every measure of input, output, transformative process and social system until they were sure that they knew how the place worked. But of course, there are already people who collectively know all that: they are the people who work there. Moreover, they already have ideas, and in many cases strong views, as to how their work sections can be changed for the betterment of themselves, their mates and the enterprise as a whole. By pooling their knowledge and initiatives for change, they themselves can redesign their workplace. *This is the essence of participative design.*

As soon as Fred realized that the workers had already conceptualized the need to move to a more satisfying and productive design, there remained only the need to create optimal conditions for constructive utilization of the mutual trust required to produce a genuine structural alternative; one that would through its processes of creation and implementation provide the conditions for continued learning and adaptation towards fulfilling joint purposes.

This again was the subject of action research. The merging of the series of DHRs (Development of Human Resources workshops) with Fred's independent efforts provided the tests which resulted in the basic refined tool box of concepts and processes that we carry today and give to others as they embark upon organizational and cultural redesign. The resulting process bears little resemblance to that conducted before 1971 and because of its advantages has spread widely.

We first published *Participative Design: Work and Community Life* in 1974. It was a slim volume of 14 pages and as it had a shiny gold cover, we called it 'the little golden book' after the popular children's series. By that stage we knew that the concepts and practices it described were worth their weight in gold for making effective organizational change but more than that, we had seen the effect of the ideas on people—even those for

14.

whom a democratic arrangement at the moment was a far flung dream. But it was not so much a dream as a vision to be realized and it thus created expectations and other undercurrents which are to this day working themselves into reality.

Concurrently we had been developing the Search Conference, a highly participative form of planning, and the early seventies were a time of great cultural excitement and change. But diffusion and change bring their own problems. By the middle seventies, Industrial Democracy (ID) became a band waggon offering a grab bag of competing ideas, speculations and practices sometimes drawn indiscriminately from the academic melting pot and flung back into the fire beneath.

While some were brave new thrusts towards a more desirable future, others had been tested exhaustively and found wanting. But many of the newcomers to the field had not done their homework and the resulting confusion did considerable damage to the original concepts and practices. Some variations on the Search Conference, for example, proved positively inimical to its goals and in some cases, the name was used without any attempt to resemble the processes involved. It is really only in the last two or three years that clarity and credibility have begun to return to the field.

One of the results of this damage done, particularly in the ID field, was that many of those who had grasped the participative concept and were intending to use it, went ahead and did so but without any great fanfare or publicity. After the first great wave of media and other attention, silence descended and the cry went up—'Industrial Democracy in Australia is dead'. In 1988, the cry is that ID has risen from the dead but the truth is that it spent many years playing possum, waiting for a social climatic change. There has been a similar pattern developing in the US over recent years but for different reasons.

These problems began to surface quite early and are illustrated by the difference in the introduction to the first and second editions of the monograph Participative Design. The first (early 1974) said simply "these two papers are meant to provide the essential 'guts and guidelines' from social science experience for raising the quality of work life". By late 1975 we felt it necessary to add the following:

There has been nothing in our experience in the last couple of years which has caused us to revise the basic concepts laid down in this little book. Our experience has further confirmed that this conceptual tool kit is effective in democratizing an increasingly wide and various sample of organizations and groups.

What we hope to do in this introduction without cluttering up the main text is to set more firmly the context into which this book fits, and to clarify a little more the concept of democracy within. Historically we have lived with two quite distinct threads of democracy. They can be described as representative and participatory. The following examples of representative forms are included to make quite clear what this book is not about.

Representative forms

Joint consultative councils
Workers directors
Works councils
Co-determination
Worker control
Town councils
Advisory committees, etc.

Such formal mechanisms for democratic consultation have been studied, analyzed (Emery and Thorsrud, 1969) and found lacking in their ability to meet the day to day requirements that can only be met by first hand involvement. This book is concerned with precisely this latter; the need for participatory first level forms of democracy which are appropriate to the nature of people as purposeful systems.

Throughout the history of the democratization of work program there have been critical phases in the development of ideas about how to introduce the concept of participatory democracy. For a long time it was believed that there might be some productive activities so tied to one-person-one-machine that they could not be democratized. It has become clear that if there is a managerial function to coordinate and control the work of a number of people then there is always room to involve them in self management of at least some of the co-ordination and control. A democratic social structure can be brought into being in so called technologically determined situations simply by this move. It is the devolution of levels of management function to a work group with the responsibility that this entails which is the critical leap from bureaucracy to democracy. *The more that a group manages itself the more it is democratic.* SDTS

Clearly participative design does not necessarily include or preclude change in the technical system. A variety of experience has shown that a self managing group can muster and implement ideas for improving the technical system it works with at a level of ingenuity not reached by others. (Minor editorial changes have been made from the original.)

PARTICIPATIVE DESIGN has been directly exported from Australia to Norway, India, Sweden, Canada, Holland, USSR, UK, USA, and NZ. In 1973 it was introduced into Norway and India and at the Summer School of the International Council of the Quality of Working Life held at Fleveroord in Holland. From there, active young teams spread it into several European countries and Israel and from there, it moved through close colleaguial and other contacts to such countries as Peru. Its diffusive potential is unlimited in the sense that minor cultural variants are the rule while the fundamental dimensions of locus of responsibility for co-ordination and control remain unchanged.

The fundamental and proven assumption of participative design is that maximal effectiveness is obtained only by designing in the unique circumstances of people and environment, in *your place*. The tools themselves have proved to be cross cultural but their application and the final product in terms of a first new design is a matter of the creativity and collective concern of the participants.

Among the benefits of a genuine participative design is that it goes a long way towards solving the problem of resistance and paradoxical inhibition. Involvement evokes powerful feelings of psychological ownership and as the interests of the involved have been taken into account, so there are less people to resist the change. This on its own is an overly simplistic statement but the principle holds. If the change proposed has been sufficiently broadly discussed to have encompassed the concerns of the potentially disadvantaged; e.g., middle management, and they have been instrumental in the resolution of their concerns, then the stronger it becomes.

This assumes that at the beginning of the process, guarantees will have been given as to the active sanctioning of the process and its outcomes. We are not discussing here talkfests, sensitivity or coping, 'how to adapt', personal development activities. We *are* talking the hard realities of structural and economic change and obviously, every participant will be in there attempting to obtain their most optimal solution. The key here, of course is strategy and that which has generally been adopted for success is that of the Indirect Approach (Hart, 1946; Boorman, 1971).

This is the broad front approach; the opposite of the single site 'experimental' or 'demonstration' strategy. Instead of a redesign taking place in one area, a redesign workshop will, for example, consist of four or more teams who work in parallel on their own areas and then compare notes, or who work with another team functioning as a 'mirror group'. In this latter case, the groups swap roles for the second round of redesign so that each has the opportunity to work on their own area with the assistance of a team which can query their unspoken assumptions and other matters taken for granted by those whose area it is. This was the basic design which we employed in the DHR workshops and it clearly provided multiplier effects for learning (see also 'Further Learning about Participative Design', Part II).

A Comprehensive Open Systems Approach

Throughout these papers there is an implicit emphasis on the integrity of the methods, their coherence and consistency. To every extent possible they have been designed and are managed to meet the criteria for effective communication and maximal learning of and for democracy. While many of these look like radical alternatives to what we have come to understand as education or learning, they are actually very simple and basic features of every day life as it is practised in informal peer and friendship groups outside the institutional infrastructure. That is, they are the fundamental forms of relational structure people choose when they are free of bureaucratic constraints. Clearly, they are of the type which employs as many of our human capacities as are necessary at the time, including the abilities to consider the past, anticipate the future and plan for it.

The conjunction of an inherently democratic group structure such as found in a group of mates (of both sexes) planning their weekend using the local vernacular, spoken language, is a pure prototype of the purposes underlying the new methods for learning to be democratic. It is a sad reflection on our culture that although everybody knows how to be democratic and still does do it, it is considered inappropriate behaviour for formal organizational business.

It is one of the great strengths of these methods that they are essentially simple, using our greatest skills as conscious communicators with spoken language. Has there ever been a culture in which people did not confer? The spoken word, dialogue or conversation is the essential glue of humanity (Ong, 1967) and all of our participative methods are built around group (large and small) task oriented discussion. These participants are doing their own qualitative research. This is a belated recognition that 'research' is an age old part of the human condition—to be curious, to learn and to pass on to others. It is also, incidentally, a recognition that humanity and its concerns cannot be adequately captured by sterile, objective 'empirical' techniques (Emery M, 1986). Learning, influencing and being influenced by conversation are intimate elements of belonging, perhaps the most basic human need (Greco, 1950).

To further this learning, the ground rules of the Search Conference ensure that no hierarchy is either built in or allowed to develop between participants, regardless of their status in everyday life. Designed to increase the effectiveness of strategic planning by giving people more control over their long term purposes and directions, each participant is there because they have in their heads a particular piece of the jigsaw puzzle which confronts them. Because they are equally necessary to the solution or restructuring of the puzzle, and they often come from quite disparate organizations, hierarchical status is irrelevant to the task.

But in a Participative Design Workshop the focus on the natural activity group with or without a deep slice team often makes it difficult to avoid established status differences. Basically the bureaucratic realities are reflected in the beginning of an organizational redesign task; it is common for many staff not to know what others really do in their jobs or how they perceive them, and here it is critical that they do know and appreciate other's positions and duties. It is necessary, therefore, for time to be spent redressing this situation, and throughout the whole of such a project which may be extended, the process managers must constantly be alert for the destructive use of bureaucratic status and therefore, their need to intervene and restore equality of relationships.

Another dimension common amongst all the various forms of participative activity is our elevation of the importance of direct perception or ecological learning. As is implied above, we all directly extract meaningful information from our environment and all our varied perceptions are valid. To adopt this stance as it is spelt out in the paper 'Educational Paradigms' is to advocate change as it is now clear that our accepted version of 'education' (teaching) has been fabricated from doubtful premises. The unitary human perceptual system does not operate as a machine in a Newtonian mechanical universe or environment. Essentially, this new understanding elevates everyone to, and equalizes them, at the status of researcher, learner, teacher and resource.

The effects of all these changing concepts filter slowly through the cultural morass and can be traced through the proliferation of citizen action groups, small political parties and schools and the resurgence of concepts such as that of the Science Shop which serves as a link between community groups needing information and specialist research. Science Shops provide free or very cheap access to the privileged resources of elite establishments.

The Australian 1987 higher education green paper (now white) is perhaps a most powerful symbol of governmental acceptance of community pressures for educational democratization. To survive, research and teaching institutions must respond to the groundswell of public confidence in their own perceptions and doubts about the value of abstract knowledge which is protected and controlled by those institutions. And despite the problems, many do respond because they too have been touched by the new forces and values in the environment.

Another dimension of these barriers involves the whole concept of 'structure' and the previously sacrosanct status of representative systems and the representatives themselves. It has been obvious to some for a long time that representative systems have failed to deliver democracy and in fact, only add to the financial and other burdens that are carried by the populace at large. Yet often when the subject is broached, the argument is put that 'we do have to have some structure—do you want anarchy?' This argument reveals the depths of the belief that dominant hierarchies are an inevitable part of life.

They aren't and the papers in Part III clarify the fact that governance structures designed on the second design principle are probably more detailed and strictly controlled than are those of the current representative system. In this they are directly analogous to the organizational level where goals, rules and conventions must be more detailed, carefully worked out, explicit and known in a democratic structure than any needed in a bureaucracy where buck passing is the name of the game. What is a representative system if it is not just a higher level form of the ubiquitous design principle 1?

In the field of education, the debate is probably more polarized and even less well understood. As the note on 'Structured vs Unstructured' (Part IV) points out, the dichotomy is inadequate, serving only to create a conceptual morass. It, the debate, is currently surfacing again under the rubric of a return to the 3 Rs and better discipline. But here there is the complication of laissez- faire. It is often difficult to establish whether those who advocate the return to 'structure' are opposing laissez-faire or democracy as they are so little differentiated. We therefore have a three way confusion.

Let us not forget either the Master Servant Act which still determines the structure of most paid employment and exerts a continuing influence on many parts of all our lives. It enshrines in law, bureaucratic structure and personal dominance. It is often forgotten in the rush by some to 'humanize' organizations that organizational structures are legal entities and that employees need to understand industrial relations and the changes taking place in their workplace. Nothing is worse than the despair of a self managing group or organization which has been successfully sabotaged because its experience had been confined to the practice and who have not been able to articulate or argue their case on conceptual grounds or with outside support. One of the great benefits of the last waves of industrial democracy is the recognition that ID or democratization cannot be taken out of the industrial relations context (Cole et al, 1986).

Genuine democracy requires widespread and contextualized conceptual and practical understanding if it is to stand a chance against the forces of autocracy.

This volume is an accumulation of our understandings of why systemic, structural change is necessary and desirable and how it can best be achieved. Participation can apply in any area and there is no longer any reason to assume that democratization applies only to the small group level. There is a general need to raise the basic and common human ideals through processes in which the people intimately involved in those decisions which affect them affirm their ideals and design their own futures. In the course of doing this, they almost always take into account their respect and regard for other humans, other species and the environmental interdependencies on which they too are dependent.

The various papers here have either been revised over time as we have learnt from our experiences or are new, and it therefore contains our most recent considerations as to concepts, tools and process. The emphasis upon process is necessary as one of the early resistances to democratization arose from the perception that you had to have a semi-autonomous work group (SAWG) now known as a self managing group, which looked like the classic text book example.

You *do* have to have democratic structures to build in such critical features as mutual support, respect and learning but most grass roots designs deviate from the schematic, abstract models used to illustrate the concept (Part II). Different groups choose different levels of autonomy for starters knowing their design will evolve according to the development of their people and the demands of externalities. Lots of workplaces have an old man who just wants to go on doing what he has always done and who has not experienced the woman who is so lacking in self confidence that she is reluctant to try anything which tests her abilities.

A Participative Design exercise done well recognizes and makes clear the value of individuality. The process not only allows but places a premium on the idiosyncrasies and circumstances of the people involved. The design must be optimal for all those involved. In time, many of those who opted to stay out of the new arrangements change their mind and gradually become integrated into the democratic arrangements. But this is a learning process for them, without compulsion. The exceptional case is that of a supervisor who by claiming the right not to change is thereby denying to others opportunities to take responsibility and grow.

Like its predecessors, this volume concerns itself with the ways in which people can begin to take charge of their own affairs and mobilize their hidden potentials. We eschew, in the main, the fashionable trend towards 'stress management' and other similar techniques and philosophies which really boil down to the message that as you cannot change the system, you had better learn to cope with it; ie, that people are powerless to change the organizational context of their lives. The basic assumption here is, as above, that there must be a bureaucratic structure. Such attitudes just make it more difficult for many to take seriously the task of learning to actively accept responsibility for basic change.

While there can be no argument against people looking after themselves, the 'I'm alright Jack (so stuff you)' attitude, so prevalent today, is a denial of the generic conditions created by organizational structures. This attitude is no more than an elaboration of the increasingly dissociative nature of our culture, an expression of responsibility centred entirely upon the self. Democratic structures provide opportunities for mutual support and respect and thus learning of the other as an essential prerequisite for preventative medicine at the cultural level. Individual responsibility must be complemented by an awakened sense of collective responsibility. The whole debate involves much broader thinking than has generally been the case up to now. A coherent framework of concepts informs this view and those interested in this more detailed underlying theory can consult the references.

This brief survey only highlights some of the consequences of a social science which appears to have neglected its responsibilities to the community. While it has not been fashionable or in the career interests of the individual social scientist to make such statements or to pursue action research which serves both academic social science and the practical affairs of people, it is encouraging that there is a revival of such concern.

Many during the seventies slowly became conscious that we were reaching a critical point in our culture, a possible turning point where subtly but collectively, the decision will be made about our future directions. As the first paper points out, there is a choice to be made: it will be made but by whom and towards what purposes? We, the authors, make no secret of our values: there are no hidden agendas here. It is better that any choice be an informed and conscious one than a slippage into dependency and dissociation or a rigidly imposed and, therefore, superficial democracy. The question is simple: do you want a democratic society or don't you? The answer is yours.

A Note on the Differences between Australia and North America

It is not unusual in Australia today for the people I am addressing or working with to assume that democratization is an American invention. Similarly, academic colleagues who are entering the field frequently quote only the most recent publications of which there is currently a flood from America. But, these rarely acknowledge sources other than American and thus ignore the roots of their work. Much of it appears to be a case of re-inventing the wheel with the replication of all the early assumptions and dead ends.

There is very little history of American origin as diffusion into the USA has, until quite recently, been slow for reasons which appear to concern a deep cultural substratum, totally distinct from that observed in Australia, Scandinavia, Europe or India, (in my experience and also from reports of colleagues). Canada appears something of a mixed bag but the recent demise of the Ontario Quality of Working Life Centre (June 1988) could be taken as a sign that trends towards Americanization have become dominant. The value trends so strongly observed in the US and competing in Canada at the moment are, of course, also observed as emergent and potentially damaging in cultures such as the Scandinavian, often to the chagrin of the native professionals in the field.

At the most superficial level one sees the immense amounts of money paid to visiting US academics and consultants. These often have no more than a passing acquaintanceship with the core of the field. They may once have interviewed a foreign manager or surveyed the 'alien' literature. But they are the well marketed, prestigious high-priced experts who grace the opening of a conference, recruiting local money and bearing gifts of easy fix-it solutions and promises.

What is this American legacy? While it is dangerous to generalize about such a turbulent nation whose regional and cultural differences are so apparent, there is still to be observed a widespread reluctance to change anything more than the superficialities: a reluctance to change the system or 'the American way'. It can be seen as a deep form of authoritarianism and ambivalence: conflict and aggression are everywhere in America from the streets of the inner city ghettos to the highest levels where newspeak is easily absorbed into thick, luxuriously, wall-to-wall carpeted minds.

It is not difficult to find remnants of the old collective culture of America but it has been so overlaid by the belief in competition, individual achievement and fear of 'communism' that individuals often have to perform intellectual gymnastics to extricate themselves from the inconsistencies and paradoxes that arise for them in confronting democratization. Frequently they fail. It is right and proper, says the rhetoric, to help one another but changing the system is something else, even though it means being better able to help others.

The problem lies in the fact that democratization is a radical change to 'the system' as we know it. It is about changing the fundamental power relationships in our societies and cultures. As such, it will automatically cause distress, anger and disbelief within anybody who has given allegiance to or has derived benefits from 'the system'. The heart of the problem is the old 'love it and hate it' phenomenon.

There are many vested interests in maintaining the status quo. Any student of the processes of changing bureaucracies knows that they breed informal or 'shadow' organizations which in many cases run the show. America is a mass of shadow organizations—they derive their power from the formal structure, the rhetoric and the paradox. They are loath, therefore, to destroy their power base. But shadow organizations do not run the show in the interest of the total enterprise; they really only look after the interests of their members.

However, 'the times, they are a-changing' and some have chosen to look fairly and squarely at the whole and its direction. They make their judgements on that basis. The successes of the British and Scandinavian experiments of the 40s, 50s and 60s, and, paradoxically, one of the first government reports to appear, *Work in America* (O'Toole, 1974) may now be bearing fruit.

That latter was a detailed exposition of amongst other things, the effects of bureaucratic work structures on people's mental and physical health. It did little at the time to change the attitude and values of the American people to their organizational system. The old was too strong and America was too powerfully insulated for the message to be heard. To distance themselves from this problem they developed and accepted the concept of QWL. In essence, QWL is a rag bag covering everything from better human relations, individual job enrichment, health and safety to genuine democratization. Hans van Beinum (1987) has detailed the problems with this concept.

A basic change required nothing less than a broad front strategy of information from the outside, the deterioration of America's place in the world and its domestic economic paradoxes and gathering problems.

For those of us who have been brought up to regard America as one of the great bastions of freedom and democracy, their struggle with their own internal authoritarian paradox has been instructive. But one thing is clear: it doesn't matter whether a regime is blatantly or subtly oppressive, human ideals are always simmering away underneath. When they reach boiling point they surface in ways which accord with the nature of the environment at the time. America has been very slow to democratize but it would appear that they are moving as prejudices break down under the weight of economic and other older cultural pressures. Recent publications such as Weisbord (1987) will help.

I have spent time on this because it illustrates the ways in which participative philosophies and methods wax and wane with cultural cycles. While Australia is tied internationally in many ways which influence our directions, we appear to have been lucky in the strength and depth of our cultural roots. Australia has been and is a leader in democratization although this has not been generally acknowledged in Australia. This is not an academic observation. Overseas visitors constantly remark on our strange every day democratic conventions, indeed, it bothers some when the waitresses and waiters of the new tourist industry decline to see themselves as servants and assert their rights to human dignity. Democracy lives in the environment ('anyone can die out there, mate') and the flesh and blood of Australia, and there is, therefore, a special responsibility for Australian researchers to describe, analyse, and diffuse their findings.

In Summary: The Path Ahead

As this historical overview shows, the track began in the world of work and the original analysis of work as the leading edge of change was undoubtedly correct. From the huge effort poured into this sector, we have learnt much. New needs arose, however, from the transition from a relatively stable to a dynamic environment, characterized by relevant uncertainty and discontinuities. These were needs for new, more effective means of planning, educating and governing. This transition phase has continued to intensify and the same needs are now more obvious and more urgent.

Over time the fragmented needs have coalesced into a coherent need, not simply for democratic workplaces or communities, but for a participative democratic culture; one that reaches into and ultimately transforms the hidden niches in our society as well as its institutions. The form of this book follows the form of the need- first to make it explicit in terms which begin to provide the means to the end. There are now well established pointers to this future and it is the most fundamental of these that we present here.

Part I details the agenda and one major means (our direct perception) we must urgently begin to practice if we are to revitalize our people's confidence in their own abilities and potentials. Without this, participative democracy is a dead duck.

Part II reviews some of the highlights of our learning from the previous waves of exploration into the world of work, but in today's context where there is still the danger that powerful concepts such as group responsibility will be interpreted and applied mechanically as job rotation and/or multiskilling.

Part III presents the major papers on extending participative democracy into the area of governance. These lessons are applicable in many fields as indeed is the modified model of democratic management discussed in 'Participative Design' (Part II).

In **Part IV** we really begin to tackle the education system, clearing up some traditional misconceptions and describing some of the means tested so far for practically transforming education into a vehicle for the realization of a more participative democracy, one which intrinsically provides more and continuing learning.

This introduction will already have alerted the reader to the track being long and fraught with dangers both of the past, present and future. And, of course, it is not difficult to understand that the learnings encompassed here are primarily the work of adult/continuing educators, those who have never really been admitted to the institutional hallowed halls of 'learning'. They have not traditionally been so subject to the academic, managerial or centralized institutional pressures which would incline them to the quick fix. Charged with the responsibility for 'educating the community' rather than the already educated elites, a freedom has been extended. This is gratefully acknowledged.

If this book does nothing else, it should also alert the reader to the diversity of effort that is needed if 'real', participative rather than representative, democracy is to be approximated in our cultures. A 'broad front' approach is now essential. Rather than being seen as a proliferation of 'ratbaggery', every effort that employs good ideas and practices must converge to increase the awareness and practical know how for the continuation of the momentum for more real democracy. It is still important, however, for idealistic practitioners themselves (for whom this book is written) to know how the whole fits together.

This book then encompasses a vision and the authors make no secret of the values they bring to this. We simply hope that we have conveyed some clear and practical guidelines for those who share at least part of that vision.

References

Boorman S A 1971, *The Protracted Game*, Oxford University Press.

Cole R, A D Crombie, A T Davies & Ed Davis 1985, *Future Directions in the Democratisation of Work in Australia*, Employee Participation Research Report No.5, Dept Employment & Industrial Relations, AGPS, Canberra.

Emery F 1959, 'Characteristics of Socio-Technical Systems', Reprinted in Emery F 1978, *The Emergence of a New Paradigm of Work*, Centre for Continuing Education, Australian National University, Canberra.

Emery F 1981, *Open Systems Thinking*, Two Volumes, Penguin.

Emery F 1989, *Towards Real Democracy*, Ontario QWL Centre, Ministry of Labour, Toronto.

Emery F & E Thorsrud 1969, *Form and Content in Industrial Democracy*, Tavistock, London.

Emery F & E Thorsrud 1976, *Democracy at Work*, Martinus Nijhoff Social Sciences Division, Leiden.

Emery M, *Searching*, 1982, Centre for Continuing Education, Australian National University, Canberra.

Emery M 1986, Introduction to *Qualitative Research*, Australian Association of Adult Education Inc, Canberra.

Greco M C 1950, *Group Life*, Philosophical Library, New York.

Hart L 1946, *The Strategy of the Indirect Approach*, Faber & Faber.

Lippit, Ronald & Ralph K White 1943, 'The "Social" Climate of Children's Groups', Ch.XXVIII of *Child Behaviours & Development*, Roger G Barker, Jacob S Kounin & Herbert F Wright (eds.), McGraw- Hill, London.

Ong W J 1967, *The Presence of the Word*, Yale University Press.

O'Toole J 1974, *Work in America*, Special Task Force to Secretary of Health, Education & Welfare, M I T Press.

Trist E L & K W Bamforth 1951, 'Social and Psychological Consequences of the Longwall Method of Coal-getting', *Human Relations*, IV 1 3-38.

van Beinum H 1986, 'Playing Hide and Seek with QWL', *QWL Focus*, Vol.5.1.

Weisbord M R 1987, *Productive Workplaces*, Jossey Bass.

PART I.

THE CONTEXT

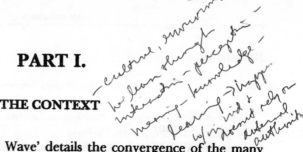

'THE AGENDA for the Next Wave' details the convergence of the many problems which confront us, to the point where we have become aware that we face not simply an economic but also a cultural crisis; a crisis of western civilization involving a choice of design principle.

It traces and analyses western history, both ancient and modern in conceptual terms, specifying the choices we have made with their consequences as above. Our choices now are outlined and it is strongly argued that we must choose a coherent set which embody our humanity and our needs for an associative society if the west is to survive as a democratic culture or civilization.

Ecological perception is one of the factors advocated in the Agenda paper and 'Educational Paradigms' elaborates this key element in the underlying rationale for the structures and processes advocated in the rest of the volume. The paper begins by examining the old paradigm, the assumptions and beliefs that for so long tied us to a mechanistic view of ourselves and defeated so many attempts at educational change. Experience has shown that while reform was only at the structural and processual level, it inevitably floundered. Only by moving the challenge to the more fundamental level of epistemology, our theories of how we learn and know, would we open the resistances and barriers to debate and hopefully change.

The basic challenges to the established paradigm entailed firstly separating the concept of object from that of the medium which conveys knowledge of it; or figure from ground. For example, radiant and reflected light are different media. Only reflected light conveys meaningful information to the human perceptual system. Secondly, Heider upped the challenge by hypothesizing that the environment was an orderly structure of information that we are adapted to directly know. Gibson confirmed the validity of this hypothesis by showing that we detect the pattern and meaning of changes in the environment. From here the emphasis had to change from fragmented, discrete bit of sensory information, at best incomplete and reliable, to direct, unmediated knowing, the product of a perceptual system. This system is attuned to the invariances or unchanging patterns evident in the constant flow of events and movement in the environment.

From this successful challenge to traditional assumptions has been derived a whole new epistemology or theory of how we know. We can see that we no longer need rely on a taxonomic hierarchy of things or abstract 'generic' concepts but 'serial genetic' concepts which are the product of continuously extracting meaning from perceived patterns. Both paradigms arrive at sophisticated theories of how the world works but those of the second paradigm are usually referred to as 'common sense' rather than scholarly knowledge. When used by the established academic elites 'common sense' conveys the devaluing of perception and the learning derived from it.

Emery goes from here to discuss with examples, the many changes this new paradigm will ultimately effect in our educational efforts. If we achieve meaningful, adaptive knowledge directly from perception, we are not reliant on mediators (teachers) and their extensive injections of abstracted knowledge. But if we are to pursue this line as part of the movement to revalue human potential and dignity, the move to a more democratic society, we need more practice in effectively using our perceptual system. The focus of the system changes from the transmission of information to educating perception.

The new methods described here in Part IV for helping people learn about participative democracy are designed on the second educational paradigm, using people's direct perceptions, experience and ideals, towards those ideals, and fostering their confidence in all of these phenomena.

Part I argues the why of a new way, in detail. As spelt out elsewhere in this volume, it can be dangerous to try to practice something without understanding the reasons for and behind it. We have many examples of how that has gone badly off the tracks. History has also proven that it is insufficient to institute democratic organizational structures without an adequate level of epistemological change and understanding. Any quiet, educational democratic cultural revolution will flounder without this latter.

If we do not appreciate the reasons for the radical changes required, we will not change what is in our heads, or more accurately, attempt to come to grips with what our heads are into. This is a major rationale for participative approaches to change. Open systems methods of learning encompass both what our heads are into (a changing and uncertain environment) and how we must begin to use our perceptual system if we are to make the changes required. These two papers, therefore, detail the perspectives from both sides of the system/environment boundary.

The Agenda for the Next Wave

Fred Emery, August 1985

MY CONCERN IS with the next agenda that must be engaged upon in the next couple of decades to overcome the essential failure of social science in the postwar years. It has failed to meet, or to contribute in any really deep way (with exceptions) to the programme initiated by Kurt Lewin in his posthumous paper 'Frontiers in Group Dynamics' in 1946.

Now if one is going to draw up such an explicit agenda, it must be based on the agenda that the society is currently setting itself. It may well be that when drawing up some sort of reasonably convincing agenda of social issues, we might look at it and say 'we are not really in much of a position to contribute to any of the important items on that agenda'; that may well be the case. Or it may be that we can identify some of the items on the social agenda that are significant and to which theoretically we should be able to contribute, but we find that we are not in a position to do so because we lack resources. Apart from our resource of a well educated population, there are also increased resources in social science now. We need only look at the post 1945 expansion of departments of sociology; psychology; psychiatry; and anthropology and biology. We do have vast resources but we may still conclude that there is no way these resources can either be released from their commitment to academic disciplinary pursuits or that for some reason the population will be reluctant to operationalize such an agenda. When a culture draws up an agenda there is an implicit sort of pressure as to when these things need to be achieved, and how they will be orchestrated.

In our considerations we should remember the extensive and radical changes that are starting to take place even in universities. Many of the major advances in what I call Open Systems Thinking (Emery F, 1981) are now being made in areas such as linguistics and ecology. By the social sciences I mean all of those sciences that contribute to our understanding of human ecology. That clearly covers even areas such as physics which is turning to ecological physics, the physics of the world within which humans live. Some physicists continue with the subnuclear quantum universe but there is another physics which quite properly applies here and which the Gibsonians have had to invoke. There is a new science of chemical ecology emerging as we learn about the human effects of pollution, for example. There's also a science of ecological biology which applies to human ecology and takes us a long way from rats in mazes.

Underlying these shifts is a basic change in the way we perceive ourselves in our world, our root metaphor. That metaphor or world hypothesis which is emerging is called 'contextualism' and we return to it below. But first, let me explain why it is becoming critical that we raise our consciousness of the emerging social agenda.

Increasingly and internationally, there is a sense of crisis. Both the economic and cultural dimensions of it can be discerned and these need to be analysed if our dimly felt and perceived crisis, and therefore our similarly perceived agenda, is to be clear and understood. For such a task, the first issue is an appropriate time horizon. Is it an agenda for tomorrow or for the 1990s?

It was only after 1970 that we detected the breakdown of our assumptions of assured economic growth. That has turned our attention to the fifty year Kondratiev economic cycles. They have been established empirically over the last two hundred years of industrial society. They are clear through all of the countries involved in the world economy (Emery F, 1978). It was also clear once that was established, that we needed to go back and examine the phases and the depth of these economic crises.

These phases of struggling out of the fifty year depressions were all characterized by a tremendous efflorescence of ideas and institutions built around ideas. Many of the ideas had in fact emerged before this period of efflorescence but people coming out of these depressions were confronted with challenges to the expectations they had had for the previous forty years or so, expectations which had guided the way they brought up a new generation of children. The ideas that were scattered around were treated almost as trivia before, as Schumacher's 'small is beautiful' was treated as faddish for a while. As Karl Marx has said "there's a time when ideas become a material force in the way a society changes". I'm suggesting that these periods following the depths of the depressions are such times.

This current economic crisis is more serious than before because more nations have been brought tightly into the international economy with the growth of the transnationals. A 'post industrial' society may emerge, but as we got further into the matter and tried to examine and identify what are the basic conditions for it in terms of infrastructure, social structure and social control, it became clear that some of those basic conditions were not present. We couldn't even see them on the horizon. Some of them were, but for the others, two or three out of the five, we could see no solution at all. A typical example is a power base. Pulling yourself out of these troughs always seemed to require the emergence and development of a new more broadly usable and cheaper source of power.

We thought we had that with nuclear energy in the sixties and the early seventies but the bottom fell out of that; it was not a cheaper source of power. It was not going to do for this depression what gas had done for the one before and steam turbines had done for the one before that. But that just meant that a much higher probability had to be given to the possibility that we were dealing with an horizon which was not a fifty year one, but something more like a two hundred and fifty year horizon. In other words, a movement from an industrial based society to something radically different which is not just a straight line projection of growth in per capita GDP.

It then became clear that the challenges that were emerging were deeper than this type of structural change: they were, in fact, cultural changes. When we tied together the series of waves of beatniks, hippies, punks, etc. and the diffusion and internalization of many of the values of the 1960s, we see this fundamental challenge to our traditional cultural assumptions (Emery F, 1978). I'm quite convinced in my own mind that what we are facing is in fact nothing less than a challenge to western civilisation itself. A challenge going back to the choice that was made when the intellectual achievements that Plato made in the latter stages of his life were overruled, turned under and buried by Aristotle's school in Alexandria. The social choice of that time set us on a path that gave us a basic pattern of civilisation and it is now that pattern which is under challenge.

Many of you would have read Stavrianos in his *Promise of the Coming Dark Age* (1976). He has suggested that the challenge might have gone back to the period of 5th century roughly, but I'm going further back because of what I think is involved in the philosophic formation of the foundations for our civilisation, prior to the Roman empire, not after.

This challenge has now to be taken seriously. The question had been raised by Nietszche and others in the crisis at the end of the nineteenth century; it's been raised by Spengler and subsequently of course by Toynbee. The reason I think it is serious is twofold— that this is the only civilisation to our knowledge—and here I'm basing myself on Toynbee's massive study of all the known civilisations—which has ever based itself or claimed to base itself on what we call design principle two. All the other civilisations, those prior to the emergence of western civilisations and those co- existent with us such as China and Japan base themselves on the first design principle (Emery F, 1977).

The first, the usual design principle for getting stability in large civilisations, which comes with the emergence of urban areas and the network of mutual reciprocal relationships that are required to enable the urban *concept/terms*

centres to emerge, involves 'redundancy of parts'. One of the ways you can get reliability in a system of unreliable parts is by building in 'redundancy of parts' so if one part fails, another is there to take over. For example, the American shuttle has four computers working in parallel with a fifth on standby. As we see reflected in the price of labour and in the life expectancy of most people in design principle one countries, individuals are prepared for a specific function in life. Enough of them are prepared so that if someone drops dead or is kicked to death, there are still sufficient to get on with the job.

"*Surplus of capacity*"

The alternative principle for getting reliability in a complex system is design principle two, building in a 'redundancy of function'. You over educate all the people who are constituent parts of the society so if any one person fails to carry out a particular function during that time, then someone else has the additional functions at their disposal; the capabilities to help out.

If you design on principle one then it is essential that you have a control body, some other specialised group of people who will decide when a person is allocated to one part of the system or another. The parts can only do their own bit, they cannot, not knowing the other bits, decide whether and when they are moved around: the epitome is the assembly line. In other words, you need some hierarchy of control, 'a dominant hierarchy' in such a society; there is necessarily a stratification of the worth of a life and an elitism.

In moving to the second design principle, theoretically all that is required is the multiple functioning parts, parts who are equipped to share a sufficient appreciation of the field within which they are mutually operating, and a sufficiently extensive but commonly known range of values to enable them to individually and collectively decide what ought to be done in certain circumstances. The second design principle should result, in large measure, in a self controlling society and not require a special control section; not require an elite or dominant hierarchy.

Differentiation of functions, heterogeneity leads, in the first design, to increasing complexity of controls and an increasing diversion of the free energy in the system to the internal control function.

In the second design, differentiation of functions (increasing heterogeneity) leads to an enrichment of the qualities of the parts without either, (a) increased complexity of the control system or, (b) diversion of system energy to the control function.

The first point is, therefore, that western civilisation is the first and only civilisation that has attempted to establish a stable and reliable society, with extended interconnections maintained over time, on design principle 2: it is the odd man out and I think that that in itself suggests that you have to watch to see whether it's a going concern. The second is that our particular experiment in time, in western civilisation, has been inherently more unstable than any of the other civilisations that we know; inherently unstable, not just more subject to climatic change or disease because the civilisation that we've had has been built on a lie from the period between Plato and Aristotle. A choice was made there and the lie is pretty simple and straightforward. It is a civilisation dedicated to the notion of the second design and yet it is a civilisation which in practice says 'there's no way all of you characters are going live within the second design. Because of the scarcity of resources it'll only be possible for key people to be in that act; the rest of you are going to have to put up with being redundant parts'. ⎣ politics : management around ...

Now we know that if we've got any situation where there are two system principles operating then we have dire trouble on our hands. That trouble was containable by us, despite our ups and downs until quite recently. While we have historically had instability, it did not prevent the second design principle providing the conditions for a culture which was tremendously more creative than was found in any civilisation built on design principle one. The only sort of thing that would motivate a civilisation built on design principle one to be creative in any significant sort of fashion, was warring against someone else. If you look at the history of technology, even through our western civilisation, you can see that war was still our major force.

The crisis we've lumbered ourselves with is that we did, by 1944, achieve a tremendous mobilisation of our productive forces on the basis of our technical knowledge. In 1944, while masses of our prime work force were in uniform wasting production, not producing, we managed to reach magnificent heights of production. We were producing more guns, tanks and planes than the admirals, generals and air force commodores were literally able to use. We were running short of willing people at the end of the European War and in the Pacific theatre but with a still vast surplus of production. From that point, there was never any question that the argument that scarcity of resources, the favourite argument of the Malthusians and the modern day economists was effectively dead right around the world. That did not prevent us reinforcing the existence of the gap between the 'haves' and the 'have-nots'. It did not lead to that gap collapsing straight away. It was still there as a primary threat because it was still possible to use the threat of warfare. It was still possible to use that argument to demand that people subordinate themselves to the interest of the nation in order to survive.

But when warfare went from atomic bombs to thermonuclear devices, any such appeal to patriotism, love of god and country wasn't worth a brass razoo to the new generations coming up. There was little point in fighting for your country if there was no country left at the end of the fight. That pulled the last plug out on that which had held together western civilisation with this inherent contradiction.

The final straw landed when we found out that the civilisation most deeply rooted in and probably the best living representative of design principle one, Japan, was beating the pants off the Americans and Europeans. The belief in the sheer ability of our cultural model to meet the needs of its people better is therefore under tremendous threat. The challenges to our western civilisation are mounting. A further problem is coming up which will only intensify demands upon it, demands that either we get our act together or we will almost certainly make the choice to revert to design principle one, and that threat of reversion is not an idle one. [This further factor is the change in climate world wide—Ed.]

In 1917 we saw a major section of our western civilisation, with the same sort of double faced dedication to design principle two, switch over to design principle one and a few others joined it behind the iron curtain. Make no bones about this; the other side of the iron curtain is in fact a reversion to design principle one. We also saw it in Germany faced with the last fifty year crisis. That is a threat as long as we have both design principles in our civilisation, and it's becoming more real. So there is a degree of choice and a question of when we make our choices.

How do we handle that challenge? Well, that is also pretty clear. The first step in meeting the challenge clearly would have to be total commitment at all levels and at every point in society to establish design principle two as the ruling design principle, the system principle. It would have to apply in every sort of group activity which one can engage; international, national, state, regional, community or small informal group. Efforts should be made to move towards establishing design principle two consistently. That's not totally impossible. Engels and Max Weber in 1895, were both convinced that you could not unleash the resources of a large major modern enterprise of the sort that emerged through the 1880s, without autocracy. We went along with that. Autocracy appeared to be the price we had to pay at work in order to live according to design principle two in other areas of our lives. Now in the past 20 odd years, action researchers coming out of the Lewinian post war tradition have shown that we can't manage and get the maximum benefit of the development of that technology without moving into design principle two. So what had looked like an impregnable area of autocracy has already been fundamentally flawed and undermined. If it can be done in places of paid employment, the practical lessons are that it can be done anywhere. One area I would never have thought it possible for these values and practices to infiltrate is the catholic church. But what happened? The catholic church blew itself apart with its Vatican Council and John XXIII. The current Pope appears to be encountering some resistance to his reinstatement of the more traditional lines.

Given the contradiction between those parts of our society that were based on design principle one and those in design principle two, we have had a pretty good run up till now. Still not enough to give us too much comfort unless we work to get more resources devoted to change. We have to have it clear in our minds what our target is: we've got to get rid of design principle 1 wherever we find it, in the classroom, in the factory, in the voluntary organisation. Also, we're not going to achieve this at any real speed until people's minds (remembering that people's minds operate between them and other people and the social ecology within which they are operating) are given a chance to crystalize out the ideas and values that they are committed to. Bear in mind that the values which carry through because of that contradiction in western civilisation have been almost totally negative. In Christian society we have the ten commandments. Some of the Ten Commandments have come to be phrased in a positive form, but biblical theologians appear to agree that they were originally all in the form of 'Thou shalt not...' (Harrelson, 1980). The idea appeared to be that if people were to hold to those negatives, then that would be sufficient orientation for them to keep a Christian civilisation.

This is hardly adequate and in as far as we have tried to move towards positive ideals, we've had the ideals of plenty, of good, of justice and of beauty. We left the economic machine to look after plenty and it's not doing a very good job of that in terms of distribution of the wealth that's been created, and it's certainly not doing any better today than in 1944. We left the ideal of good to the churches and that seems a good recipe for war. We left justice to the lawyers and the courts and we have seen similar sorts of results. In other words, we've assumed because of this contradiction that positive ideals are carried in and looked after by our institutions. With truth for example, we really believed in universities organising and running themselves in order to look after truth. They are supposed to be the guardians of truth. But we know perfectly well that if there is a challenge to the continued economic wealth of the universities, truth is not the first thing on their agenda. It is their survival. The way the universities acted immediately for the Nazis in 1934 is one example. It tells you about institutions. Now we've got to do better than that.

I have tried to formulate ideals which are appropriate to a culture based on design principle 2, not a mixed bag of principles. I've suggested such ideals were those of humanity, homonomy, nurturance and beauty (Emery F, 1977) They are those which ignore dominant hierarchies and apply across the whole human spectrum. As well, we require a different world hypothesis, from the Aristotlian, the Newtonian and Organicism. Organicism, just like Newtonianism and Aristotlianism, denied that people could have direct knowledge of the world around them. It promoted the belief that information has to be processed by special elite groups before it became meaningful knowledge. It's only with the emergence of the notion of *contextualism* that we've got a world hypothesis that starts from naive realist notions of direct perception and knowledge of the real world. It's the first world hypothesis of that type that we've had although it was and is the foundation of the so called primitive cultures of the hunters and gatherers. Contextualism was rejected when formulated by Pierce (1932) in the 1890s crisis, and again in the last crisis when Pepper (1942) formulated it explicitly as an alternative world hypothesis. It was then given some credence but as soon as we started to recover economically and the old powers got back, it was beaten down again. But it's coming up again.

You'll find contextualism around the fringes of all of the sciences, particularly in those dealing with child development, ecology and perception. This has to be our paradigm because it's the only one that's appropriate to what is happening culturally and in action research. It's the only paradigm based on an epistemology of realism. It is based on *common sense*. It's the only paradigm which has ever taken change as the reality from which we start, the others have all started from static substance as the real world. Contextualism starts from change in the emergence of quality and if we don't consciously work as action researchers within that, two things follow—we're not going to look at the world around us, the one containing the crisis we are confronting, and we're not going to be able to accumulate our findings, the results of our actions.

In making this case for the priority of educating for a change in design principle, I am of course, arguing for a shift from representative to participative democracy. This is but another way of presenting the major focus. What we've done in developing new educational methods, which we didn't realise at the time, is to work implicitly from those realistic contextualist assumptions. Search conferences would be ineffective unless these assumptions about perceptions and realism were correct. Search conferences, Participative Design Workshops and further development of matrix type organisations involve non dominant hierarchies. You may have a 'hierarchy of functions' as some functions will need to be carried out at a regional or national level, or on a different time scale but that does not imply that we need 'dominant hierarchies', where some have personal dominance over others as in the master servant relation.

Within the learning environments created by the 'deep-slice' groups of the Participative Design workshops and the ground rules followed in the Search Conference and related methods, people can actually experience the conditions for effective democratic discourse and purposeful work. We've made some progress in designing and developing these methods so that both experiential and conceptual understanding of the alternatives is gained; but we've got a lot more to do.

One element in particular involves the status difference between spoken and written language which needs addressing and redressing. Spoken language is probably as old as humanity itself, but written is still an innovation which needs further evaluation. We are hard-wired to speak but not to read and write. It is possible to sustain an argument that the elevation of the written was not more than another highly successful ploy by the already successful to exploit their advantage in a stratified society. Continuous complaints about the destruction of the English language (as it was spoken and written by Chaucer, perhaps?) neglect the fact that any living language is precisely that, living and changing in direct correlation to the changing circumstances of the times.

Written language, text, has been used to keep the great unwashed in their place. Peirce's work has shown how treacherously the rulers can put down the 'unlettered' people who use only their spoken language to communicate their reality. 'If we can prevent them coming together and also believing that their conversations have validity, we can maintain control'. Perhaps the greatest power inhering in spoken language lies in its spontaneous generation of metaphors and these are most dangerous when they are immediate and apart. Far from the abstract form, people use day-to-day metaphors which are immediately recognizable and which they can also draw up as simple diagrams and/or other iconic forms of communication; e.g., the cartoon. Critical and rigorous distinctions can be made at this level and rather than the academic conclusion that these do not convey precise meaning, they show that people can engage in debates and analysis of highly complex matters by metaphorically illustrating the essences of such debates.

of Professional
Commones
course

Clearly, if we are to pursue the elevation of design principle two and participative rather than representative democracy, we must also work to return spoken language to its proper place as the prime form of human communication. That can only be achieved by discourse under the conditions of openness and equality laid down by Asch (1952). Only then do we find association rather than dissociation, or any of the other maladaptions (Emery F, 1977).

References

Asch S E 1952, *Social Psychology*, Prentice Hall.

Emery F E 1977, *Futures We Are In*, Martinus Nijhoff, Leiden.

Emery F 1977, 'Youth—Vanguard, Victims or the New Vandals?', In Emery F E 1978, *Limits to Choice*, Centre for Continuing Education, Australian National University, Canberra.

Emery F 'The Fifth Wave? Embarking on the Next Forty Years', In Emery F E 1978, *Limits to Choice*, Centre for Continuing Education, Australian National Univ., Canberra.

Harrelson W *The Ten Commandments and Human Rights: Overtures to Biblical Theology*. 1980. Fortress Press, Philadelphia.

Lewin K 1947, 'Frontiers in Human Dynamics', *Human Relations*, I.

Peirce C S 1932, *Collected Papers*, (Vol.2), Harvard University Press.

Pepper S C 1942, *World Hypotheses*, University of California Press.

Stavrianos L S 1976, *The Promise of the Coming Dark Age*, W H Freeman & Co, San Francisco.

Educational Paradigms
An epistemological revolution

Fred Emery, December 1980

Introduction

In any process of increasing participation in workplace decision making one inevitably comes to a social barrier between skill based labour and knowledge based labour: between what is properly blue collared labour and what is white collared labour.

This is typically interpreted as the line where participation should sensibly cease.

In what follows it is suggested that this is a social barrier: not a barrier dictated by inherited natural differences.

The inspiration for this paper came from two sources. After delivering the presidential address to the new ANZAAS section on Communications, in which I expressed my concern at finding, for twice running, that a major medium for mass communication had proven, on close examination to be quite contrary in its nature to what seemed obvious I came across, on the same day and in the same city, a copy of Northrop Frye's *Fearful Symmetry*. It had long seemed to me that McLuhan must have had a central vision in order to have been so insightful, so often, about the role of the media (See Taking Stock of McLuhan, Chapter 12, Emery and Emery 1976). I had in vain followed McLuhan's suggestion that it lay in the work of Harold McInnis. In Frye's *Fearful Symmetry* I had my answer. McLuhan's vision was Blake's vision. Blake had seen, with great clarity the fearful implications of the Locke/Newtonian view of the world: 'May God us keep from single vision and Newton's sleep'. Frye wrote this work during the throes of World War II and McLuhan was his student shortly thereafter.

To my mind Frye provided an answer to the question of why engineers kept fouling up the design of electronic communication systems—they were asked to design for a Newtonian world,

The second stimulus came from Michael Gloster. He was deeply into the study of non formal education, he was aware of our earlier work on educational processes but asked whether there were not problems about the educational process itself, not just the democratisation of educational settings. This paper is a response to that question. I have written a number of times about ways in which we could democratize the educational process. It was only with Frye's insight and Gloster's goading that I realized that the problem was a fundamental problem of epistemology.

Some readers may feel disappointed that I did not draw on the works of Paulo Freire, Illich, Piaget and Polanyi. These writers have been convergent with the path I have taken here in (a) their criticisms of the old paradigm, and (b) their search for an epistemology ('tacit knowledge', 'structural concepts') that does not deny ways of knowing that we clearly possess. However, it has seemed to me that only Heider and Gibson put their fingers on the assumptions that have led us for so long to deny the evidence of our own perceptions. Only they put us in a position to systematically demolish the so-called scientific foundations of those assumptions.

Without the contribution of the Heider-Gibson paradigm the educational reformers can expect to be denigrated, as once Chambers did to Illich for claiming that knowledge is naturally gained and giving as an example the prodigious feat of learning a new language ('prodigious' according to the assumptions of the old paradigm):

> It is also massively misleading to draw an analogy for learning in general from his claim that 'normal children learn their first language casually'. Learning a native language is a very different business from learning the discipline and forms of knowledge that are built up late by using that language as a tool. The learning of a native language is of a unique kind. Indeed Chomsky suggests that the only way of explaining the ease with which children acquire their native language in all its depth and variety is on the postulating of innate structures of mind that '...permit the constitution of rich systems of knowledge and experience on the basis of scattered evidence'. That something like innate structures needs postulating is backed up by such facts as that...the number of sentences in one's native language that one will immediately understand...is astronomical; and that the number of patterns underlying our normal use of language and corresponding to meaningful and easily comprehensible sentences in our language is orders of magnitude greater than the number of seconds in a lifetime. Out there are no such innate structures that can help with the acquisition of disciplines and forms of knowledge. These have been built to the stage we now have them only through minute and painful intellectual increments by the great minds of the human race over thousands of years.

In what follows we will examine the assumption that 'there are no such innate structures': in doing so it is as well to bear in mind that Chomsky's point has only very recently gained acceptance.

It seems quite probable that Chomsky has not got things quite right the first time around. It is highly probable that a gift for language and gifts for most other forms of knowing about our world and our fellow beings are what the infant human being starts with: the evidence which we will review forces us to that conclusion.

'May God us keep from single vision and Newton's sleep!'
(Wm Blake 1802)

Educational practice over the past hundred years and more of mass education has shown a remarkable degree of continuity. This continuity of practice has flowed over from mass primary school education to mass secondary and tertiary education, to adult education, industrial training and to management education.

The tremendous growth, in the last sixty years of psychology, sociology, linguistics and anthropology appear to have re-enforced rather than shaken traditional educational practices. The erosion of educational practices that is commonly attributed to the influence of the modern social sciences seems to be much more an incidental effect of affluence and a tolerance of wastefulness.

The other aspect of this continuity is the remarkable ability of educational institutions to shrug off repeated demonstrations of better educational practices and to live with damning indictments of their inefficiencies.

When better methods are demonstrated they are ignored or, if debate is unavoidable, they are discredited by any available means, in line with the folk saying about 'any stick to beat a dog'. When evidence is produced which questions the established practices it receives similar treatment.

WHEN ineffectiveness takes on public and scandalous proportions the standard defence is that there is nothing wrong with the practices that could not be cured by better text books, better trained teachers, more highly rewarded and hence more highly motivated teachers, better classrooms, better teaching aids. This situation has all the earmarks of an established paradigm.

In this kind of situation we have learned that the established paradigm is, for all practical purposes, unchallengeable at the level of practical evidence. Until the paradigm is directly challenged by a new paradigm it will continue to rule. People are simply not prepared to jump from the frying pan to the fire. (Even when a challenging paradigm emerges, people are more prone to prefer the devil they know. Only those who are marginal to the established institutional arrangements are likely to see the furthermost fields as greenest.)

As current public pressures mount for a return to the fundamental 'Three R's' we have to ask *why the modern challenges to the traditional paradigm have proven so ineffective*; amongst teachers as well as amongst parents and employers.

If we look to the paradigmatic struggles that have taken place in other fields of human endeavour; e.g., science and industrial organisation, we find that there is no real battle until there is a challenge to the critical ground occupied by the traditional paradigm (what I referred to above as a direct challenge).

How can we directly challenge traditional educational practice, or even know whether grounds exist for such a challenge, unless we can identify what is at the core of that paradigm? What is the critical ground that it occupies?

Most previous challenges, and here I think of Montessori, Dewey, Neill, and Lewin, have failed to constitute a direct challenge because they have failed to see that the core of the educational paradigm lies outside of educational practices. That core does not lie in the character of the teacher-pupil relation; it does not lie in open classrooms, teacher teams, group project work and not even in the balance of rewards and punishments. Traditional educational practice can and has accommodated all of these innovations, particularly in times of affluence when efficiency in educational practice mattered little, or when the educational goals are over ridden for other purposes; e.g., child minding or instilling the sense of being one of a privileged elite. These things have been accommodated when and where they have been necessary and then expelled from the system when 'real' education has been re-established as the goal.

The core of the traditional educational paradigm lies in epistemology, not in educational practice.

That is, it lies in assumptions about how it is possible for people to gain knowledge. Once the possibilities are defined the practice is prescribed.

Throughout the two hundred years of industrial civilisation educational practice has been cocooned within the empiricist epistemology that was sorted out by Locke, Berkeley and Hume. These gentleman sorted out, in the most rigourous fashion, what it was possible for human beings to perceive in the world as it was defined by Newton. Herbart spelt out in detail what this implied for educational practice. Helmholtz and Muller reaffirmed the world of Newton in their studies of the physics of optics and Thorndike, after Einstein and Dewey, re-established the Newtonian world as that in which people transact their daily lives.

Science has been cocooned within the same empiricist epistemology and each advance of science has acted to render the paradigm more impregnable. So much so that in 1980 we can find curriculum design referred to as an applied science (Pratt, 1980).

The core of the traditional educational paradigm is to be found in the basic assumptions of the Lockean tradition of empiricism, namely:

° the individual mind is a *tabula rasa*, a clean slate, at birth;

° the perceptual world of the new-born is a 'buzzing, booming confusion';

° percepts arise from the association of stimuli;

° concepts of an object or belongingness or of causal relation are inferred from associations of stimuli.

These assumptions were not casually arrived at. Locke, Hume and Berkeley argued very soundly that if the world was as depicted by Newton then the transfer of information from an object to a viewer had to obey the Euclidean geometry. Within that geometry, the light reflected from an object to the retina of the eye could yield only a chaotic two-dimensional representation of reality. Any perception, and hence any useful knowledge of a three dimensional world (such as stops one falling off cliffs) would have to come from some sort of intellectual inference. This inference from the chaotic, disordered stream of energy impinging on the sensory organs could only find a firm base in the associations that happened to occur, in time and space between different sensory feelings, including internally generated feelings of hunger, pain, euphoria, etc.

Thus, any perception of *similarity* would have to come from common associations; e.g., the redness and sweetness of both Jonathon apples and pomegranates.

Any perception of *object constancy* would have to arise from contiguity in time of similar, associated sensations.

Any perception of *causality* is impossible because in a Newtonian world an actual causal relation between A and B could not generate stimuli that were any different from those created by the chance concomitance of A and B. The laws of physical optics in a Euclidean space simply do not allow it.

Perception of *depth* could only arise from inference and calculation.

In a Newtonian world, based on Euclidean space, there was no way that the stimuli impinging on any living organism could yield direct and immediate *information* about a three dimensional world of solid, persistent objects and serially related events (transformations such as those we refer to as causal relations and musical melodies).

Locke, Berkeley and Hume proved that scientifically speaking, we could have no sure knowledge of such a world outside of us, at least, not as individuals. At the same time, Newton had released a great upsurge in the growth of scientific and technological knowledge which we firmly believed to be knowledge of a solid corpuscular world, 'out there'.

The question was, "How did we acquire that information and how was it possible to accumulate and distribute (communicate) such information?" With only the evidence provided by the chaotic array of energies impinging on our sensory organs we would be like the people in Plato's cave with no more knowledge of what was taking place 'out there' other than what we could infer from the flickering shadows on the walls.

Kant brought even more rigour to the questioning of how we gain knowledge. In *Critique of Pure Reason* (1781) he did not question the existence of the world and he did not dispute the fact that knowledge was being achieved. He questioned the assumptions of the British empiricists. Locke and Berkeley had proven that in a Euclidean world our senses could yield no direct knowledge of either things or events, they could only be inferred from *contiguity* of sensations. Hume had proven that we could not directly perceive causal relations if the stimulating energy flows obeyed the laws of Euclidean space, but allowed that the impression or idea of causality could be gained from the close succession of sensations. Kant, pushing the same logic even further, proved that in a Euclidean world we could have no perception of either *contiguity* or *succession* unless our nervous systems were designed so as to apply the Euclidean assumptions to the incoming sensations: the sensations themselves could provide no such ordering in time and space. This created no special difficulty for the empiricists as it was then inconceivable that the world was ordered in any way other than that described by Euclid; it was easy to assume that the human nervous system was so designed as to be an integral part of Newton's world of Mechanics, Statics and Optics.

Herbart took over Kant's chair at Konigsberg and proceeded to lay the systematic basis of pedagogy for modern society. Herbart explained how we can gain knowledge from noting what stimuli tend to occur together; i.e., associate in our intuited time and space. Herbart's Laws of Contiguity seem rather presumptuous in the light of today's knowledge but they were seen in the nineteenth century to provide a foundation for a science of pedagogy—a basis for the rational inculcation of knowledge in systems for mass primary school education. This foundation was preserved through the contributions of Pavlov, Thorndike, Hull and

Skinner. These contributions from experimental science preserved the Lockean-Herbartian paradigm by allowing that a special role might be given to the contiguity of stimuli, response and internal stimuli indicating good or bad feelings (reinforcements). These extensions enabled the paradigm to be preserved in the face of Darwinian challenges as to how such incompetent perceptual systems could have had survival value.

Throughout all these historical variations in the support base of the traditional paradigm there persists a common definition of what is sound knowledge. Sound knowledge, truth, is approached by eliminating what is idiosyncratic. The oneoff perception by an individual of an association of stimuli is the treacherous, unstable material from which knowledge must be processed (like gold from an orebody). Knowledge is approached only as the vagaries of individual perception are replaced by repeated observations under experimental conditions or the effects of the individual nullified by a random sampling of observers. Replicability by others is the final test of whether these procedures had added to the accumulating body of truths. Each observed association that survives this testing program is another accretion, another brick added to the knowledge structure. There is not, of course, one structure. Each observed association must be checked against the observed associations most similar to itself. As these delete or subsume each other they define a special knowledge structure—a discipline.

This process of accumulation of knowledge in an Euclidean world has special characteristics. It has the characteristics of *analytical abstraction* and *logical inference*. The knowledge gained by association of stimuli is useless if we cannot generalize to something other than the properties of the immediate, transient, experienced stimuli. From our experience of similarity (supposedly the gross similarity of identical stimulations) we infer the existence of classes of objects and from our knowledge of the associations of classes of objects we infer that there are relations such as those of cause and effect. We progress from constructing a picture of the world which tells us it is 'as if' to one in which we can, with varying degrees of success, assert that 'if...then...'.

In this world the key role in the accumulation of tried and true associations necessarily goes to those who understand the intellectual processes of abstraction and logical inference. It is they who, by association, discover that some forms of abstraction (classification) are more productive of good feelings than are others; that some modes of deriving logical implications are more rewarding than others. The same people find that they are better able to specify what kinds of association are most likely to be sought for, under what conditions (eg, design of experiments or surveys). They are better able to do this because they are familiar with the contradictions that emerge at the higher levels of abstraction. They have the further responsibilities of ensuring that garbage does not enter the system and that knowledge does not flow out of the system unless there is clear understanding of the degrees of uncertainty associated with the layers of knowledge that underpin it. Attempts to popularize knowledge are regarded with suspicion.

The task of education is primarily that of distribution of the accumulated knowledge. Given the tiered structure of abstractions that characterises each special branch of knowledge the educators must take care that no layer of knowledge is distributed until the underlying knowledge has been distributed and absorbed.

Three general requirements must be met if this distribution is to lead to a successful transfer of knowledge.

First, the educational system must insist that the 'fitful, random individual experiences of association' are totally inadequate as a source of knowledge. Such experience is first and foremost the source of error and the educator must brook no competition between the claims of individual experience and the proven status of accumulated knowledge. The path to knowledge is the memorization of established associations and the knowledge of the rules of classification and the logic of implication. Educational progress is then measured by tests of memory and of one's ability to apply the rules of classification and logical inference. The classical measures of 'Intelligence Quotient' are primarily measures of the latter abilities (Olson, 1975).

Everyone coming into an educational system possesses some of the sensory organs and hence all must be taught to distrust their personal experience as a guide to knowledge. Only a few have the high IQs that go with the ability to make higher order abstractions and determine logical implications. Only these can carry the burden of building on, maintaining and controlling access to the knowledge structures. The rest, having found that they cannot learn to be scholars or scientists are returned, enriched solely by whatever established associations they have memorised.

Second, it is not enough to just, as it were, poke the eyes out of the would-be learner. The educational process also required disciplined students (just as the industrial revolution created the need for a disciplined work force). At the heart of the disciplinary process is the need to create in the mind of students a measure of independence between their judgements of 'where' and 'when' education is best pursued. The natural tendency of any human being, or for that matter any living system, is to act as if there is 'a time and place for everything' (the evidence for biological cycles is quite overwhelming). Within machine-based industry the clock is set to fit the requirements of the machine regardless, more or less, of the biological clocks of the workers. Similarly with learning settings. The process of distributing knowledge is 'time independent'. This peculiar circumlocution simply states that the time for teaching is independent of any question of whether it is the 'right time and place' for the student. The right time for teaching B is when A has been learnt. C can be taught only when B has been learnt. The disciplined student accepts that the appropriate time for studying is that laid down by the curriculum, which in turn is presumed to be dictated by the nature of the socially accumulated body of knowledge. From the earliest times, according to Marrou (1956), the pedagogue was the layer-on-of-the-cane who forcibly adjusted the student's clock to the tempo of the learning process; the controlled delivery of stimulations to ensure the student's learning was originally thought a more menial task that could be left to others.

The **third** pre-requisite for learning within the traditional educational paradigm is *literacy*. Only when one has mastered the competencies required to record in writing and to read writing can one master the processes of abstraction and logical inference:

> ...The form of human competence involved in drawing logical implications from statements of unknown trust-value or plausibility is a form of competence tied largely to literacy. It may be argued that for logical analysis to occur the *statements themselves must become the reality*. (Olson, 1975, p.370).

The central role of literacy in the advancement of knowledge, in this paradigm, does not derive only from the need to pin down what we think we have perceived, it is also to pin down what is reported:

> ...while speech is an ephemeral and transparent code that maps onto a picture of reality that we called commonsense knowledge, writing changes speech into a permanent visible artifact, a reality in its own right. (Olson, 1975, p.370)

Within this paradigm *numeracy* is but a special branch of literacy. It took more than a century of failed teaching before the need for a 'New Maths' was accepted.

These three pre-requisites pretty well define the aim of this educational paradigm—to produce the *critical, disciplined* and *literate* mind.

The significant variable beyond the control of education was seen to be that of intelligence. People appeared to be innately different in their abilities to abstract and infer from propositional statements in a textual form. As these abilities were essential to all of the specialized bodies of knowledge, it came to be common place to assess the IQ of a person as a basis for deciding whether it was worthwhile trying to educate a person beyond a certain level (eg, the eleven-plus exams in the UK).

The emergence of a new paradigm of learning

The basis of the traditional paradigm was at risk from when Einstein displaced Newton's Euclidean world with that of Reimann and Lobachevski. However, Newton's *Optiks* lived on, thanks to Helmholtz's prodigious studies, as that branch of physics and psycho-physics that studies the properties of light per se and its detection by the human organism. The limits to this context were not apparent and little impact was made when Alfred N Whitehead, in 1926, pointed out that Bishop Berkeley's problems with the apparent constancy of perceived shapes disappeared if one allowed that perceptual organs were geared to Reimann's timespace and not to Euclid's. In the world of middle-sized objects and moderate speeds that humans lived in these considerations seemed esoteric.

The fundamental challenge to Lockean epistemology, and hence to the traditional paradigm of learning, came when Fritz Heider in the same year as Whitehead, stated that:

> the question has never been raised whether something that serves mainly as a mediator (eg, air for light) has not from a purely physical point of view, characteristics which are different from those of an object of perception. (Heider, 1959, p.1)

Heider was correct. From Newton through Helmholtz to even the present day; e.g., R K Luneberg's *Mathematical Theory of Optics*, 1975, this seemed an irrelevant question. The properties of light had to exist in its particulate or wave-forms and the perception of light had to be based on the properties of the rods and cones that formed the retina of the eye. This was all we needed to know in order to determine whether something was 'perceivable'. Content was irrelevant to the perceptual stage. Following the Lockean school it seemed obvious that content, the meaning of the perceptions, could only emerge at the stage of cogitation.

The observations made by Heider sustained the relevance of his question. First he noted that in the perception of objects we are dealing with ambient, reflected light, not the radiant light that is so central to the studies of optical physics. Reflected light, except for mirrored light, has the property that:

> the order of the direction of light rays is changed at the surface of an object. All rays, whatever directions they come from, are absorbed to produce the one vibration which conforms to the surface of the object at each point. The rays are not reflected independently of each other as far as direction is concerned. With an object which has not the properties of a mirror, however, the kind and direction of incoming light rays are more or less irrelevant, if only enough energy reaches each point to set its free vibrations in motion... the waves at the single points of a solid body are independent of each other, nevertheless in a certain sense they form a unit, because the many points themselves are part of a unitary object... If an illuminated body moves, all the vibrations on it move in a certain order...the light rays are coupled because they are reflected by coupled points. These light waves always appear together, although changed as a result of their illumination, position, etc. *They contain an order* which becomes meaningful only if one refers them to the corresponding object. (Heider, 1926, 1959, pp.16-17)

The order in the reflected light rays is still there as we change our viewpoint, turn our head, move around or touch the object. This is the truly critical point that Heider made. In the sea of changing sensations we see the unchanging, invariant order that is imposed by the object on the light rays that reach the eyes. It is misleading, however, to suggest that we have to refer them to an object for them to be meaningful. The object or event is the order we are directly given in our perception, no more and no less. Nothing corresponding to this transmission of information about order is the subject of physical optics or physiological studies of the eye. With the recognition of this transmission the so called paradoxes of size constancy, colour constancy, depth perception, etc simply vanish. Kant, it turns out, was solving a problem we had caused for ourselves by an inadequate theory of perception.

The critical step that Heider took in this paper was to "explain some of the characteristics of the 'sensations' on the basis of the characteristics of the correlates among physical events" (p.34). With this step he laid the basis for 'ecological optics'. With his next paper, 'The Function of the Perceptual System' (1930), Heider completed the foundation of the alternative scenario of how we learn to know. He established that the environment had an informational structure at the level of objects and their causal interactions, and that the human perceptual systems were evolved to detect and extract that information.

Nothing was done by physicists to build on these foundations, they were into lens systems and the micro-world of electrons and photons, not the everyday world of ecological optics. Psychologists were uninformed or unimpressed. Heider's circle in Berlin was broken up in 1933-4 and his papers not translated into English until 1959. More seriously, Egon Brunswik launched a serious and very public program of research along these lines in the 1930s. His program got nowhere. Assuming that the coupled information at the source of reflected light was being transmitted to a perceptual apparatus designed for a Euclidean world he could not see how any other than doubtful probablistic information could be received—as Bishop Berkeley could have told him.

The program of research indicated by Heider's work could not come to fruition until the assumption of Euclidean space was dropped, at least in the consideration of visual perception. This was done by James J Gibson. In 1938 he published *A Theoretical Field-Analysis of Automobile-Driving* which presupposed a projective geometry freed of Euclid's Fifth Postulate, that parallel lines never meet. He showed that the critical information required by a car driver was present in the flow of light rays reflected from the environment to any point at which there was a potential driver of a moving vehicle. Given the properties of reflected light and the nature of reflecting surfaces, that information would still be there even if no one had invented fast moving surface vehicles, or no one in a car had ever driven on that course. A tumbleweed blown along that same course would not have picked up the information as such a pick-up presupposes perceptual organs evolved to do so. Through the forties and fifties Gibson was deeply involved with such perceptual problems as controlling high speed landings on aircraft carriers. This provided a critical practical test for his theory of perception in a non-Euclidean world. Within the Lockean framework perception of depth required calculation and inferences from cues given by binocular vision. Within Gibson's perspective geometry depth was directly given in the flow patterns of the visual field—one eye was all that was needed to pick up the flow patterns. The test, in whose design and execution Gibson had no part, was simple. Pilots barrelling down to a pitching flight deck at 140 odd knots had vision of one eye blacked out. This did not increase the accident rate.

Twenty years after the first paper, Gibson published *Visually Controlled Locomotion and Visual Orientation in Animals* (1958). With this publication it could no longer be doubted that the Lockean paradigm had to go.

Heider had established that the Lockean paradigm was incompatible with the notion of the perceptual systems having survival value. Walls (1942), had shown the remarkable relation between the various eye structures that had been evolved and the ecological demands upon the species having those different structures. Gibson determined the non-Euclidean geometries which allowed for the direct transfer of light-borne information from the environment to eyes such as those possessed by human beings and other living beings. As of 1958 he had only proven the case for visual orientation and visually controlled locomotion. However, for organisms that can only survive and reproduce by moving toward 'goodies' and away from 'baddies' that was no trivial achievement. If the concept of Euclidean space had to be dropped in order to make that achievement what grounds existed for hanging on to the Lockean paradigm? On the face of things there were no such grounds. In all the other areas of perception—taste, smell, touch, auditory etc—the assumptions of the Lockean paradigm had created problems as insoluble as those of depth and the constancies in visual perception (Gibson, 1966).

The striking features of this Heider/Gibson paradigm are:

° the environment is recognized as having an informational structure;

° this informational structure of the environment is embodied in the invariances that exist in the relations between energy flows despite fluctuations in the individual flows and regardless of whether they impinge on the sensors of an organism;

° the perceptual systems of living species have evolved so as to detect and extract this information from their environments despite a great deal of 'noise' at the sensory level;

° our conscious feeling of sensations is all but irrelevant to the role of the senses as discriminating perceptual systems (Johansson, 1975).

This new paradigm allows us to think in strict and non-mentalistic terms about perception, not just sensations. It is also a paradigm that forces us to think in non-mentalistic terms about 'things' and 'media'. Such considerations were extraneous to the old paradigm of perception but now they are to be seen as intrinsic to the questions of what we perceive and how we perceive, and hence intrinsic to questions of human communication.

This paradigm rejects the two assumptions that underline the traditional paradigm:

° Locke's assumption of the *tabula rasa*, the blank tablet of the mind at birth (1690);

○ Johannes Muller's doctrine of the specific qualities of nerves (1826), implying the "booming, buzzing confusion" of the infant's perceptual world.

The puzzles about how we build up the associations enabling us to 'unconsciously infer' three-dimensionality and perceptual constancies (Helmholtz, 1865) go by the board.

Sensations are not, as we have always taken for granted, the basis of perception.

When the senses are considered as perceptual systems ('systems of detection', p.1), all theories of perception become at one stroke unnecessary. It is no longer a question of how the mind operates on the deliverances of sense, or how past experience can organise the data, or even how the brain can process the inputs of the nerves, but simply how the information is picked up. This stimulus information is available in the everyday environment, as I have shown. The individual does not have to construct an awareness of the world from bare intensities and frequencies of energy; he has to detect the world from invariant properties in the flux of energy. Such invariants, the direction of gravity for instance, are registered even by primitive animals who do not have elaborate perceptual organs.

Mathematical complexities of stimulus energy seem to be the simplicities of stimulus information. Active perceptual systems, as contrasted with passive receptors, have so developed during evolution that they can resonate to this information." (Gibson, p.319)

Johansson and the Uppsala school have confirmed Gibson's finding that the physical correlates of the perception of visual motion are the invariants in environmental stimulus flows that are described by projective geometry and vector analysis of the components of those flows. They have established, alas, that there is no conscious choice involved, "...the observer is evidently not free to choose between a Euclidean interpretation of the changing geometry of the figure in the display and a projective interpretation" (p.86). In computer language, the visual system is obviously 'hard wired' to extract this kind of higher-order information from the stimulus flux before it reaches consciousness.

In the field of colour vision Edwin Land and his colleagues have been able to demonstrate that "... the stimulus for the colour of a point in an area is not the radiation from that point". (Land, 1977, p.115)

They have gone beyond this to establish that:

Whereas the initial signal produced in the outer segment of the receptor cell is apparently proportional to the light flux absorbed by the visual pigment, the final comprehensive response of the visual system is 'lightness' which shows little or no relation to the light flux absorbed by the visual pigment. (p.110)

The information people extract to establish the biological response of "lightness" turns out to be a complex mathematical function of absorption and reflectance properties of the surface, and the properties of the illuminates; and not of their absolute values but of their ratios as established for each of three levels of wave-length reception,

After the three lightnesses of an area have been determined by the three retinex systems (something between retina and cortex) no further information is necessary to characterise the colour of any object in the field of view...for each trio of lightnesses there is a specific and unique colour. (ibid, p.115)

It goes against the grain to grant such complex analytical capabilities to the perceptual systems. Why, however, should we readily accept this order of capabilities in organs like the liver and the kidneys and expect evolutionary adaption would be successful with any less capability in the perceptual systems?

The other side of this biological picture of the perceptual systems must be noted. Much of the information present in the environment of the evolving species must have been irrelevant to survival and "...accordingly the perceptual machinery provides no means for their extraction" (Julesz, 1975, p.3). Julesz has discovered such a limitation in the extraction of information from the 'ground' in figure-ground perception. Those things that take on figural properties can be distinguished at very high orders of complexity but 'grounds' take on the properties of textures and:

Whereas textures that differ in their first- and second-order statistics can be discriminated from each other, those that differ in their third- or higher-order statistics usually cannot. (ibid, p.35)

He has established that this is not a learnt effect. It appears to be a limitation we share with other forms of animal life (as witnessed by their evolved forms of camouflage). In dyslexia and in the figure-ground reversal of high speed motor racing we appear to approach our perceptual limits. The implications of the Gibson/Heider paradigm go beyond our perception of the physical environment.

Asch has made similar advances in analysing the informational properties of face-to-face social environments (Emery & Emery, 1976, pp.20-

26). Heider and the socio-linguists have made real beginnings in the analysis of the invariances that carry the informational properties of conversational fields.

This latter has probably been one of the most striking challenges to our everyday conceptions and bids fair to revolutionise our ideas about speech as a medium compared with text.

In keeping with the traditional paradigm we have tended to assume that in listening to speech the sounds we hear are assimilated to learnt vocabularies and grammars and that we make use of other clues to infer what the other is meaning. For a long time psychiatrists, particularly those working in small group settings, have had their doubts about this. They have become convinced that sometimes they can hear another level of communication, what they call the 'music' of the conversation, and that it is out there to be listened to and not at all like the process of making conscious inferences from a few clues. Studies such as that by Labov and Fanshel (1977) leave us in no doubts about that. They show that perceivable invariances in conversational fields directly yield us information about invariances in the dynamics of interpersonal interaction (see also Heider, 1958). They find this so compelling that they insist that speech must be seen as an action that directly changes the environment of the other (Emery, 1980).

These findings have been generalized to cover music as well as speech by Jones (1976) using the mathematics of invariances found in group theory. In this, and in Gibson's most recent work (1979), we find that our perceptual systems appear to have evolved to cope with a world that is remarkably similar to the world to which modern physics subscribes: a world which is a nested hierarchy of spacetime events structured by invariant relationships of relations. The world in which we perceive is, like the world perceived by modern physicists, inhomogeneous, an-isotropic and discontinuous. So long as we thought that the problems of epistemology were the problems of how we perceived objects in a homogeneous, isotropic and continuous Euclidean space, existing as an absolute, independent of objects, and of how we perceived change in a time that was independent of space and objects, then, for just so long, we were bound to be defeated in our task.

The convergence with modern physics extends to the very concept of 'object':

For now, we regard the object as an abstraction of a pivot or invariant structure, but not as a basic element, which exists separately, and serves as the source of casual action on other objects, and which is in turn the recipient of casual actions by these other objects. Thus, it would be wrong to think of the centre of a vortex as a separately existing entity, capable of exerting 'forces' on other centres. And more generally, such centres, pivots or invariant structures do not do anything at all; they just are invariant. In other words, *it is the movement that possesses a certain invariant, and not the invariant that creates the corresponding movement.*

Our customary mode of using language tends to confuse us on this problem, for it is based on the conception of what is as a set of objects, as symbolized by our words. (Bohm, 1963, p.49)

As a theoretical physicist who has made significant contributions to the history of science David Bohm has explicitly considered the import of the Gibson paradigm (1965). In this light he sees science as an extension of our perceptual activity of extracting information from the invariant features of our environment and not primarily as an activity to accumulate a body of verified knowledge. The latter is in his terms only an adjunct to the process of extended perception (p.228).

Extraction vs Abstraction

In discovering how we perceive, Heider, Gibson et al did not only lead us to a new ontology. If that is all they did, it would not challenge the traditional paradigm of education. We could, as we did with the New Maths, teach it as a subject in the old paradigm.

It is the new epistemology that emerges with Heider/Gibson that constitutes the challenge to the traditional education paradigm. I will later discuss ways in which this challenge has emerged in educational practices but first it seems desirable to consider the challenge at the most general level. This is the level at which we conceive of moving from perceiving to knowing, any kind of knowing, and of moving from 'percept' to 'concept'.

The traditional paradigm took over from Aristotle and the medieval Schoolmen the assumption that this transition is achieved by a process of abstraction. The process of abstraction provides the bridges, in the traditional paradigm, from sensation to the higher levels of thought about the nature of inferred reality. It is essential in the process of getting from the flux of sensations to the concept of thing; it is equally essential in getting beyond this to generic concepts of classes of things and classes of classes. The advancement of knowledge is seen quite literally as a ladder of abstraction, as these bridges all lead away from the impossibly rich flux of sensations to levels of conceptualization that are increasingly more general in their reference to larger and larger classes of things and decreasingly specific about the qualities of the things to which they refer; i.e., more abstract—less concrete.

This is the process, that is identified with Aristotle, of *abstracting the universal from the particular*. This is a process that depends upon association of sensed similarities, some storage of these experiences in memory traces and some interaction between these traces and subsequent experiences of the particular association. The traces and the new experiences have, of course, to find each other for a strengthening of the memoried association and presumably this is because the traces retain an image of similarity.

So long as we start from the basic assumption that information about the outside world is conveyed by radiant light in a Euclidean world then this is indeed the only way we could have built up our scientific and other bodies of knowledge. Even the Gestaltists who firmly asserted that we had a knowledge of a structured world 'out there' were stuck with the problems of similarity and memory traces. The best they could do was to suggest that the 'brain fields' that transformed the sensory inputs were like electrical fields with non-Euclidean properties (Brown and Orbison, 1939).

Adopting a new language, the language of computers, has not freed thinkers from this traditional paradigm (Weimar, 1977, pp.269-70).

As we have come to expect in paradigmatic conflicts this persistence has occurred in the face of quite startling contradictory evidence. In a long series of experiments Erich Goldmeier showed that our primitive assumption that 'we knew similarity when we saw it' was certainly true but it conformed in no way to what the traditional theory of abstraction required—similarity of retinal images. The dimensions within which he was able to demonstrate perception of similarity were such that "In general it is not possible to rotate the space and refer it to rotated axes, as can be done without restriction in Euclidean spaces... Besides not being Euclidean, similarity space is unusual in another way: it is far from continuous." (1972, p.125)

It was also assumed that for the brain to perform the abstraction process, incoming information had to go from the projection areas of the brain to the so-called 'association' areas where they would link up with similar memory traces. However, destruction of the tissues connecting these areas does not prevent concept formation (Pribram, 1971).

Within this paradigm one would also expect that the more stable one could hold the retinal image (by eye movements, turning the head etc) the stronger would be the impression that one gained. Imagine the surprise when, after techniques to experimentally ensure stability of the retinal image had evolved, it was found that a stabilized retinal image rapidly breaks up and is lost to sight (Pritchard). Carefully controlled experiments with the development of vision in kittens led Pribram to a strong conclusion: "the tuning of the cortical cells to the environmental situation which remained invariant across transformations of head and eye turning was behaviourally effective; the tuning of the cortical cells to consistent retinal stimulation had no behavioural consequences" (1977, p.93).

The deep-seatedness of this part of the traditional education paradigm cannot be over-stressed and it is intimately entwined with literacy at the core of the paradigm.

In his study of our historical concepts of *Substance and Function* (1923) Ernst Cassirer noted that:

In the historical beginnings of logic this fact is most evident. Concept and form (images) are synonyms, they unite without distinction in the meaning of eidos. The sensuous manifold is ordered and divided by certain spatial forms, which appear in it and run through all diversity as permanent features. In these forms we possess the fixed schema by which we grasp in the flux of sensible things a system of unchanging determinations, a realm of 'eternal being'. Thus the (Euclidean) geometrical form becomes at once the expression and the confirmation of the logical type. The principle of the logic of the generic concept is confirmed from a new angle; and this time it is neither the popular view of the world nor the grammatical structure of language, but the structure of a fundamental mathematical science upon which it rests. (1923, pp.68-9; my inserts).

The reference to grammatical structure is emphasized in Olson's remark that "...while the Greeks thought that they were discovering eternal truths about reality, they were in fact merely reflecting on the logical structure of ordinary (written) language". (ibid, p.367; my insert),

Within the new paradigm *the universal is grasped in the grasping of the particular:* the universal is not achieved by a separate intellectual process of abstraction. The kinds of concepts that represent this perceptual achievement are serial-genetic concepts—the concepts yielded by the perception of the serial order generated in nested spatio-temporal events. They are not the generic concepts yielded by a process of abstraction and naming; e.g., of naming species and genus.

Ernst Cassirer, in 1923, was able to show that the advance of modern physics and chemistry was founded on the use of such serial-genetic concepts. By reference to one of Helmholtz's observations he was able to point to the perceptual activity that yields such concepts:

> From the standpoint of logic, it is of especial interest to trace the function of the concept in this gradual process of construction. Helmholtz touches on this question when he affirms, that even the presentation of a connection of contents in temporal sequence according to law would not be possible without a conceptual rule. 'We can obviously learn by experience what sensations of vision, or some other sense, an object before us would give us, if we should move our eyes or our bodies and view the object from different sides, touch it, etc. The totality of all these possible sensations comprehended in a total presentation is our presentation of the body; this we call perception when it is supported by present sensations, and memory-image when it is not. In a certain sense, although contrary to ordinary usage, such a presentation of an individual object is already a concept, because it comprehends the whole possible aggregate of particular sensations, that this object can arouse in us when viewed from different sides, touched or otherwise investigated.' Here Helmholtz is led back to a view of the concept that is foreign to traditional logic and that at first appears paradoxical even to him. But in truth *the concept appears here in no mere extravagant and derivative sense, but in its true and original meaning as was the 'serial concept', in distinction from the 'generic concept'*, that was decisively revealed in the foundations of the exact sciences, and that, as is now seen, has further applications, proving itself to be an instrument of objective knowledge." (Cassirer, 1923, pp.292-3).

Helmholtz is referring here to what we perceive when we act as a percept-generating system with two eyes, a head for turning, a body for moving about and overlapping sensory modalities. Unfortunately the paradox between the yield of this perceptual system and the yield of the retina in isolation did not budge him from his dedication to Newtonian optics. Ironically, Cassirer also failed to make the jump. He was in Berlin at a time when the psychology of perception was literally in a ferment, thanks to the emergence of the gestaltists, but he could conceive of no theory of perception that would encompass Helmholtz' insight. He settled for an objective idealism somewhat like Kant's: some sort of thinking was achieving the structural concepts, not perception. Lewin was emerging in the same heady Berlin atmosphere and was deeply influenced by Cassirer but also became locked in by the Lockean assumptions to a near soliptic 'life space'. It was left to Heider to complete the foundations of the new paradigm and exorcise the 'ghost of abstraction' that still lurked on in the work of Cassirer and Lewin.

Some of the contrasts between the two paradigms may be summed up as follows.

Traditional paradigm	New paradigm
abstraction	extraction
generic concepts	serial-genetic concepts
permanence-change	relative persistence
achieved by thinking and memory	achieved by perceptual activity

The implications of the challenge to the logic of abstraction are substantial. In the first place we can consider the implications for the social ownership of knowledge. There are bodies of 'knowledge' that have been built on the logic of abstraction. Cassirer has shown how they have necessarily used structural concepts to determine what will be abstracted out. These tacit 'rules of abstraction' are the inner mysteries of the various bodies of scholars and theologians. They provide a ready operational definition of an 'outsider'. Such boundaries abound in science. However, as Bohm has pointed out, there is, in the new paradigm, no such boundary between perceptual and scientific activity:

> ...fundamentally both can be regarded as limiting cases of one overall process, of a generalized kind of perception, in which no absolute knowledge is to be encountered (1965, p.230).

In this new paradigm it is pointless to speak in absolute terms of the advances of science; it becomes necessary to speak of advances relative to the perceived knowledge of invariants available to the 'non-scientific' members of the community. With regard to bodies of knowledge that are more akin to theology it is necessary to ask whether they measure up to what is known to people through their direct perception. I suspect that little, for instance, of the psychology of personality and interpersonal relations would stand up to such a test (Heider, 1958). The general and undeniable consequence of the new paradigm is that no firm barriers can be drawn between common sense and bodies of scientific or scholarly knowledge.

Concepts

The so-called special skill of identifying the universal (the invariances) through logical abstraction and logical inference is a myth. It was of course a convenient myth for preserving social hierarchies.

This is not entirely correct. It is certainly true that we have direct perceptual access to a good deal of the order present in nature (and by the leverage of instrumentation to a very great deal of the order that our perceptual systems have not evolved to directly detect). Finding order in our symbolic representations of our observations is a very different kettle of fish: particularly when those records are contaminated by the ordering principles invoked to create our symbolic systems. The dominant symbolic systems are written languages and numbers but there are hosts of minor ones such as regimental insignia for military bodies. There are special skills in logical abstraction and inference within those symbolic systems, and they can be tested and measured. Furthermore there appear to be significant and relatively stable individual differences in ability to exercise this class of skills (e.g., the studies of IQ). The point is that these skills in identifying and handling abstract similarities are:

o not predictive of ability to identify serial-genetic invariances in non formal systems; i.e., to detect order when we see it. (Formal education is of little help to the tracker or the policeman on the beat. It is possible, however, that skill in identifying serial-genetic invariances in formal systems; e.g., the number series and graphical representations of chemical structures, is predictive of ability to identify such invariances in non formal systems. The reverse need not hold because of unfamiliarity with or disdain for formalized systems);

o highly dependent on long periods of motivated engagement with formal (symbolic) systems. Otherwise known as 'schooling'.

Less abstractly, a high IQ does not indicate an ability to behave intelligently outside the narrow world of academic scholarship although higher average IQs can be expected from social groups that spend more years in academic studies and/or are more involved in handling formalized, symbolic systems. Therefore, being governed by the more schooled, higher IQ strata of society does not ensure more intelligent government. That is a point that could be made even about the government of universities.

It is important to look closely at both of these points.

Regarding the first the critical question is that of 'intelligence'. We do not know what intelligence is but we do know that behaviour is more or less intelligent insofar as it reflects "the apprehension of the relevant structure of the total behavioural field, relevance being defined in terms of the immediate and presumptive future purposes of the actor" (Chein, p.115). A vast amount of empirical study has been devoted to the development of tests of intelligence and the results of these tests have been widely used to select who shall be given further education; e.g., the English 11+ exams. They have been extensively used for selection of potential officers, managers, etc. on the unproven grounds that those who were est able to benefit from schooling were also those best able to learn in non academic settings, and therefore most likely to develop into effective officers or managers.

From the very beginning IQ tests were constructed so that they predicted, as well as possible, the results that could be expected from examination of schooling. They were designed to reflect the requirements for success in schooling.

Success in schooling depends primarily on being able to learn from being lectured to. This requires:

° an ability to sit still and attend to the narrow range of stimulation provided by, and dictated by the teacher (range of attention and degree of concentration);

° an ability to remember what is not understood (ie, to find a frame of reference that is not provided by one's own experience);

° a willingness to engage in the repeated rehearsals necessary to establish such an independent framework.

The ideal of such rote learning is clear and exact reproduction of the lessons that have been taught or prescribed. The ideal qualities that are sought in the student are obedience (first and foremost), diligence (constant and persistent application to the set tasks) and conscientiousness (striving to meet set standards of performance). The second qualities are truthfulness, straightforwardness and stoicism. These are secondary only in that they relate to the student's acceptance of the coercion of the teaching relation. It is helpful to that relation when the students accept that they must not seek to avoid the compulsions by lying, deceit and evasion, and it is easier to maintain those pressures if they accept their punishments 'like a man'.

Performance on IQ tests directly measure ability to master the unnatural tasks of abstracting and inferring with man-made symbol systems and indirectly measure the extent to which the student has been able to internalize, or systematically cheat, the coercive relation of teacher and student. The student-teacher relation absorbs one aspect of the child-parent relation. It is obvious that no child would willingly opt for the coercive relation that traditional education (schooling) demands. It is equally obvious that this relation will not be effectively imposed unless the family gives its active support or the student-teacher relation is granted significant autonomy, as in boarding schools.

What is clear is that the 'educational reproduction' that we see with our formal educational systems has as little to do with the natural reproduction of intelligence as eunuchs have to do with sexual reproduction.

In the second place we can consider the implications for education in general. We have conceived of education as a filling up of minds with information and a training, where suitable, in the logic of abstraction and inference. We are now confronted with the fact that people are equipped to directly achieve information for themselves and they achieve that in conceptual form—the same form of serial concept that stands as the highest achievement of modern science. The central problem for education is no longer which minds can achieve conceptual knowledge and undertake conceptual operations. In the new paradigm the central question is what kinds of environments best enable all minds to exercise their ability to perceive deeper orders of invariance. Educationalists will be in the business of manipulating the L21 not the L12 (Emery, 1977, p.90; McLuhan, 1977).

> When the behavioural situation is too simply structured the organism tends to behave in a stereotyped fashion and learning takes place by a blind conditioning process; when it is over-complex, the organism tends to display random behaviours and learning is by vicarious trial-and-error. Organized behavioural sequences and insightful learning presuppose a degree of structure that is optimum for the particular organism. (Emery, 1959, p.66)

This is quite contrary to our traditional practice of minimizing environmental variations by standardising schools, classrooms, teacher training, text-books, curricula and grade-work.

Confronting the challenge

In theory, that is, in the theory of the Lockean paradigm of knowledge and education, the Heider/Gibson contribution should have led to the ransacking of the established stores of knowledge and a massive re-thinking. In theory, the program for accumulating knowledge and distributing it is controlled by impersonal criteria of validity and consistency. The criterion of validity has an important modifier, generality; it is not expected that a new truth will necessarily displace an accepted truth at a higher order of generality. This new paradigm was proven more valid in critical areas of perception: it had consistency where the old paradigm was riddled with long-standing and apparently insoluble paradoxes and, more significant, it challenged at the highest order of abstraction of the old paradigm, its geometrical model of the world.

History, not theory, is a better guide in these matters. The challenge is so profound that we have to accept that we are confronted with a clash of paradigms.

As an historian of science Thomas Kuhn documented the lengthy strife that has accompanied past conflicts of paradigms. He was not optimistic enough to think that this process of radical change could be accomplished more easily once we were aware of what we do to each other. He was not, on the other hand as pessimistic as Max Born, a celebrated leader of the new paradigm of quantum physics, who suggested that the fight was over only when the believers in the old paradigm were buried, literally.

In this case we are dealing with a paradigm that has effectively structured the allocation of statuses and resources throughout the lifetime of industrial society, in education, science and the arts. There is more to the reallocation of statuses and the shifting of institutionalized priorities than the validity, consistency and generality of scientific findings. Persons and institutions will seek to defy any down-grading of their standing; as the eminent representatives of an order of knowledge that has long served the society they will always be well placed to powerfully oppose change. Against this there are forces in a rapidly changing society toward gaining a better understanding of what it is doing.

We have noted how the development of airborne weapon systems gave a powerful impetus to Gibson's line of thought. Untoward developments in the telecommunications industry gave rise to convergent challenges to the Lockean paradigm that had guided the telecommunications engineers (Emery & Emery, 1976, 1980).

The critical confrontation of the paradigms that we see today is not a direct result of the scientific work of Heider and Gibson nor a flow-on from military research. The confrontation arises from the mass utilization of electronic means of communication; e.g., television and visual display units. Within the Lockean paradigm these should constitute remarkable advances on the information communicating capabilities of speech and text: they do not. Theoretically, again in the Lockean paradigm, they should have transformed education; they have not.

Clearly something was wrong. Something is wrong. The Lockean paradigm has been proven to be a thoroughly misleading model of how we gain knowledge. In the field of education Herbart, Thorndike, Hull and Skinner built on the assumptions of that paradigm. Our programs of mass education are premised on the assumptions of the Lockean paradigm. Dewey, Montessori, Neill and Lewin were not able to challenge the epistemological assumptions of the Lockean model, the Euclidean geometry assumed by Newton, and hence their efforts were as futile as Blake's poetic fulminations against 'Newton's single vision'.

We are now faced with the stupendous task of redesigning a system of mass education that is powerfully supported by entrenched social interests. The task of redesign is not idealistic. As pointed out above the existing educational systems are fatally flawed. They blind, not educate their students. In a bureaucratized society this may be a stabilizing factor. To quote from de Bono, "A headmaster once told me that it was *unfair* to teach people how to think. He said that most of the pupils from his school were going to spend their lives at factory benches and that thinking would only make them dissatisfied." (1978 p.20)

In a society trying to cope with turbulence, the pressures toward participative forms of work, planning and governance are building up a ground swell of resentment against an educational paradigm that does little to develop the confidence or competence of most people. The emergence of the new paradigm shows that this is not inevitable and it points to the directions in which changes can be made.

Some Educational Implications

Some of the educational implications of the new paradigm can be spelt out. **First,** since limitless information is present in our environment then any person with some intact perceptual systems can access as much or as little as he or she needs for as long as they live. Access is restricted only by habits of and lack of confidence in perception. The pretence that knowledge can be accessed only through years of schooling in certified educational institutions is a sham.

The claims that the real knowledge is locked up in the storehouses of knowledge that are so jealously guarded by a priesthood of scholars and scientists is also a sham. There is some kind of knowledge in those storehouses and there are extensive social and economic limits on what can be accessed but these are not the fundamental limits on knowing implied by the traditional paradigm; limits that denied to most people the knowledge that they could gain valid knowledge without being schooled in it.

Second, education is first and foremost the education of our perceptual systems to better search out the invariant characteristics and distinguishing features of our personal, social and physical environments. It is an education in *searching* with our own perceptual systems not an education in how to someday *research* in the accumulated pile of so-called social knowledge. An education in searching is an education in generative thinking (these are de Bono's terms. Elsewhere I have characterised it as 'open systems thinking' (Emery, 1967). An education for research is a schooling in bodies of organized knowledge, in the workings of formal logic and in fluency of textual expression. Whilst Edward de Bono appears to be unaware of the revolution wrought by Heider and Gibson he very clearly locates generative thinking in their paradigm. Drawing on his remarkably extensive experience he has shown that generative thinking about our environment and our place in it is a matter of perception, of seeing things more clearly and of seeing things in context, not a matter of puzzling over images and abstract ideas in our mind:

> Perception is the processing of information for use. Thinking is the processing of information for use. We have defined thinking as the 'exploring of experience for a purpose'. That is why perception and thinking are the same thing (ibid, p.82).

> Thinking arranges and re-arranges perception and experience so that we may have a clearer view of things (p.41).

> The teaching of thinking is not the teaching of logic but the teaching of perception... I wish to make this point very strongly... In its proper place logic is a tool of perception" (p.77).

In the traditional paradigm it seemed obvious that "thinking itself was not possible without a repertoire of language-based concepts; that language was the very stuff of thinking and not just the means of expression (p.36). It was easy in this context to "...regard thinking as semantic manipulation and all errors in thinking as semantic mismanagement" (p.37).

This has not been without its consequences, "...it is a very bad mistake —for which our academic institutions are solely responsible—to equate semantic tidiness with thinking skill... It could be said that the main obstacle to our development of a more effective thinking system has been our obsession with semantic thinking" (pp.40-1).

In the new paradigm "Thinking does not have to take place in words. Nor are concepts limited by the availability of words to describe them. Thinking can take place in images and feelings which are quite definite but too amorphous to be expressed in words" (p.36). "The very first step in teaching thinking must be to provide a bypass to (this) instant judgment by requiring the thinker to direct attention to all the relevant and interesting points in the situation" (p.42).

De Bono has demonstrated that thinking is a skill which can be learnt by anyone prepared to learn, that is, anyone not too conceited about their innate cleverness. He has shown that it is a skill which improves the performance of young or old, bright or dull, literate or illiterate.

It could appear from the above that I am saying that if we recognize the human potentials for perception revealed in the new paradigm, and proceed to teach thinking along the lines developed by de Bono, then we will raise the intelligence of people. In the context of the long standing debate about IQs and genetic inheritance this would certainly seem to be a reckless claim.

However, as Olson (1975) has pointed out IQ tests are overwhelmingly measures of how well the person has mastered the arts of abstraction and logical inference from textual propositions . These tests certainly correlate well with performance in schoolwork (and so they should as the items in the test are selected because they show such a correlation or are highly correlated with items that do) and they show lesser but stable significant correlations with social class, ethnic status and other such variables that are correlated with spread of literacy.

The nub of the matter, however, is the definition of intelligence as 'thinking abstractly' or 'ability to learn'. In this debate learning, or the evidence for such an ability, is always pushed back to an ability to learn from texts or the blackboard so that 'thinking abstractly' is the issue. We need go back only thirty-five years to find this issue thoroughly disposed of in Isidor Chein's conceptual analysis *On the Nature of Intelligence*:

> If 'thinking abstractly' were to define intelligence, it would follow that intelligence could only be manifested in thinking behaviour and that the more abstract the thinking the greater the intelligence. Neither of these conclusions accords with usage; they do not apply to all of the facts that have been meaningfully described in terms of intelligence.

> Of two people confronted with the same problem, not the one thinking most abstractly, but the one thinking most to the point is thinking most intelligently. It is not the degree of abstraction in thought, but its quality that makes the difference. Moreover, the possible implication of this definition that it is the frequency of indulgence in abstract thought that differentiates between greater and lesser intelligence also carried with it the further implication that a single thought cannot be intelligent, an implication that cuts us off completely from

the observable referent, the behavioural act. This definition in terms of abstract thought is clearly beside the point. (1945, p.115)

As Chein develops the point it is clear that when we talk about intelligence we must be careful to identify what it is we are talking about, namely, intelligent behaviour. We then have little difficulty in seeing that "an activity is as intelligent as it occurs with reference to all of the relevant factors in the behavioural situation" (p.115). We then find that *"Intelligence is the apprehension of the relevant structure of the total behavioural field*—relevance being defined in terms of the immediate and presumptive purposes of the actor" (p.115).

It will be now seen that I am claiming that with the emergence of this new paradigm and guidelines such as those worked out by de Bono, we will find significant increase in intelligent behaviours. This will not necessarily be reflected in greater skills in textual analysis, and hence IQ measurements. It is a conclusion I find very easy to accept after three decades of experience with the effects of participative democracy at the work-face.

Third, the new paradigm leads to a 're-centering' of the teaching process. It seems appropriate to examine this in the context of the basic skills of thinking, conversing, reading, writing, arithmetic and motor skills. The world wide expressions of dissatisfaction with the educational process have been focussed on the failure of the educational systems to establish the basic skills. Not unnaturally these expressions of dissatisfaction have been accompanied by an insistence that the educational practices return to a more rigourous practice of the traditional modes of education.

This is a simple minded solution that would get no marks in Dr de Bono's book but it puts the educational systems in a dilemma. In a world that increasingly frowns upon the use of the stick and allows children unlimited access to television it simply may not be possible to return to pedagogics. If they could return it is by no means sure that they could, by those traditional educational practices, produce people who have a command of the basic skills and yet be productive members of self governing communities or of the 'quality control circles', project teams and self managing work groups that industry increasingly demands. The problem is even more complicated than that. The demand for the rigours of pedagogy typically come from the backward employer who sees himself producing in the bureaucratic mode for years to come. The employer who has seen that more participative modes of production are required sees some part of the problem, but finds no way to express his demand. The self employed are practically voiceless in a society which is overwhelmingly bureaucratised.

The recentering of teaching in the basic skills is necessary as we can now see that the essential skill, in each case, lies in the perception of invariant relations and distinctive features that are present in characteristic stimulus arrays to be found in each skill area. This contrasts sharply with what is seen as appropriate teaching if knowledge is only that which has emerged from the logical, abstractive layouts of others: in this latter case the methods of rote-learning and stimulus-response (S-R) reinforcement are efficient. Eleanor Gibson, life-long co-worker with James Gibson, has formulated what this re-centering means:

> The S-R formula does not apply to perceptual learning because it is not a response that is learned but a distinctive feature, an invariant, or a structure that makes order out of chaos and produces information. Collating of features, finding, permanent, invariant attributes of things and places and predictable relations in events, is adaptive and achieves cognitive economy. (p.34)

> ...R D Bloom (1971) concludes, 'There is surprisingly little clear-cut evidence dealing with the ability of operant techniques to alter such covert features of reading as comprehension or the formation of inferences' (pp.7-10). We know of none and expect none, for a schedule of reinforcement cannot even be imposed on let alone produce, comprehension or inference. They must come from within the learner. (p.275)

> Because a learning process that involves abstraction of invariants or inducing rules is of necessity largely internally regulated, the question of motivation and reinforcement becomes very important. If the child must essentially 'do it himself', what will make him do it, keep him at it, and tell him when he has perceived a useful relation? (p.265)

The issue is put into the broader context of education as a social institution by a study that was simply concerned with measuring what actually appeared to be going on in a primary school:

> The child's relationship to the learning materials is given little opportunity to develop into a spontaneous interest relation because it is overshadowed by the teacher-child relationship. The teacher generally decides what material should be worked on, the relative importance of the different aspects, how it should be worked, the standard of achievement and when work should cease. It is only rarely that the child's behaviour is spontaneously oriented towards problems posed by the material itself or guided by the demands implicit in the structure of the material. Because the initiative and guidance comes from the

teacher the *behaviour of the child is oriented primarily towards the teacher and not towards the material to be learnt.* (Emery & Oeser, 1954, p.182).

In the old paradigm the perceptions of the student were a useless and potentially dangerous distraction from the task of instilling proven knowledge and the authority of the teacher had always to be preserved. In the new paradigm this is destructive of learning. If the student is caused to be looking over his shoulder at his teacher he is distracted from attending to what is before his eyes. In the new paradigm the teacher must act so as to vary what is before his student's eyes whilst his own presence passes unnoticed.

Such a different concept of teacher is implied that it might be wise to speak just of the educator.

Some understanding of the role of the educator may be gained from close study of three of the most developed educational practices within the new paradigm Hughes, Catherine Stern's *Structural Arithmetic*, and de Bono. De Bono, working with highly literate adults as well as five-year olds, found it necessary to provide tools that would block, or at least hinder, the established perceptual practices of taking a quick sampling of the perceptual offering, making a snap judgement about what was offered and retreating into further abstraction and logical inference. To devise these tools he had to abstract from the invariant features of perceptual differentiation. He did not see himself in the business of providing concepts that generalized the contents of the subject-matter his students were thinking about. He depicted the contrast in the following two diagrams.

The tools are contrived to help the learner by blocking his easy slide into perceptual error or making snap judgements. In effect they are reminders to look again, to inspect the broader context over a longer time span, to look for higher order invariants than might emerge from a casual glance. A teaching role is sometimes necessary in order to convince people who have been brought up in the old paradigm that there is information to be gained from perceptual work that cannot be gained by the mental processes of abstraction, classification and generalizing. The blocks make them conscious of processes that are normally habitual.

In Catherine Stern's *Structural Arithmetic* we find the emphasis is upon discovery not on unlearning old habits. The tools she has created allow children to perceive for themselves those invariances and distinctive features that we associate with arithmetic and our number systems (see following page).

Structural Arithmetic provides materials to be used in experiments that reveal

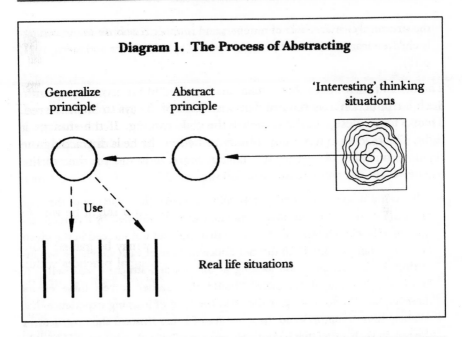

Diagram 1. The Process of Abstracting

Generalize principle

Abstract principle

'Interesting' thinking situations

Use

Real life situations

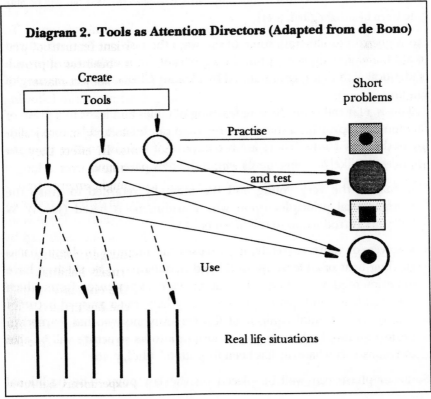

Diagram 2. Tools as Attention Directors (Adapted from de Bono)

Create

Tools

Short problems

Practise

and test

Use

Real life situations

the structural characteristics of numbers and number relationships. Accordingly children learn arithmetic by insight and not by drill. (Stern and Stern, 1971, p.15)

The teacher introduces these materials for the child to experiment with. Such introduction may require demonstration of the task to be mastered. Thanks to the design of the materials the child can see when he has got it right. The teacher can not only observe whether the child is grasping the relations but also when they are failing. Stern indicates the role of the teacher when the child in failing as follows:

> What can a teacher do when pupils fail to perceive the structure of the stair and cannot succeed in this task? Some may even be satisfied by a random sequence of blocks. Others are able to see that they did not succeed in the given task. For example, one child did not notice the size of each step as he was inserting the blocks, but upon looking at the finished structure said sadly, 'It looks bumpy, bumpy! No Stair!' Should the teacher correct these errors directly? No, this does not give the child the kind of learning experience that will help him to comprehend the structure of a stair. Instead she re-structures the task in such a way that he not only can see what to do next but will be able to learn by insight. (ibid, p.41)

Stern goes on to illustrate some of the ways the task can be restructured to aid the child gain insight but the significant point is that the approach is identical with that recommended by Eleanor Gibson for the learning of reading.

This is a far call from the rote learning of tables and leads to a grasp of mathematical principles that is clearer than can be gained by rote learning of the New Maths. There are two important lessons for us in trying to appraise the likely achievements within the new paradigm:

○ it enables the very young and the mentally retarded to grasp the mathematical principles upon which arithmetic is based (see W W Sawyer's Introduction to the Stern book);

○ it solves, or more correctly, it by-passes the memory problem that is the bug-bear of all learning in the old paradigm—"The children have experimented with materials that provide experiences from which they can learn and grow. Whatever they have once grasped becomes part of their mental equipment forever. Anyone who has learned to perform a task by having gained insight into its structure will be able to reconstruct whatever has been forgotten." (ibid, p.46)

Some emphasis can well be placed on the last point. The traditional paradigm of learning is also a paradigm of memorizing. Within that paradigm great stress is necessarily placed on forming and strengthening associations and examinations that supposedly test the continued existence of those associations. On the assumption that there are no directly perceivable structures 'out there' this dependence on memory is unavoidable. On the same assumption the prototype of the memory process is the memorizing of nonsense syllables that have no previous associations attached to them and the most important means for building associations is repetition, drill. The fact that the human memory is highly unreliable and prone to forgetfulness and that drilling de-motivates people have to be put up with as some of the unpleasant facts of life.

A great deal of evidence has accumulated to support everyday experience that a lot of learning does not seem to involve such a memory process (Rock, 1958; Asch, 1960; Katona, 1940). This evidence makes sense within the Heider/Gibson assumptions. When structure in the environment can be directly detected, as children detect the principles of arithmetic in Stern's material, then learning is not dependent on drilling and memorizing. In learning to detect the higher invariants in that material they do not have, as it were, to store away 'memory traces' and subsequently engage in some mysterious process of 'retrieval'. Having learned how to detect these invariants they can more easily detect them again in some other setting where that information is needed. The problems of memory, like those of thinking are problems in perception. We are not designed like computers but it may well be that computers are designed on a mythical image of man.

To round out our picture of how the basic learning tasks might look in the new paradigm we turn now to reading and writing. Fortunately a good deal of the groundwork has been done. Eleanor Gibson and Harry Levin have completed an exhaustive study of *The Psychology of Reading*. Doman and Hughes have evolved a teaching practice that, like Gibson and Levin, takes these tasks as tasks in perceptual learning.

Learning to read and write is, in the traditional paradigm, critical to gaining access to the stores of knowledge in society. Without such literacy education could hardly proceed. Conversely any studies, such as the arts, craft, sport and rhetoric, that did not require literacy could hardly be regarded as serious studies.

However, learning to read and write appeared to be truly formidable tasks. It was a fact that practically every child had learnt to comprehend and to produce comprehensible speech before they began their formal schooling. This was not seen as lessening the task of learning the alphabet, developing a vocabulary, learning to spell, learning the rules of grammatical construction and, of course, the skills of writing. All of these appeared to require years of drilling to build up the necessary mass of remembered associations. The complexities were such that it is little wonder that experimental psychologists left the matter alone for the first sixty years of this century (E Gibson, p.xi). It is also not surprising that major attention was given to the question of when a child's nervous system might be sufficiently mature and robust to undertake these tasks.

In the new paradigm these matters no longer have the same relevance. The appropriate question becomes, 'what information is present in the visual and auditory structures of speech and writing that enable us to extract constant meanings regardless of the sensory modality and regardless of the wide variations in the stimulus array?' When we ask this question it becomes obvious that the unschooled toddler is already well versed in extracting information from his physical and social world. In learning to comprehend speech *and* to produce comprehensible speech the toddler has demonstrated a grasp of the world-with-symbols. The critical passage from a world-without-symbols to a world-with-symbols has been made before formal schooling even begins.

It is as well to pause here and consider how that particular transition is so frequently achieved with so little apparent effort at teaching - this might tell us something about what could be expected with reading and writing if we are not blinded by epistemological assumptions.

First, it is very relevant that the Wernicke and Broca areas of the left cortex "seem to be organized explicitly for the processing of verbal information" (Geschwind, 1979). The audible component of speech, but not other kinds of sounds, and the visual signals of writing are both apparently processed in the Wernicke area and proceed to the Broca area for speech production. Obviously people have evolved for speech in much the same way as musk rats have evolved pheronomes for intra species communication.

Second, "The list of distinctive features that exist in the languages of the world is supremely restricted" (Jakobson, 1971, p.7). All of the known languages have evolved to use a finite and limited set of perceptually distinctive features for their phonemes and their morphemes. These features are clearly based on the inherited capabilities of the human species for modulating, sustaining, starting and stopping the flow of air in their air pipes, in a limited set of ways (Studdert-Kennedy, 1974).

And, as noted above, there is an ability to extract these kinds of sounds from the auditory field. "There is a directness in perception that makes it difficult to hear the sounds, even of a totally foreign language, as purely auditory events. We hear them instead phonetically. That is to say, we hear them as sounds generated by the vocal organs of humans...this level is no longer one of sound, but rather of some intricate, abstract derivative from the initial auditory analysis" (Studdert-Kennedy, 1974, p.2351). The distinctive features that characterise speech are invariant over a wide range of differences in conditions of production (eg, in a party). These three characteristics, economy, reproducibility and detectability, are what we would expect of a communication system that has evolved to support survival of a species.

One further question remains. The ease of transition to spoken words would be readily explained if the spoken words shared some of the distinctive perceptual features of the objects or events that they symbolize. In onomatopoeic words, such as choo-choo for steam engine, such a direct mapping of phonemes to a distinctive feature of the referent is obviously present. Such instances are rare and probably misleading. Nevertheless the study of poetry and the pathbreaking work of Heinz Werner on the physiognomy of words, particularly with non literates, are an insistent reminder that there is probably something there. Since Jakobson has shown that phonemes are unique clusters (combinations) of a few distinctive features it would seem that if we are to disclose the mapping it will be at that level. We would not expect all spoken words to have strong physiognomic features because of their own evolution to provide context for each other, but awareness of those that have might make it easier to introduce children to the perceptual task of 'seeing through hearing'.

To resume the main trend of this discussion: we are discussing how easily young children make the transition from *seeing through hearing*. The next transition, the transition to literacy, is to *hearing through seeing*. This transition is greatly facilitated by the fact that the young learner is already skilled at producing speech. He or she is thus able to test whether they can uniquely match what they see in a grapheme with a morpheme or phoneme. Initially, of course, a child is introduced to the written word by someone who is already literate in that language. The first learning task is then to produce a phoneme or morpheme that matches the speech sounds that someone else matches to the particular visual symbol. Remember that they are already well-versed in producing speech to match the speech of other. The only problem they face is that of identifying the uniqueness of the visual symbols before them. Thus, for instance, they already know dogs and they know they are the invariant referent of the spoken word dog (a dog does not get called cat although lots of other things might occasionally get called dog). The visual symbol of 'd o g' is novel only in that it is a certain kind of visual symbol; it is not novel to find a symbol referring to dog.

In the traditional paradigm we confronted this as another task that required the build-up of a massive apperceptive structure of stable associations. We seem to have made a mountain out of a molehill.

If we regard this as a perceptual task all we have to do is help the learner to perceive what is unique and invariant:

o identify those few distinctive features that, in combination, define the uniqueness of graphemes and encourage the learner to look for these;

o present the graphemes writ very large so that the distinctive features are readily perceivable to young people who have developed no strategies for searching text (Hughes, 1971);

o introduce only a few grapheme at a time. Rock's studies and Asch's, demonstrated quite clearly that what we have called an association is a perception of a unique relation; this perception is retarded by undue clutter or too many conflicting perceptual demands just as surely as it is by absence of obvious distinctive features (the above two points).

Repetition *per se* has no role in making this transition to 'hearing through seeing'. The role of repetition is practice in detecting the unique relation in differing contexts.

This seems ridiculously simple, but that is the message coming from the meticulous study by Eleanor Gibson and Harry Levin and the down-to-earth practice of Doman and Hughes.

By basing this education on the perceptual capabilities that children already have we are able to achieve a simple self-motivated transition to reading as soon as spoken language is learned; i.e., well before the age of formal schooling.

The further transition to writing offers little problem if the distinctive features of graphemes have been grasped in learning to read. As might be expected in such a perceptual task the transition to a 'world-with-symbols' is heavily influenced by the extent to which the child is growing-up in a world-with-symbols: "Children seem to develop tremendous sensitivity to differences in graphic materials simply by having plenty of graphic displays around to look at" (E Gibson, 1975, p.239). Nevertheless there is "some early, painless, and apparently self-motivated learning about the writing system for the school to build on later" (ibid, p.233). In a review of studies of the development of children's spontaneous scribbling Levin concluded that by three years of age they are producing forms that "contain features that are characteristic of writing and not of pictures" (ibid, quoted, p.233). By the age of three children, even those in environments that were impoverished with respect to symbols, distinguished writing from pictures (ibid. p.239).

The evidence indicates that the written word is processed in the same area of the left cortex as the spoken word; i.e., the Wernicke area. It seems difficult to imagine that any evolution of the central nervous system could have occurred in response to the very recent emergence of writing. It is not difficult to imagine that writing systems evolved to take advantage of the particular set of distinctive characteristics utilized by the Wernicke.

In the traditional paradigm the achievements of Doman and Hughes in teaching preschool children to read and write had to be regarded as freakish and treated with the same sort of reserve as Stern and de Bono. They were, in effect declaiming that 'the emperor has no clothes'. In the new paradigm their achievements are only what one would expect.

The achievements in this field need not stop with cessation of the self-defeating educational practices of the old paradigm and the introduction of the simple search and display strategies suggested above. A major task within the new paradigm would be to explore the physiognomic properties of the semantic relation *and* the relations between the written word, the spoken word and the referent, as a set. We know enough to know that this exploration needs to be at the level of distinctive perceptual properties and not at the level of phonemes and graphemes. We know also, from the poets, that some written words have a 'fittingness' to their spoken equivalent and to their mutual referent that is not possessed by other words. Such words offer a royal road from one system of symbols to another. Aphorisms and folk-sayings offer frozen capsules of meaning, invariant over time, and to some extent over cultures, that serve similar functions.

These explorations have been deliberately focussed on the primary tasks of education. The thought was that if the new paradigm has substantial consequences for the teaching of the three Rs it could hardly not have a similar magnitude of effect on subsequent learning. I should have learned better. When we engaged in the democratization of work we figured that if we could show a beneficial transformation in such places as coalmines, mills and factories then the possibilities for places of relatively privileged white-collar work would be obvious. We found instead that Weber's theory of bureaucracy created a special form of blindness. Sure enough, we find special reasons for not regarding the transformations at the level of the three Rs as evidence for what could be achieved at the higher levels of education. The three Rs is now seen as 'really a training in skills'. 'Real learning' is defined at some point beyond where mass learning finishes—somewhere beyond first degree level. This redefinition of learning is very convenient but not sustainable. Pioneering work, such as that done by Stern and Hughes, has already been done at the higher levels of education (Ackoff, de Bono, Emery, Williams). At the higher levels of education there is the same reliance on abstraction, classification and generalisation. Memory has the same central role in learning and examination. What we have had to say in contrasting searching with researching applies with as much force at this level as at the level where children are learning the three Rs. More so. The weight of evidence is that educated; i.e., literate, adults find it particularly difficult to use the evidence of their own perceptions, We have become particularly sensitive to this problem in the past decade or two and come to espouse a 'continuing education' that goes beyond normal education and somehow or other comes to be described as *'learning to learn'*.

The implications of the new paradigm for this emergent field of continuing education need to be considered because this is par excellence the field that concerns the serious education of adults so that they can better understand and advance their most serious purposes in life.

Continuing education emerged from widespread recognition that social traditions and authority structures were changing at such a rate that:

° the need for education now continues long after formal schooling ends as important social changes occur that were hardly conceivable in the minds of those who designed the old curricula;

° the appropriate aim of such education should be 'learning to learn', not just more schooling.

'Learning to learn' was an idea that was not in anyway referring to the traditional concept of study habits. The core referent was to learning for oneself, not teaching oneself from text books.

In my own attempts to dissect this new concept I was much taken with the extent to which it centred around *unlearning* and not just learning of new contexts and new details (Emery, 1975). It did not matter whether the learnings concerned local planning, corporate objectives, work organization or the like: the critical learning problems seemed to lie in unlearning habits of thought and cognitively restructuring or recentering what was already known. This parallels de Bono's experience with trying to teach adult people to think.

When what one has been taught has also been taught as *The Truth* then there are no built-in stop commands, as there has to be on a computer program. In some parts of experimental science there are such signs but this is the exceptional case and not always very effective there. In the traditional paradigm knowledge adds on knowledge and the progress of knowledge is simply assumed to be an inevitable process of accretion. Details will have to be corrected, sometimes a rush of details will have to be added, but the notion of serious restructuring belongs to the prescientific era when people could believe in things like phlogiston and witches. That is, the notion of restructuring or recentering is alien to the traditional paradigm of knowledge and to the people who have absorbed this paradigm as a world view. It is the most difficult of learning tasks.

To enable people to achieve a capability of learning to learn we have had to devise ways in which they can cope with the boot-strap operation of unlearning (for it is that kind of operation in the traditional paradigm).

To this end we gradually evolved the tools that are labelled Search Conferences and Development of Human Resources Workshops. These are tools of the same nature as the tools that de Bono had to devise to help adults learn to think. The effect of these tools was to enable people to achieve in joint activity what they could not achieve alone; i.e., to accept that their pooled perceptions disconfirmed their assumptions and provided alternative conceptions of reality. These practices, which we evolved for adults concerned with their continuing education, do not differ significantly from what Paulo Freire evolved for the same purposes with illiterate peasants of the 'Third World'.

The new paradigm allows us to identify the referent for the slogan 'learning to learn' (and slogan it was becoming because within the old paradigm it was close to gibberish). The new paradigm gives meaning to the phrase 'learning to learn'. In learning to learn we are learning to learn from our own perceptions; learning to accept our own perceptions as a direct form of knowledge and learning to suspect forms of knowledge that advance themselves by systematically discounting direct knowledge that people have in the life-sized range of things, events and processes. This is hardly a learning activity that is reconcilable with the concept of learning that is embedded in our current institutions of learning. They are committed to the view that learning is an indirect, esoteric and tortuous path of research with a split off element concerned with transmitting the results to students. What is unavoidable in the study of nuclear particles and galaxies has become the prototype of learning, as did the study of unobservable homunculi in the middle ages. I suggest that in these cases the form dictates the content. Real knowledge, and hence real learning, is taken to be that which fits the ruling paradigm. Knowing ourselves and the world we experience and live in takes a poor second place.

There is a certain irony emerging here. In the historical period in which continuing education has been emerging there has also been emerging a massive growth in electronic computerization and communication. The latter has been seen as the inevitable source of an *information revolution*. These new technologies have been designed on the assumptions of the Lockean paradigm and Newtonian Optics. They are providing a paralyzing flood of signals from which human beings are finding they are unequipped to extract information, or in the case of the telephone, unprepared to make use of the information that is transmitted (Emery, 1980). The real information revolution lies in the emergence of the new paradigm.

As everyone with some intact perceptual systems becomes a selfconfident source of information generation will we be faced with a real information explosion?

There seems little room for doubting that with the emergence of industrial society, the mass society, we offered mass education in the same way as we offered popular democracy—the appearances without the reality.

We have discussed above how this particular feat was accomplished. We also discussed how the new paradigm could transform the learning of the basics, the three Rs. These transformations, and the methods of de Bono for teaching thinking, would all help to restore confidence in the direct access to knowledge that is available to young and old alike. To make only these transformations would be to render obsolete the dichotomies in learning potential that have been enshrined by the old paradigm. We should, however, be thinking beyond this.

If perception is so central to thinking and learning should we not be reconsidering the roles of art and poetry in education? Should we not be giving thought to the education that is to be gained from allowing that we might learn from the other sense, the haptic and those of smell and taste?

One has simply to raise these questions and the direct concerns are expressed about the educational implications of the new paradigm. It is yet another excuse to land us back with the earlier suggestions that the serious business of education be replaced by permissive playfulness? Is it not an education in sensuality?

However, the seriousness with which we proceed to replace the old paradigm will probably be best measured by our answers to those questions. The move from one paradigm to another is literally a figure-ground reversal. We will have to notice that a child trying to capture on paper an invariant that he perceives is more given to frowning, a puckering of the lips and other signs of intense concentration than a child trying to recall an algebraic formula. More than anything else we will have to notice that humans, regardless of their educational levels, achieve creative thinking by grasping 'the universal in the particular'. This they do by perceiving the higher order invariants presented to their own perceptual systems. These higher order invariants are embedded in the total context of objects, events and their environments. They bear no necessary relation to the higher order abstractions that are based on qualities that appear to be very frequently associated with particular classes of objects or events; e.g., that swans are white and all people are selfish.

The figure-ground reversal we are confronting is one in which the education in the three Rs can be safely left to parents and elder siblings. The professional role of teachers will be centred on the complex task of guiding children, and adults who have been blinded in the old paradigm, into the multiplicity of ways in which they can enhance their capabilities for extracting information from their world.

To summarize:

Our perceptual experiences are engagements with an environment that is already informationally structured. They only begin to approximate the traditional notion of sensory impressions when we are engaged in trying to perceive ourselves perceiving (Chein, 1972, pp.136-7).

Our perceptual systems have evolved so that we, and other animals, are, at birth, attuned to detect invariances in the available flow of energy and particles that are ecologically significant sources of information. "Furthermore, there is ample evidence that the senses are not only generally preattuned but *become* more sensitively calibrated to pick up those exigencies of the environment that bear directly on the survival, success and well-being of the perceiver—what has sometimes been called the *education of the senses*." (Shaw and Pittenger, 1977, p.107)

This in-gathering of information takes place in non-Euclidean space. If it was transmitted through media that behaved as Euclidean space most of that information would be garbled beyond retrieval. Admittedly, "There are what might be called 'Newtonian oases' in perceptual space. Within a frontal plane, space is approximately Euclidean; and up to a few yards from the observer, shape and size are actually seen as unchangeable" (Arnheim, 1974, p.290). Even within that flat place we cannot always 'see straight', as is demonstrated by the well known Muller-Lyer and Ponzo illusions. Viewing beyond the first few yards, it is almost impossible for someone not trained well to 'see in perspective' to see things as if they were just a distortion of a Euclidean scene.

Despite the evidence of the senses, schooling, within the old paradigm, appears to move us a long way toward the assumptions of Locke and Herbart. The preschool child's concept of space is topological; by twelve it is Euclidean (Piaget and Inhelder, 1956). Within the new paradigm one would hope that by the age of twelve a child would have as many geometries as his world requires, if it is to speak to him or her.

IN THE FOLLOWING TABLE (opposite) I have tried to summarize the differences in education practices and experiences that have been or are likely to be observed in the different paradigms.

I have not attempted to contrast the effects on the personal development of those adults whose lives are committed to teaching. This is only because I am not sure that a life-time commitment is necessary or desirable in the new paradigm. In the old paradigm, Charles Dickens' Mr Gradgrind is still very much with us. The poets tell us more about the new 'teacher'; and little wonder that Plato would ban the poet from his Republic!

> If he [the teacher] is indeed wise he does not bid you enter the house of his wisdom, but rather leads you to the threshold of your own mind. (Gibran, 1923)

> It must go further still: that soul must become its own betrayer, its own delivered, the one activity, the mirror turn lamp. (W.B. Yeats)

Summary Table

The Practice

	Traditional Paradigm	The Ecological Paradigm
Object of learning	Transmission of existing knowledge, abstraction of generic concepts	Perception of invariants; discovery of serial concepts; discovery of universal in particular
Control of learning	Asymmetrical dependence: teacher-pupil; competition of pupils	Symmetrical dependence: co-learners; co-operation of learners
Co-ordination of learning (a) Behaviour settings (b) Timing	School/classrooms, age-grading/school calendar, class time-table	Community settings synchronized to and negotiated with community settings
Learning materials	Text books, standardized lab. experiments	Reality-centred projects
Learning activity	Paying attention, rote practice, memorizing	Discrimination, differentiation, searching, creating
Teaching activity	Lecturing, demonstrating	Creating and re-creating learning settings
System principle (after Abrahms 1953)	Pedagogy: 'the mirror'	Discovery: 'the lamp'

The Experience

	Traditional Paradigm	The Ecological Paradigm
Cultural mode	Work/Religion: 'serious drudgery'	Active leisure: 'exciting, frustrating'
Dominant group emotions (after Bion, 1691)	Dependency: flight-flight	Pairing
Personal development	Conformity; bullying Divorce of means and ends; cheating; self-centredness; hatred of learning (and swots)	Tolerance of individuality; depth and integration; homonomy; learning as living

References

Abrahms M H 1953, *The Mirror and the Lamp*, Oxford University Press.

Ackoff R L 1968, 'Towards an Idealised University', Management Sciences, 15 B, pp.121-131.

Arnheim R 1969, *Visual Thinking*, Berkeley University of California Press.

Asch S E 1960, J Ceraso & W Heimer, 'Perceptual Conditions of Association', *Psychol. Monograph*, 74 No.490.

Bion W 1961, *Experiences in Groups*, London, Tavistock.

Bohm D 1963, *Problems in the Basic Concepts of Physics*, London, Dillons.

Bohm D 1965, Appendix 'Physics and Perception' in D Bohm, *The Special Theory of Relativity*, New York, W H Benjamin.

Cassirer E 1923, *Substance and Function and Einstein's Theory of Relativity*, Chicago, Open Court.

Chambers J H 1980 (Nov) Review of I. Illych 'Deschoolong Society', *Unicorn, Journal of the Australian College of Educators*, p.133.

Chein I 1945, 'On the Nature of Intelligence', *J. Gen. Psychol.*, 32, pp.111-126.

Chein I 1972,*The Science of Behaviour and the Image of Man*, New York, Basic Books.

De Bono E 1979, *Learning to Think*, London, Penguin Books.

Doman G 1968, *Teach your Baby to Read*, London, Pan Books.

Emery F E 1959, 'Characteristics of Socio Technical Systems' in *The Emergence of a New Paradigm of Work*, F E Emery (Ed), Centre for Continuing Education, Australian National University, Canberra.

Emery F E 1969, (Ed), *Systems Thinking*, Harmondsworth, Penguin Books.

Emery F E 1972, 'Research and Higher Education', Chapter 9, in G S Harman and C Selby Smith (Eds), *Australian Higher Education*, Melbourne, Angus & Robertson.

Emery F E 1975, 'Continuing Education Under a Gum-tree', *Aust. J. of Adult Education*, XV, pp.17-19.

Emery F E 1977, *Futures We're In*, Leiden, Martinus Nijhoff.

Emery F E 1980, 'Communications for a Sustainable Society', *Human Futures*, Autumn, pp.1-7.

Emery F E & Emery M 1976, *A Choice of Futures*, Leiden, Martinus Nijhoff.

Emery F E & Emery M 1980, *Domestic Market Segments for the Telephone*, Melbourne, PA Consultants.

Fyre N 1947, *Fearful Symmetry*, Princeton University Press.

Geschwind N 1979. *Scientific American*. September

Gibson E 1969, *Principles of Perceptual Learning and Development*, New York, Prentice-Hall.

Gibson E & H Levin 1975, *The Psychology of Reading*, Cambridge, Mass., MIT Press.

Gibson J J 1958, 'Visually Controlled Locomotion and Visual Orientation in Animals', *British J. Psychol.*, 49 pp.182-194.

Gibson J J 1966, *The Senses Considered as Perceptual Systems*, Boston, Houghton Mifflin.

Gibson J J 1979, *The Ecological Approach to Visual Perception*, Boston, Houghton Mifflin.

Goldmeier E 1972, *Similarity in Visually Perceived Forms*, New York, International Universities Press.

Heider F 1958, *The Psychology of Interpersonal Relations*, New York, Wiley.

Heider F 1959, *On Perception and Event Structure and the Psychological Environ-*

ment; selected papers, New York, International Universities Press

Helmholtz H 1925, *Physiological Optics*, Optical Society of America.

Hughes F 1971, *Reading and Writing Before School,d, London*, Pan books.

Jakobson R 1971, *Selected writings II: word and language*, Mouton, The Hague.

Johansson G 1975, 'Visual Motion Perception', *Scientific American*, June.

Jones M R 1976, 'Time our Lost Dimension: toward a new theory of perception, attention and memory', *Psychol. Rev*, 83, pp.323-355.

Julesz B 1975, 'Experiments in the Visual Perception of Texture', *Scientific American*, April.

Katona G 1940, *Organising and Memorising*, New York, Columbia University Press.

Kuhn T 1962, *The Structure of Scientific Revolutions*, Chicago, Phoenix Books.

Labov W & D Fanshel 1977, *Therapeutic Discourse*, New York, Academic Press.

Land E H 1977, 'The Retinex Theory of Color Vision', *Scientific American*, December.

Marrou H 1956, *A History of Education in Antiquity*, London, Sheed & Ward.

McLuhan M et al. 1977, *City as Classroom*, Agincourt, Ontario, Book Society of Canada.

Miller G A & P N Johnson-Laird 1976, *Language and Perception*, London, Cambridge University Press.

Olson D R 1975, 'The Language of Experience: on natural language and formal education', *Bull. Brit. Psychol. Soc.*, 28, pp.363-373.

Piaget J & P Inhelder 1956, *The Child's Conception of Space*, London, Routledge & Kegan Paul.

Pratt D 1980, *Curriculum Design and Development*, New York, Harcourt Brace, Johanovich.

Pribram K H 1971, *Languages of the Brain*, Englewood Cliffs, New Jersey, Prentice-Hall.

Pribram K H 1977, 'Some Comments on the Nature of the Perceived Universe', Chapter 4 in R Shaw & J Bransford, *Perceiving, Acting and Knowing*, New York, Wiley.

Pritchard R M 1961, 'Stabilized Images on the Retina', *Scientific American*, 204, pp.72-78.

Rock I 1958, 'Repetition and Learning', *Scientific American*, August.

Shaw R & J Pittenger 1977, 'Perceiving the Face of Change in Changing Faces', Ch.3 in R Shaw & J Bransford, *Perceiving, Acting and Knowing: towards an ecological philosophy*, New York, Wiley.

Stern C & M 1971, *Children Discover Arithmetic*, New York, Harper & Row.

Studdert-Kennedy M 1974, 'The Perception of Speech' in T A Sebeak (ed), *Current Trends in Linguistics*, Vol.12, pp.2348-2385.

Turvey M T 1973, 'Contrasting Orientations to the Theory of Visual Information Processing', *Psychol. Review*, 84 pp.67-86.

Walls G L 1942, *The Vertebrate Eye and its Adaptive Radiation*, Cranbrook Institute of Science.

Weimar W B 1977. 'A Conceptual Framework for Cognitive Psychology: Motor Theories of the Mind'. *Perceiving, Acting and Knowing*, Shaw R and Bransford J (eds), pp 267-311. Lawrence Erlbaum Associates. Hillsdale N.J.

Werner H 1961, *Comparative Psychology of Mental Development*, New York, Science Editions.

Whitehead R N 1946, *Science and the Modern World*, Cambridge, The University Press.

Williams T 1975, *Democracy in Learning*, Centre for Continuing Education, Australian National University, Canberra.

PART II.

PARTICIPATIVE DESIGN AT THE ORGANIZATIONAL LEVEL

THIS PART DISCUSSES the concepts, practices and outstanding issues in changing design principle as it applies at the level of the discrete organization. Many of the issues are also relevant at other levels but they usually surface first and are certainly more frequently debated within the context of a discrete group or organization. Regardless of the size of organization, community or governmental system, the second design principle and the small self managing groups it creates remain as the basic building block upon which the more extended forms (Part III) of democratic apparatus rests. It is important, therefore, that these blocks are brought into being by the most congruent methods available, those which will help ensure their strength and stability while not impeding their evolutionary life.

This part begins with an argument which confronts one of the central purposes of democratization. 'The Light on the Hill' puts the whole issue squarely on the board of current political and professional thinking about industrial democracy, productivity and economic development. Emery (F) argues that the elevation of multiskilling and retraining above the need to change the design principle from 1 to 2 is misplaced. Multiskilling will not deliver the goods unless there is a form of work organization that demands, motivates towards and creates new or higher levels of skills. One of the crucial advantages of democratic groups over the one person-shift as the unit of bureaucratic structures is that it provides learning and the conditions for continuous learning. This is of course one of the six criteria for psychological satisfaction and also one of the reasons that participative design workshops have become a basic tool of many adult educators.

'Participative Design: Work and Community Life' has been rewritten to incorporate the intensive research done in the last few years on both clarifying its concepts and tightening up the structure and process of the workshop itself. Its current form with three briefings in even more structured than in the past and is highly effective in producing learning and excellent, implementable designs. This report of it leaves few loopholes for misunderstanding or confusion with other methods.

In 'Further Learnings about Participative Design', Emery (M) describes and analyses a much broader range of practical variations in the application of the workshop. As use of the workshop has intensified, so has experimentation for systemic change. There has been conscious attention paid to ever greater efficiency and value for money in the introduction of change. Tolerance for methods which do not deliver learning and change within reasonable timeframes and budgets is dwindling rapidly. Above all, there is an increasing demand for methods which produce organizational self sufficiency.

This is one reason for including the paper on the difference between PD and STS. STS for sociotechnical systems is now enshrined as a *method*, particularly in the USA. But it is the old method used by social scientists in the experimental phase, to establish that joint optimization of social and technical systems constituted an alternative to autocracy (a sociotechnical system without joint optimization).

STS as a method is an inefficient and expensive method of introducing the change of design principle, and actually fails to explicitly educate about the design principles.

When awareness of the design principles is lacking, various Human Relations type methods can produce unstable pseudo solutions, such as changing the role of the supervisor. That this translation of the supervisor from 'cop to coach' (TLC—Trainer, Leader and Coach) is popular is an indication that it is the easy option, i.e., it doesn't change the design principle and the location of responsibility for co-ordination and control.

The paper 'Management by Objectives' contains a table setting out the differences between organizations designed on the two principles. The extent and mutual exclusivity of these justifies describing them as separate organizational paradigms.

There are plenty of organizations, however, which are taking a fundamental approach to change and it is particularly for these organizations that this edition contains the new papers by Fred Emery focusing on management after the change to democratic structures. As he argues, managers must also be prepared for major changes in the content and amount of management as well as radically changed relationships within management and between management and other levels of a non-dominant hierarchy. The underlying theme is that when organizations change from design principle 1 to design principle 2, the change is *systemic*. It cannot be sustained merely as a change on the shop floor, or even to middle management.

In 'Matching Effectivities to Affordances in the Design of Jobs', Emery (F) explores the six psychological job requirements of work (not necessarily paid employment) within the framework of ecological psychology, thereby enlarging our understanding of these basic factors, and tying more closely the design and epistemological dimensions of organizational change.

Two other small papers conclude this part by arguing against two of the often perceived alternatives to participative design workshops. 'Laissez-faire vs Democratic Groups' presents the most recent evidence to confirm Lewin's finding that 'doing your own thing' is not design principle 2, nor a half-way house to democratization and does not, therefore, provide learning about the alternative to autocracy. It is part of a continuing argument with those within the profession who do not see the light on the hill and/or do not realize that productivity is intimately tied in the long term only to shared responsibility for co-ordination, control and planning; those functions which provide the conditions for continued learning, commitment and, ultimately, productivity.

'Getting to Grips with the Great "Small Group" Conspiracy' is part of the same argument as it outlines the distortions and paradoxes which are inherent in the wave of efforts to teach people how to be democratic and communicate, without changing the structure to which they must return, or even without teaching them how to recognize and deal with it. The misconceptions involve the nature of 'small group', laissez-faire as an alternative and deeply socialized needs to maintain the status quo. They also touch upon some fundamental misunderstandings about human communication. We are, by nature, excellent 'communicators' but only when it is in our interests to communicate quickly and accurately. Design principle 2 organizations provide a perfect setting and reason for effective communication (see 'Training Search Conference Managers', Part IV) and most 'communication problems' can be solved by the implementation of a participative design.

The Light on the Hill, 1988
'Skill formation' or 'democratisation of work'

Fred Emery, October 1989

FOR THE PAST TWO YEARS the notion of 'Work Restructuring' has been at the centre of national debates. With the recent decisions of the Industrial Commission it would seem that the die is cast—the nation is set on the course of Restructuring. Having set course, all that now remains is to take off and proceed in that direction.

Unfortunately, little attention has been directed to how we take off and fly. The major focus is discussions to date has been on skill formation and the opposition of short-sighted managers and craft unionists. In focussing on this they have directed attention away from what, I will argue, is the prior and central question of why industry persists with forms of work organization that demonstrably lead to de-skilling, low productivity and chronic unconcern for quality.

The simple fact of the matter is that industry employs the mix of skills that best suit its dominant form of work organization. Industry feels no need to adapt its employment structure to the mix of skills produced by the educational systems (except insofar as it might give preference to Arts Graduates for clerical jobs or give preference to degreed engineers for draughtsmen's jobs). By the same token, industry is not at all motivated to invest in creating or materially rewarding skills that cannot be used by their forms of work organization.

If one insists on skating over the surface of the matter, then it seems sensible to suggest to politicians that they restructure the educational system so that it pours out the skill mix that industry should have in the future, and offer monetary incentives to industrial concerns to retrain for this future. The reality is that employers will use graduates for their purposes; e.g., engineers as draughtsmen or classy sales representatives, regardless of the purposes of their educational curriculum. If employers introduce training schemes because of a monetary incentive, then one can be sure that most will degrade training to turn the scheme into a profit earning subsidy scheme.

There is no doubt that a different skill mix will be needed for a high technology industry. It is not at all sure whether this requirement can be met by a small core, skilled force and a mass of unskilled workers or robotic machines.

There is also no doubt that skill formation is not the critical problem. The critical problem is the introduction of a form of work organization that both demands and creates new skills for an obvious return in higher productivity.

It is the critical problem because unless it is solved there is no way that investments in skill formation will lead to higher productivity. Such investments will have the unintended consequence of protecting and bolstering the old form of work organization; of sustaining low productivity and congealing the islands of poverty and unemployment. Those investments will certainly do that because, if the demand for skilling does not arise from the felt demands of industry, of the sort that would arise from adopting the new principle of work organization, then the investments will flow down through the bodies that have educated and controlled training for the old form of work organization.

It is the critical problem because, if it is solved, we find that enterprises and companies quickly discover the value of training and education, and quickly discover the most expeditious and cost effective ways to give the self managing work groups the knowledge and skills they need to do their job, and go on doing it despite the absence of individual members due to illness, holidays or absenteeism. Due to the learning that can be shared on the job, when employees find it in their interest, the demand for specially financed training is usually considerably less than what industrial trainers deem to be necessary, or what industry training levies, as in the UK, provide for.

The problem is critical not only for industry and its productivity but also for the structure of the labour market and, hence, the shape of society. If a modern economy like Australia's remains tied to the old form of autocratic work organization then productivity will continue to yield lower returns to capital than interest rates. Naturally new capital will not flow into industry. Existing investments will be protected by cannibalization of the lower grade assets and minimizing the steady haemorrhaging through wages and salaries. The unions, unless they have extraordinary political clout, have little option but to protect their institutional stability by concentrating on the interests of the diminishing number of employed, fee paying members. These will tend to be the skilled workers who are hardest to replace if there are temporary business upturns. On the other hand, the employers still wish to free themselves from the organised power of the traditional skilled craftsmen. They will seek, in the new technologies, to concentrate technological decision making in the hands of the new tertiary educated technologists; people who are very willing to associate professionally but eager to strike personal employment contracts with their employers.

The picture we have drawn here is not a futuristic picture. It is what has been happening in most of the major corporations for the past twenty years (with some exceptions, to which we will come later). Over this period they have consistently shed labour whilst increasing the proportion of employees with tertiary educational qualifications, and increasingly shed, to subcontractors, the unskilled work. Subcontractors are usually less controllable with respect to conditions of employment; wages, hours, compensation etc. The net effect of these changes has been a polarization of the work force to a smaller full-time educated or skilled group and a growing mass of part time and unskilled or unemployed workers.

If this restructuring of the skill mix continues, then the social results are fairly obvious. Those with steady jobs and the incomes that go with skilled or educated employment status will gravitate to suburbs and dwelling areas of like placed people. They will live and be serviced in a social world that has minimal contact with the other more populous but poverty ridden world of the unskilled, uneducated. But it will be in a social economy that is faltering and dying.

The alternative form of work organization is the democratization of work. Quite simply it means that decisions about co-ordination of work should, as far as possible, be made by those who are performing the work. Not made by non-working supervisors.

This is the form of work organization that the science based corporations started to recognize as the necessary future in the sixties and early seventies. They have not changed course in the eighties because they have found that it is the path that leads to increased productivity.

Moving along this path produces a different social world. It is puzzling, and disturbing, to see 'skill formation' now being singled out as the royal road to productivity.

This is not quite the direction that one would have expected from a Labor Government. It is certainly not the direction taken by the first Frazer Government when it formed a Dept of Productivity under the ministerial guidance of Mr Ian McPhee. It is not the direction envisaged in the unanimously adopted resolution of the 1976 ACTU national congress on industrial democracy.

The evidence that is brought forward to justify this position is less than satisfactory. It is contended that Australia needs the sort of skilled work force that exists in Sweden, West Germany and Japan. It is forgotten, or overlooked, that those countries had that sort of skilled work force in

1970 but found that they could not get commitment to productivity from their work forces, and hence turned to democratisation of work.

Are we so blind to history that we have to invent an Australian wheel? At a time when productivity is a national necessity, and capital is in flight from industry, it does not make sense to divert operating capital (and in the case of the teaching institutions, investment capital) to the training and education of people who are not committed to using their abilities in order to increase productivity. And the training and education provided by the institutions (and professional trainers?) will be very little related to the immediate requirements of industry. This can be summed up.

Proponents of 'skill formation' as our primary path appear to be assuming the following causal pattern:

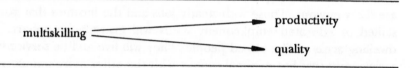

If the traditional work organization remains in place, then this is a thoroughly disproved hypothesis. Within that structure industrial engineers know that profits come from following Fred Taylor's dictum about specializing and de-skilling the work force, and paying accordingly. The skilled workers know that their economic security rests on having a mass of unskilled labour. We are simply back where the Swedes, Germans and Japanese were before circa 1970.

In the 1960s, that is almost thirty years ago, the Swedes, Germans and Japanese had already seen that the basic causal structure was as follows:

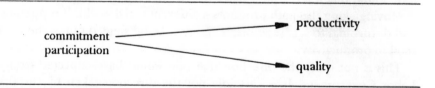

It would be foolish to pretend that this was the first time that this understanding was widely accepted. It was very prevalent after World War 1 and even more so after World War 2.

In both cases an over riding national need for greater industrial productivity brought about an awareness that production was critically related to employee attitudes. The first major solution was to extend to employees the right to vote for representatives to present their views to management; Works Councils, or, in the British Civil Service, Whitely

Councils (1923-). This was seen as 'industrial democracy', and in many European countries after World War 2 was introduced by legislation for government owned and large private enterprises. The causal model this proposed was as follows:

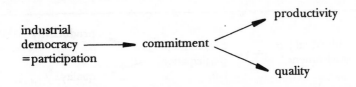

These schemes actually produced commitment; commitment of a new breed of worker politicians to gaining and preserving positions on the Works Councils as a desirable alternative to time otherwise spent in labour, without any recognition as someone special. No one has been able to document improvements in productivity or quality that could be surely attributed to the establishment of these representative worker parliaments.

After World War 2 there were two alternative and very popular hypotheses about how to create employee commitment, and hence raise productivity and improve the quality of output.

The first, owing much to Elton Mayo, the famous Western Electric experiments and the so called Human Relations movements, was that the humanization of the foreman—worker relation would create the desired level of worker commitment:

This idea got nowhere. Whatever the foremen learnt in their human relations training had then to be adapted to what was demanded of them on the job. The best of the foremen responded to the training and then resigned in disgust at the managers who had sent them on the training courses but had no willingness to change the traditional work organizations.

The 1960s fad, after 'Human Relations', was 'individual job enrichment' usually associated with the name of Fred Herzberg. Herzberg had accepted the experimentally established facts that humans are more prepared to commit themselves to completing a task if the task offers a variety of challenges and opportunities to learn new things. (Conversely, that they are turned off if the task is simply a repetition of well learned skills.) He hypothesized that if employees were given enriched tasks (requiring multiskilling!) they would be more committed to doing better and more productive work:

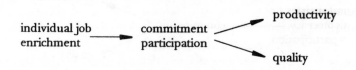

Herzberg's ideas were widely applied because at that time, the mid-sixties, the decline in productivity was becoming very apparent to the major corporations, particularly those with high investment to labour ratios.

Job enrichment schemes often produced good initial results. There is not a well documented case of any such schemes surviving the honeymoon period.

These schemes always accepted the basic framework of the traditional work organization (which might explain their temporary popularity in the United States). Within that framework they sought to equalize task benefits by robbing Peter to pay Paul. That was bad news for the Peters of the skilled labour fraternity. It was also an arrangement that could be overturned by management overnight. It was no basis for an employee to respond with any deep lasting commitment to company goals, let alone concern him, or herself, with productivity or quality.

It was out of this series of false starts that there emerged the hypothesis that employees might accept commitment to the achievement of corporate goals of greater productivity and better quality if they knew that they had a real say in how their part of the job was done (whether their part was production, storing, R & D, accounting, delivering, marketing or managing).

Here the concern was not to ape the forms of representative democracy. It was not a call for a replay of so called Industrial Democracy, a proven false path, but a call for the democratization of work itself.

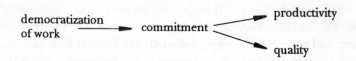

The democratization of work can only be achieved by allowing to those who are responsible for doing a job the power to decide how they can best coordinate their efforts. If they are denied that power then they cannot be held responsible for the outcome of their joint efforts and hence can take no responsibility for the outcomes. They can often be made responsible for their part but not for whether it fits the other parts.

The matter does not stop there.

If groups of workers are given responsibility for a group task, then they will usually require a degree of multiskilling that is far beyond what has been required for traditional work organization. In the absence of adequate multiskilling their commitment to work goals will normally lead then to far outstrip traditional work forces in productivity and quality. With multiskilling the difference should be multiplied.

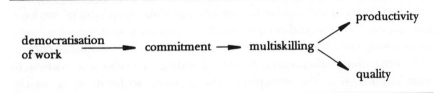

We are now focussed on a pattern of causal determination that is well proven in practice. There are here none of the gaps in explanation that characterize fads in organizational development. There is no scientific problem about what should be done to rectify the social problem of low productivity and poor quality of products.

There is obviously a social problem in the changing of traditional work organization; right here in Australia, 1988. It is obviously a problem of 'who is going to bell the cat?'.

In response to the views outlined above it has been argued that I have failed to grasp the new dynamics in the workplace that follows from the Restructuring Agreements:

> 'broadbanding' agreements → structured career paths → then, 'enterprises can make their own decisions about job design..'

The point I argued is that agreements about broadbanding of job classifications are spurious agreements unless there is a prior agreement to democratize the workplace. The spuriousness of broad-banding agreements that are not underwritten with such a commitment will quickly appear in the hard realities of the workplace. People in the workplace, managers as well as workers, will just become more cynical and distrusting of their leaders; of the Arbitration Courts for registering such agreements and of the politicians who dictated the process.

If the politicians and civil servants involved in forcing industrial restructuring 'down from the top' were serious then they would insist that the Arbitration Courts not register such agreements until they were satisfied that there was a genuine commitment to new forms of work organization. The traditional forms of work organization would simply become slacker and less efficient if they adopted broadbanding. Any gains from elimination of old restrictive work practices and erosion of the prerogatives of skilled workers would be short lived as the costs of worker compensation and quality defects rose.

I have argued that the new forms of work organization need to be more democratic so that they will generate a workforce committed to productivity and quality of the product. It would not seem appropriate that the Courts be directed to favour any particular new form of work organization. They should simply insist on evidence that whatever new form is suggested it will produce gains in productivity and quality control that more than offset costs of broadbanding. If valid alternatives to democratization of the workplace emerge, then so be it, as far as the Courts are concerned. Others can confront the implications.

It could well be that the Arbitration Courts will be proven to be incapable of assessing whether broadbanding agreements are genuine. Under the restrictions of what were termed to be 'managerial prerogatives' the Courts have always, in the past, excluded consideration of such matters and developed no relevant expertise. If the Courts fail in this, then it will soon become apparent and, in any case, it would simply mean that the matter returns to the enterprise level, and that yet one more 'revolution led by politicians' has failed. How then should we proceed?

Within my perspective multiskilling is usually, but not necessarily, an element of job redesign. Where multiskilling emerges there may emerge a skills based career path. At lower levels of technology multi- skilling means no more than training on the job—no special agreements or training investments are needed. Even at higher levels of technology that require some off the job training in techniques or skills (e.g., forklift truck driving, repair work and word processing) the range of work may justify nothing more than payment for possessing a range of proven skills. Those considerations fall far short of defining a career.

If we look at this matter from the position that I am espousing what do we find? We will find that multiskilling, reward for skills possessed, and possibilities for career structures emerge as elements of job redesign, at some levels of technological complexity. There are four steps which I would consider as essential if restructuring is to achieve its stated aims:

Step One

Before even considering what award amendments they will submit to the Courts, management and workers need to explore, in very concrete detail, what could be achieved in the various parts of the enterprise from transferring some managerial responsibilities and authority to the workforce; i.e., from moving toward an organization based on self managing work groups. Generally speaking this will require some form of 'participative design workshop'; for the simple reason that there is no traditional form for such consultation.

Step Two

If there is agreement between the workers and management in the enterprise that there are significant gains to be had from a redesign then, there needs to be further agreements with respect to:

- the degrees of autonomy that should be allowed to each work group (it will vary). The limits will usually be specified in terms of production and quality targets and controls over group membership;

- the levels of multiskilling required for the group to meet its targets at minimal levels of manning and labour reserves.

- how the increases in profitability are to be shared. There are only two practical ways to approach this problem. A group bonus system can be established, leaving it to the group to decide on the distribution; or, payment can be reviewed regularly, as it would be in ordinary labour negotiations, and levels of attained skills would determine distribution within the group.

These are matters that have to be considered together. They cannot be dealt with in isolation of each other.

Step Three

If, and when, such agreements or understandings have been arrived at then consideration can be given to seeking binding agreements from the Courts.

Step Four

Regardless of whether Court Agreements are gained on broadbanding of job classifications the enterprise agreements on the other matters will require management to re-define career structures for foremen and, most likely, for middle management. (I simply note, in passing, that officers in the Norwegian merchant marine fleet practically always came up through the ranks. That fleet competed rather well in the international market.)   *Japanese mgmt. model*

It seems quite crucial for these developments that the role of supervisor be not only re-defined in terms of content; i.e., from control to co-ordination but re-defined in status as the first step in a managerial career. We will also confront a marked reduction in middle management positions and hence a reduction in promotional opportunities. The reduction in middle management positions is not forecast as a consequence of the new information technologies, although that might be a factor. It is forecast as a consequence of the shift from bureaucratic to democratized work organizations.

The 'system principle' of bureaucracy is that the decisions about co-ordination are always located at least one level above that at which the work is actually performed. Only thus can the work of each subordinate be subjected to the control and judgement of his superior. This applies at every level in a bureaucracy and hence we find that a large proportion of middle management jobs exist simply to supervise subordinates without contributing materially or directly to the work of the organization.

In these remarks I have simply tried to point out that whilst the arguments for focussing on skill formation can be elaborated at length the fact remains that such discussions are academic unless we can define the context in which people are motivated to use the skills they have, or command. I am not criticizing the political decision to offer wage incentives for those who engage in industry restructuring. I am critical of industry consultants who recommend the short cut of skill formation with the wishy washy expectation that job redesign will naturally follow.

Reference

Neumann J 1981, 'Why People Don't Participate when given the Chance', *Industrial Participation*, No.601, Spring, pp.6-8.

Appendix

Research undertaken by the Tavistock Institute of Human Relations challenged the usual assumption that people always welcome participation. The reasons why it makes sense to an employee not to participate were investigated; several categories of explanations, other than personality, were identified. These broadly were structural, relational and societal. Some examples of when people do not participate are when: the organization's real decisions are made outside the participative forum; rank and status continue to be more important than competence and mastery; past and present adversarial politics have led to protection of self and others.

Comment

The first two examples confirm our long standing belief that people can tell when they are being deceived and manipulated. Under such circumstances they would be crass optimists or mugs to go along with management's plans.

The third example simply confirms the decision we, and the Norwegian employers and trade union leaders made in 1962—you can forget about democratizing work if matters of gross 'industrial injustice' are still unresolved.

Participative Design
Work and Community Life: 1974, 1975, 1985, 1992

Fred and Merrelyn Emery

Section A: The Content — Organizational Design Principles

BUREAUCRATIC STRUCTURES and the systems of management associated with them have been unable to systematically provide for the learning and personal growth and development of their members, in particular the large numbers at the base of the pyramid. They may be downgraded and de-skilled by their work experiences (e.g., assembly line workers). The traditional conception of management's task has been inhibitive of learning and growth. Representative remedies such as joint councils and workers directors have also failed (Emery & Thorsrud, 1964).

> The philosophy of management by direction and control is inadequate to motivate because the human needs on which this approach relies are today unimportant motivators of behaviour. Direction and control are essentially useless in motivating people whose important needs are social and egoistic... People, deprived of opportunities to satisfy at work the needs which are now important to them behave exactly as we might predict — with indolence, passivity, resistance to change, lack of responsibility, willingness to follow the demagogue, unreasonable demands for economic benefits. (McGregor, 1970)

The Six Psychological Requirements

Cumulative investigations in Europe, Scandinavia, Australia, North America and India have enabled social scientists to identify a number of important determinants of the psychological requirements of productive activity, located both in the dynamics of person-task relations and in the social climate of the work situation. There is a core of six such requirements.

It is clear that particularly the first three of these requirements which refer to the content of the job need to be optimal for any given individual and flexible to meet variations in individual need; e.g., from day to day, or morning to afternoon.

- Adequate elbow room. The sense that they are their own bosses and that except in exceptional circumstances they do not have some boss breathing down their necks. Not too much elbow room that they just don't know what to do next.

o Chances of learning on the job and going on learning. We accept that such learning is possible only when people are able to (a) set goals that are reasonable challenges for them and (b) get a feedback of results in time for them to correct their behaviour.

o An optimal level of variety; i.e. they can vary the work so as to avoid boredom and fatigue and so as to gain the best advantages from settling into a satisfying rhythm of work.

o Conditions where they can and do get help and respect from their work mates. Avoiding conditions where it is in no one's interest to lift a finger to help another: where people are pitted against each other so that 'one person's gain is another's loss': where the group interest denies the individual's capabilities or inabilities (as in the bull gang system that used to characterize Australian dock work and New Zealand's meat freezing works).

o A sense of one's own work meaningfully contributing to social welfare. That is, not something that could as well be done by a trained monkey or an industrial robot machine. Or something that the society could probably be better served by not having it done or at least not having it done so shoddily. Meaningfulness includes both the worth and quality of a product, and having a perception of the whole product. Many jobs which are meaningful in the first sense have been downgraded because individuals see only such a small part of the final product that its meaning is denied them.

o A desirable future. Put simply, not a dead-end job; but hopefully one with a career path which will continue to allow personal growth and skills increase.

Experience has shown that these psychological requirements *cannot* be better met by simply fiddling with individual job specifications; e.g., job enlargement, rest pauses, supervisory contacts (see 'The Light on the Hill' herein). If the nature of the work allows room for improvement this will be best achieved by locating responsibility, for *control* over effort and quality of personal work and for interpersonal *co-ordination*, with the people who are actually doing the job.

The Design Principles

The reasons for the proven superiority of the 'group solution' have emerged, rather painfully, over the past forty- five years of laboratory and field experiments. The differences in the structural relations of people, tasks and supervisors is the key, e.g., Figures 1 and 2.

These figures illustrate the organizational building blocks which result from design principles 1 and 2 respectively.

For organizations to behave flexibly and adaptively, they must contain a degree of redundancy. There are two basic ways that redundancy can be built in.

1. by adding redundant parts to the system; each part is replaceable; as and when one part fails another takes over;

2. by adding redundant functions to the parts; at any one time some of the functions of any part will be redundant to the role it is playing at the time; as and when a part fails in the function it is performing, other parts can assume the function; so long as a part retains any of its functional capabilities (i.e. functional relative to system requirements), it is of some value to the system. (Emery, F., 1977, p.92)

The first way gives us design principle 1 which translates into a building block where responsibility for co-ordination and control are located one level above where the work is being done. The second gives us design principle 2 and its basic module is a group taking responsibility for its own co-ordination and control, the *self-managing group*.

Because they are taking responsibility for their own work and behaviour, a design principle 2 organization is called democratic, in contrast to the first autocratic or bureaucratic organization which is the operationalization of the master-servant relation.

Figure 1 (see over) precisely defines what has become the dominant bureaucratic form of organization that has been enthusiastically installed by production engineers and 0 & M experts alike. It is scientific management. Control and co-ordination, the two dimensions of human organization, are vested in the supervisor. S/he controls the subordinates by specifying what the individuals A, B, C, etc. will do vis-a-vis the task allotted to them, X, Y, Z, etc. Co-ordination is the supervisor's preserve. Achievement of the section's task will almost certainly be related to the adequacy of co-ordination because of either interdependence between the tasks themselves (as exemplified in process industries) or variations in optional work loads between individuals (as exemplified in typing pools).

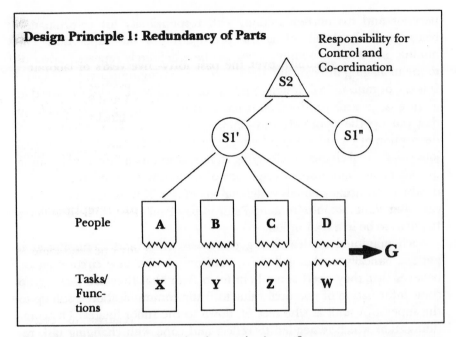

Design Principle 1: Redundancy of Parts

Responsibility for Control and Co-ordination

The short term fluctuations in the section's performance are not easy to manage as the supervisor increasingly loses the right to hire and fire. Co-ordination is the variable the supervisor can manipulate and hence manipulate the image his or her supervisor has of them. This is not without its difficulties. Tight job specifications to give supervisors greater control on subordinates can also be used by them, particularly if they are unionized, to cramp the supervisor's style when s/he seeks to use idle time to help out on other jobs. Amongst employees so organized, there will be an almost universal tendency to develop an 'informal system' to turn the requirements of co-ordination to their advantage; e.g., 1. 'Dargs' and other restrictive but informal production norms to reduce the productive potential with which the supervisor might do some shuffling; 2. Cliques whereby subgroups in the section ease their jobs by collaring for themselves the productive potential in co-ordination. Because the purposes of these cliques are personal they tend to organize themselves around bases for common trust; e.g., religion, race, old school. They do not tend to organize themselves around the interdependencies of task and personal work capabilities that particularly effect the supervisor's concern, namely the section's productive capability.

We can easily sum up this description. The building brick for this type of organization is the one person-shift unit. Controls might be sloppy or tight but the principle is the same. The organizational module is the supervisor and his or her section; with responsibility for co-ordination being jealously defended as the prerogative of the supervisor. The module and its basic building brick can be indefinitely repeated upwards to the managing director and the directly reporting functional managers. It is the organizational design that has been used by the western world to go into large scale production. It happens to he the organizational form that put up the pyramids and China's Great Wall. This rather wordy description of Figure 1 might help to show why redefinition of individual jobs has no real chance of changing things, is so much favoured by some managements and arouses suspicions of some unions. Enrichment of individual jobs usually entails switching bits of task X from A to B etc. This can easily generate into 'robbing Peter to pay Paul'. Very difficult if Peter happens to be in a craft union.

Such manipulation leaves the power structure and communication pattern basically unchanged. If A, confronted with new circumstances, believes that they need some help from B or that they are picking up some information of potential value to B the communication is still up to the supervisor and, as s/he sees fit, down to the subordinates. The communication which is needed to reflect and cope with changing task requirements is being channelled through a filter/amplifier system that is labelled on one side 'us' and the other side 'them'. The goals of the supervisor are those that concern the section's overall performance and explicitly no business of his or her subordinates, A, B and C. The subordinates' goals concern the performance standards set for sub-tasks X, Y, Z, etc. This means that communications are going to be amplified and attenuated in the same task related channel, by different criteria. The 'us's' will amplify what makes them look good vis-a-vis their own task performance or relative to their 'colleagues'. They will hear as little of the downward communication as suits them and they can get away with. The supervisor will be anxious to hear and remember what will sound good to his or her supervisor, including excuses for malperformance.

The power structure is similarly unchanged. Someone once said that 'What Caesar can do, Caesar can undo'. The redefining of individual job specifications for 'job enrichment' is very much within the traditional managerial prerogatives. Come the usual crisis and demands to tighten up, the same managerial prerogatives enable the individual jobs to be screwed back to tight, specialized, supervisable performances that will yield a guaranteeable performance level. The variation seems little different to the fluctuations between sloppy and tight rates in the individual incentive schemes we see in light engineering works. Little wonder that the engineering unions have been foremost in expressing scepticism about 'job enrichment'.

The **democratic organizational module** (Figure 2) has markedly different potentials. The first and obvious feature is that it is not restricted to just redistributing jobs X, Y, Z, etc between A, B, C, etc. It allows for A, B, C, etc to share and allocate amongst themselves the requirements for control and co-ordination of their task-related activities. Thus it is not just the sum of the individual

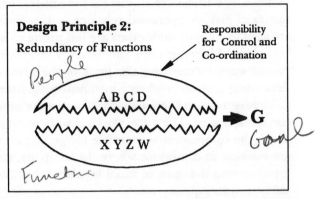

tasks X, Y, Z, etc that they take responsibility for. It is also all the task inter- dependencies (interactions XY, XZ, YZ, XYZ...). Also, and of critical importance in the kind of jobs produced by the widespread adoption of the bureaucratic model, is the fact that the group must share the tasks of monitoring and controlling the contributions of its own members, and organizing their mutual support to cope with individual and task variations. In this module individual 'job enrichment' has a qualitatively different scope. As a desirable flow-on it provides the individual with a human scale of organization (a work 'home', 'family' or territory) whereby people feel they fit into the corporation, no matter how large that may be. It provides the individual with an on-the-job defensive and offensive group of colleagues such that his/her work life will not easily be degraded at the whim of a new, go-getting manager, or because the corporation has run into yet another of its budgetary crises. Communication and power within these groups take on markedly different characteristics to what we find in bureaucratic organizations (Emery & Emery, Part III, 1976). This is why communication and power cannot be taken as basic variables of organizational design. They are universally present attributes of organization, but they do not tell us much of relevance about what is communicated, what is commanded.

Changes in organizational design affect the nature of communication and power but the reverse does not hold. Provided we have a group and not just a collection of individuals or a mob, and that the group has accepted responsibility for a group task, then it will seek to make its life easier (or more productive for their ends) by: (a) communicating quickly, directly and openly the needs for co-ordination arising from task or individual variability; (b) by allocating tasks and other rewards and punishments to control what they consider to be a fair contribution by members. Such groups can get a sense of an over riding group responsibility only if they have at least four members (with three it is too often a matter of just interpersonal relations — two against one). If the groups are kept to eight or under they are less prone to 'group emotional' (mob) behaviour. Larger groups can be very effective if they share a deep rooted work culture and the parts of the group task are highly interdependent (e.g., the eighteen man Australian Rules team of footballers).

These groups are self managing, not autonomous as they often were in cottage industry. They are working with materials and equipment for which the company is responsible for getting an adequate return. They are working in conditions where the company, not they, are responsible for observing the mass of social legislation laid down for basic pay rates, safety, product quality, etc.

Differing organizational circumstances will determine the range of responsibilities for different working groups. At the lowest level of self management, the groups may simply have the right to decide on working methods and allocation of work between themselves. At a somewhat higher level they may control some of the conditions from which they start; e.g., membership of their groups, equipment and tools, maintenance, support, quality levels for acceptance of inputs. At an even higher level they may even be involved in redefinition of work goals. Groups may proceed to a higher level which involves them more deeply in the longer range concerns of the company (e.g., product development, selection, training) and increases the autonomy that is possible at lower levels. Thus, regarding the latter, involvement in product specification can be associated with innovations in tooling up, staffing, training and also in work practices. Involvement in starting conditions may have a considerable effect on the methods of work that they can choose.

People cannot be expected to accept responsibility as a group unless a number of conditions are met. The psychological requirements that individual workers have of their jobs are just about equally relevant for a face-to-face group of workers. They must know that they can aim at targets that are explicit, realistic and challenging to them; and they must have a feedback of group performance.

In setting and agreeing targets care must be taken to avoid lopsided simple minded targets that might encourage shoddy workmanship, unsafe practices or a 'bullgang' atmosphere where group members come under pressure to go for target levels that are only really suitable for the young, the strong and the greedy. The group must set a comprehensive set of goals, including human, social and environmental as well as the purely economic and technical. It is important that the group has first go at setting its goals, but these must be negotiated and agreed with management.

They must feel that the membership of their group is to some degree under their control. They must also be free to organize their own spokespeople and internal group structure generally. Leadership and training roles usually move around the group as circumstances and needs change. These are rarely appointed formally but arise from daily group working.

Naturally, group integration will be low unless there is sufficient multi-skilling to allow flexible allocation of work within the group, to both individuals and subgroups. How they allocate the work should be their responsibility, with explicitly agreed limitations to protect plant, safety, etc. This includes on-the-job training which the group will have considered in its initial analysis of the skills it holds as a group. Once constituted as a self managing group, they will normally work to increase the extent and level of skill in the group to improve both their performance, adaptiveness and cohesion.

It will be noted that these steps toward setting up self managing work groups requires more explication of goals, methods and responsibilities than is usual. The commonsense and good judgement of a supervisor is no longer enough. If these things are not worked out there is a danger of drifting into a laissez-faire atmosphere. Groups agree on mechanisms for decision making for co-ordination and control.

It is absolutely critical for the continued good functioning and adaptiveness of a group that they have conceptual knowledge of the design principles and what is involved in self management. With this they can deliberately evolve their design towards greater group responsibility and effectiveness. Without it, the design can evolve over time, regressing towards design principle 1. Simply setting up groups and calling them self managing without their appreciation of what is entailed in responsibility for co-ordination and control, and without an opportunity to agree as a group on the 'how', can induce frustration and short-lived cohesion.

A Democratic Modified Form—Multiskilling Not Feasible

The alternative organization discussed above implies that a fair degree of multiskilling is possible and hence that people can make real decisions about the switching of jobs. However, there are important areas of work where multiskilling is not feasible. In research and development projects one may have to have such diverse skills as mathematical statisticians, chemists, marketers. Each has their own special contribution to make and while the overall success of the project depends on the effective co-ordination of their activities, one cannot expect to achieve this along the path of each person becoming expert in all of the required disciplines. In the management of enterprises we confront the same dilemma.

Beneath the managing director are usually functional managers for such things as production, finance, marketing, personnel and administration, R & D. They are typically chosen for their expertise and it is not expected that the production manager will be as good at financial matters as the finance manager. They in turn expect to be judged and rewarded for their expertise in their function.

Organized bureaucratically these work sections show the same shortcomings as are described above. Concern about this has been manifested in the rash of efforts at 'matrix' and 'project' organizations for R & D work and 'team building' for management. A lot of these efforts have been described as creating pockets within persisting bureaucratic structures where this is an 'open culture', 'trust' and 'understanding'.

In many ways they seem like laissez-faire policies to let special kinds of people 'do their own thing in their own way'.

A more prosaic but effective solution is to change to design principle 2, *locating responsibility for co-ordination clearly and firmly with those whose efforts require co-ordination if the common objectives are to be achieved.* While control, the vertical dimension, cannot be shared, there is no reason why they cannot accept group co-ordination.

The change we are proposing can be represented diagrammatically as follows, using the management example:

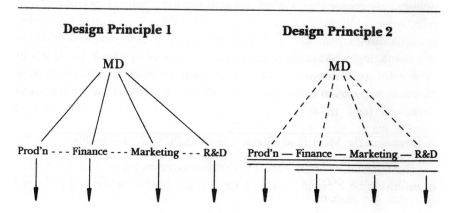

Design Principle 1   **Design Principle 2**

In the normal bureaucratic state (Design Principle 1) the functional managers will be primarily jockeying for influence with the MD so that s/he comes down in favour of their functional policies. This does not exclude temporary informal alliances between some functional managers to better ward off the threats of others. All rather suggestive of palace politics.

In the team concept (Design Principle 2) the functional manager is judged and rewarded, or punished, as much for his or her effective coordination as for the ability to propose and implement policies in their division of the organization. If an unresolved conflict arises between the managers, the MD must sort out whether it is because one or more of them is incapable or unwilling to find a suitable compromise or whether the framework of policy that s/he is responsible for creating is inadequate. In the first case the MD must decide on some re-education or redeployment; in the second, s/he must move from the normal operating mode, where they are relatively free from ongoing intraorganizational commitments, into a policy forming mode. The MD and managers need remain in the 'policy mode' only long enough to create an adequate framework of operating policies (I have been inclined in the past to write off the style adopted in the 'policy mode' as rather irrelevant; MDs form a very small proportion of the work force! This now seems an unfair reflection of my experience. Admittedly, a relevant and acceptable body of overall policy must come into being, no matter how. However, MDs who deny their managers' involvement in formulating the principles they must use to coordinate their efforts must be dangerously conceited or charismatic).

Respecifying job responsibilities in line with diagram B would seem to be a simple matter. In fact, it seems from my experience, that only time and a few exemplary experiences are needed before the changed nature of managerial (or project team) responsibilities is grasped. More difficult is the transition backward and forward from the 'policy forming mode'. If this is too frequent the 'time span of responsibility' of managers or researchers can be so reduced that they are, once again, just cogs. If it is to be as infrequent as possible and yet adequately reflect the rate of change in the organization's environment, objectives and resources then the team will have to adopt means of exploration and search (see Part IV) that are not now commonly used.

A final point should be made about this modified design. This is with regard to the emergence of leadership (a problem that is not quite so pressing at the occupational level where multiskilling is feasible; at least not until it is realized that the royal road to management is not necessarily through prior tertiary education). The bureaucratic system (diagram A) makes it very difficult to identify a potential leader. Is the next MD or project leader to be a person who was just so good (or lucky) at their specialist contribution that he or she put their colleagues in the shade? Is such a person the one best fitted to ensure the overall objective? It is difficult to know in that type of organization where a person is paid for putting their best effort into their speciality.

In a genuine team structure (diagram B) it is relatively easier to see who is best capable of grasping the overall structure within which they better make their specialist contribution. It may be, for example, the production manager who recognizes that s/he must accept a suboptimal solution to the length of the production runs if marketing requires a greater range of products; to accept a suboptimal level of stocks with all the difficulties it makes for managing production if the company needs a higher level of liquidity. It is the ability to work in this way that would indicate a potential for overall leadership.

Section B. The Participative Design Workshop

If groups of people are to be expected to take responsibility for self management, it is important that they have designed their own section of the organization. For many years, particularly in Norway, we felt that this involvement needed only their right to choice in matters of detail, a genuine democratic vote by them whether to go into the new scheme of working and real guarantees about their right to opt out, individually and collectively.

We have learnt that this creates an unhealthy reliance on outside experts and hinders the emergence of a self sustaining learning process in the groups. We have found that the most fruitful way to proceed is to involve workers and management in participative design (PD) workshops.

The aims of the design are spelt out to the participants as in the above statement of psychological requirements and they then proceed to: (a) analyze how the job is now done; (b) assess how far this falls short of meeting the human requirements; (c) redesign for a better way of doing the job (if such is felt to be needed); and (d) work out how the new design could be implemented.

The basic strategy and its underlying assumption described here depart radically from those employed in the UK and Norway. The reasons for these basic changes are simple.

The experimental phase for changing organizational structures from design principle 1 to 2 finished with the success of the Norwegian Industrial Democracy project (Emery and Thorsrud, 1975). All that remained was diffusion.

Diffusion is an educational process and the most effective learning comes from an experience of integrated theory and practice. Organizational members have by far the most detailed knowledge of their sections of the organization and require only the concepts and tools of organizational design in order to redesign them.

At the beginning of the diffusion phase in the early seventies there was learning to be done, but it was learning about how to most effectively design the settings within which people could learn to redesign their own organizations. Those learnings accumulated over many years are described here.

The role played by social scientists in PD workshops today is much more congruent with the philosophy and ideals of democracy than was the earlier role. This is brought out most clearly by the ways in which analysis is handled, the involvement of relevant workers in the process itself and the resource role of an external agent. The learning environment created in these workshops is therefore itself a working example of the second model of organizational structure.

Within the process of participative design there are problems and questions common to all technologies. Only the most common and fundamental of these are included here. Although the PD design workshops themselves are often not the appropriate time for resolution of some issues which arise from structurally innovative designs, an awareness of negotiation and action is developed.

The basic assumption underlying the methods described here is that the most adequate and effective designs come from those whose jobs are under review. It is only from people pooling their various and usually fragmented, but always detailed, knowledge that a comprehensive and stable design can come. More than that, it is only when the people involved work out their own designs that the necessary motivation, responsibility and commitment to effective implementation is present. The difficulties which are almost inevitably met in the initial phases of implementation may be found to be overwhelming if designs are imposed from above or by external agencies such as social scientists. The people must 'own' their section of the organization.

As will become obvious from the following discussions the philosophy of participation as spelt out in practical detail is considered appropriate not only to industrial and white collar/clerical work sites but also to communities and educational institutions (Williams, 1975). All organizations explicitly or implicitly contain one of the design principles.

Basic Design of the Workshop

(a) Introductions and running through the workshop

(b) Briefing 1

(c) Groups fill in matrices for 6 criteria and skills held

(d) Reports and diagnostics

(e) Briefing 2

(f) Groups draw up workflow and organizational structure and redesign the latter

(g) Interim plenary

(h) Briefing 3

(i) Groups finalize redesign and do additional tasks

(j) Final Reports

The day begins with general introductions and a run through of the plan, explaining the purpose and process of each part. This is essential even when teams have had prebriefings. It provides a unity of context for the time and because it stays up on the wall everyone can see how the work is progressing relative to time constraints.

The first briefing deals with explanations of design principle 1 as above, its inverse relation to the 6 psychological requirements of an organization and to skills. It concludes with detailed instructions for creating and completing the two matrices.

Presentation of this content appears to be most effective when it is simple, brief and visual. It is infrequent that clarification of basic concepts is requested. They seem to be readily grasped, regardless of the educational level of the participants.

Groups work on these and report their findings. Their patterns are used as diagnostic tools, the results to be taken into account in the redesign phase.

Table 1. Matrix for the 6 Criteria

Psychological Criteria	Names of Participants				
	Mary	Jim	John	Alice	Joe
1. Elbow room for decision making	-2	0	-1	-3	-2
2. Learning:					
(a) setting goals	-4	+3	-2	-3	-3
(b) getting feedback	-3	-4	0	-4	-4
3. Variety	-3	+5	0	+4	-3
4. Mutual Support and Respect	8	4	2	8	8
5. Meaningfulness:					
(a) socially useful	9	9	9	9	9
(b) seeing whole product	4	10	7	3	4
6. Desirable Future	3	7	6	2	2

Because the first three criteria need to be optimal for each individual, these three are scored from -5 (too little) to +5 (too much), with 0 being optimal, just right. As the second three criteria are things you can never have too much of, they are scored from 0 (none) to 10 (lots). The final *group product* will express the realitivities of scores across the section.

The pattern in this matrix is fairly typical. Sections organized on design principle 1 typically show a majority of low scores on the first three criteria. Scores on the second three are more unpredictable. From the above pattern, if you didn't know at the time, you could deduce that Jim was the supervisor, very happy with his autonomy, but having to look after too many things at once (variety and setting goals). Because he is an S1, nobody gives him much feedback and he doesn't see himself respected or supported. He does, however, gave a fairly desirable future.

You could also deduce that John is probably Jim's offsider (or favourite) and suffers for this by low levels of support and respect. As Jim may be grooming him to take over, he sees he has a fairly desirable future. Mary and Joe both have single or simple functional jobs. Alice comes across as a general dog's body for the section. All three are aware that they have little by way of career path or improving chances on the job market. Mary, Joe and Alice stick together and look after each other. All recognize that the work of the section is socially useful, but only Jim and John are in a position to really see how their bit contributes to the whole.

This is only an example of what can be deduced from such a matrix. In a real workshop, much of this is already known by participants and the diagnostic use in the report session confines itself to noting the major problem areas for rectification in the redesign.

The other advantages of this first analysis are, firstly, that any misconceptions of the criteria are hammered out by the group and a common and well founded understanding is established; secondly, this first task is usually sufficient for members of the team to become acquainted with each other if they have not worked together closely on site, and to become a group. This is necessary because of the fragmentation that has taken place, but a cohesive work group is formed fairly fast under these circumstances, where involvement with such a personally important task as the organization of one's own job is very high.

The second task for the groups is to draw up and fill in a matrix of skills currently held. Firstly, they must list the essential skills required in the section to make it work. Then, using a simple scale of 0 for none of a particular skill, and one tick (✓) for a sufficient level of skill to back up and two ticks (✓ ✓) for a high level of skill, the groups compile a collective picture of their skill resources.

Table 2. Matrix for Skills Currently Held

Essential Skills	Mary	Jim	John	Alice	Joe
A	✓✓	✓	0	0	0
B	✓	✓	✓	✓	✓✓
C	0	✓✓	✓✓	0	✓
D	✓	✓✓	✓✓	0	0
E	✓	✓✓	✓	0	✓
F etc.					

It is clear from Table 2 that only on skills C and D is the section covered for a high level of skill in cases of an emergency. If Mary is sick, only Jim can cover for skill A at a lower level of skill, and Jim already has too much to do. The group can probably muddle through in the short term on skills B and E. The basic rule for a multiskilled section is that there must be at least two people with a high level of a particular skill with a backup or two.

In the discussion of this report, the group would mark skills A, B and E as requiring further training. In the final session they would return to this analysis and from it spell out who should receive what training for which skills and whether it can be done on the job or not, the time involved, etc.

In the example above, it is easy to see why Mary, Joe and Alice rate their desirable futures low. Mary and Joe are stuck with basically single functions and Alice has few skills at all, and little opportunity to learn. With the change to a design principle 2 structure the section has the chance of moving to career paths based on payment for skills held. Using the same skills matrix, sections have a first go at designing a career path of skills. Such a career path is democratic because movement through it is determined by the motivation of the individual rather than by the imposed structure of the organization.

The second briefing deals with design principle 2 and its relations to the 6 criteria and skills. If there is possibly a need, this briefing will deal with the modified model as well as that for multiskilled working. It similarly ends with instructions for drawing up the workflow and organizational structure and for redesigning the latter.

Groups begin on this phase allowing sufficient time for them to consider options for redesign. The interim plenary has been found to be essential, as groups learn from each others' efforts and compare notes on options. When the plenary discussion makes clear that they are ready to finalize a design, the third briefing is given.

The third briefing outlines a further series of tasks which will help the groups ensure that their designs will work. It includes instructions for spelling out

○ a comprehensive and measurable set of goals and targets for the section;

○ their requirements for training and other things, such as equipment, arrangements for internal co-ordination and external relations;

○ a career path based on payment for proven skills held and broadbanded and

○ an explanation of how their design will improve the scores on their matrix for the 6 psychological requirements.

Groups then finalize their redesign and get as far as they can with the additional tasks. Completing these in the workshop is not essential. It is important, however, that they get a feeling for the tasks which can be finalized later and then negotiated with management.

Final reports are given and it is useful if management is present to hear these, particularly if groups give, for instance, notice of significant needs, changes to existing goals and targets or ideas about merging of existing sections.

Preparation and Planning

Like any other venture, democratization will be only as successful as the quality of its planning. Obviously, nobody is going to embark on PD workshops for a serious effort at democratization until

° the enterprise has made the decision to change the design principle; and

° if the enterprise is unionized, there is at least a draft agreement in place specifying the terms of the change. This agreement needs to have as its core only an 'in-principle' clause relocating responsibility for co-ordination and control at the level where work is being done, as in design principle 2.

Participative design workshop can also be used, however, as an educational medium for organizations which want to learn what democratization means and entails. In this case, it is important that everybody involved is open and explicit about its nature and limitations. It is vitally important that members of a natural section agree to participate, knowing that there may be no follow-up.

In both the cases of serious democratization and simply learning about it, the selection of persons to do the redesigns is critical.

Selection of Persons to be Involved in Design

Generally, the most important criterion to be observed is the size of the design group. Given a small discrete or well defined section or unit, say 4-10 persons, it is best that everybody in that unit work together on the design. This can be pushed up to 15 or so.

In large sections it is necessary to take at least one 'deep slice' through the section. The 'deep slice' was used as a strategic technique for the first time in Australia in 1971. It was tried as a response to a receptive and anti-expert oriented climate where the demand for visible and self generating change was strong. This climate and awareness of the need for change with its attendant sense of urgency would appear to be another of the factors leading to this further democratization of seminar design.

In the case of SAMCOR, the Yearling Hall selected as its deep slice two labourers, two slaughterers, the rover and the floater (first line supervisors for slaughterers and labourers respectively), the broadwalker (superintendent of the Yearling Hall), and the fitter. Present also for part of the time were the Secretary of the Meat Workers Union, the General Manager of SAMCOR and the Worker Director of the Board. One each of the labourers and slaughterers were union delegates on the floor.

It is obviously not a feasible alternative to have separate groups working on part solutions or aspects of a section design.

In large units or sections there are various ways of getting wide participation through workshops. Mixed teams from the same unit can work in parallel in the same workshop on an overall design which can be integrated, *or* different teams can do designs for the whole unit in different workshops which can be compared and integrated later on. *The basic rule is that no designs can be imposed.* Even if circumstances dictate that only one vertical slice team can attend a workshop, they have a responsibility, and are instructed, to take home, most importantly, the concepts and process, and secondarily, the tentative design in order to genuinely, participatively produce a final design from the whole unit.

The criteria for choosing a team must specify a 'deep slice' plus people representing as many functions or skills as possible across the section. But the actual choosing of the individuals according to these criteria must be done by the section itself.

It is also critical that the ratio of workers to supervisors and middle management be kept as close as possible to the real life ratio. If a particular design team for a section is top heavy with supervisors and above, it is possible that the needs, ideas and very efficient designs of the worker/operator level won't come through.

In large organizations with many levels of dominant hierarchy and diverse operations and products, it will be necessary to run PD workshops which have overlapping membership of the middle ranks. This increases the options for middle management as well as ensuring greater coherence of design and learning up and down the old hierarchy.

There is itself a design art in the ways in which PD workshops are put together—with parallel teams or with mirror groups, sorted with different organizational purposes in mind. These options are elaborated in 'Further Learnings about Participative Design'.

Note on Participation of Unions and Supervisors

The industrial conditions pertaining to, and general cultural awareness of these matters is radically different today from what they were when the original Participative Design paper was written. However, there is still the same need for ownership and understanding of design principles and their implications by both union representatives and supervisors. Both groups must be involved from the very beginning and continue to be involved until a new stable design principle 2 organization is achieved.

For unions there are new enterprise agreements and awards to be negotiated. They should be aware of the advantages or disadvantages of various means of sharing the increased productivity.

After the initial period of settling down into a new work organization, some increase in productivity usually results. It is the joint responsibility of managements and unions to anticipate this increase and prepare to negotiate new agreements for sharing when the new rate of productivity becomes stable. It is one of the responsibilities of management that can be made clear at the start. Regular reviews of flat awards have been found preferable in incentive bonus payments, even on a group payment basis. Where bonuses have been established as policy, it is still preferable to institute regular renegotiation and maintain bonuses only at a nominal or symbolic level. Individual incentives are almost impossible to allocate within the framework of self managing groups and group bonuses become difficult when there are strong interdependencies between the tasks of groups in a complex plant.

For those whose level of the design principle 1, dominant hierarchy has been abolished—and this will almost inevitably include first line supervision—there must be multiparty discussions and negotiations. Thinking about possible options will begin long before the PD workshops, but it is essential that the natural section design teams finalize a design before any other actions are made. It is in the process of doing the design that the widest range of options will be considered and the new design will cover the problem anyway.

If, for example, guarantees have been given that:

○ there will be no forced redundancies as a direct result of changing the design principle and

○ there will be no going backwards in terms of pay

then ex-supervisors are often happy to work as members of a group. In a large section, several exsupervisors and miscellaneous specialists may become a self managing resource group for the other senior managers. Again, there is often a need for experienced people to work on special issues which nobody has got around to. Groups will often be aware of such projects.

If none of these sorts of options can be agreed to, then the question must be addressed externally (to a section). With today's emphasis on training and education, some enlightened enterprises have already offered their exsupervisors and middle managers places in an introductory university management course. Those who succeed and find it to their liking are then available to move into the ranks of management proper.

Other Issues

Participation of other managers. It is assumed that the sanction of and approval and understanding of consequences by top management have been assured before the event of the seminar.

It is similarly assumed that management has a set of policies or organizational guidelines which can be used by design groups in the joint setting of goals.

This understanding in particular will be furthered if management can participate in the design process itself, at beginning and end.

Any remaining suspicions of union and operators will be further alleviated if management in person can at the time of the seminar reiterate either by word or deed its encouragement of the purposes of the design team. Top management should not be present throughout the process, except perhaps as observer, but they should be encouraged to come in at the beginning to state organizational purposes.

Management will better appreciate the organizational implications concerning, for example, training requirements and possible costs thereof, manpower situation, recruitment strategies, etc., if they are present at the end to hear the team sum up their design efforts. Remember, they will be involved in their own PD workshop.

Training and other costs may increase significantly in some technologies. This is a separate but related issue to that of revision of awards to payment for skills, where this is not already in effect. Members of multi-skilled groups are paid to the highest level of skill they hold, although this skill may not be in constant use. It is to the advantage of management to use this scheme as it helps to ensure that the benefits of multi-skilling will be retained. Deskilling has been one of the results of moves towards Scientific Management. Democratized groups work effectively, given traditional schemes of pay and classification gradings. However, it appears to be only a matter of time before groups begin negotiations for more appropriate forms. These issues have been found not to present intractable problems.

Selection of group members. Established working groups must be allowed some say in the composition of the group. This can be arranged in terms of a trial period for new members after choice from a short list prepared by management. Incompatibility of individuals with groups is often simply resolved by the individual choosing to look elsewhere for a more appropriate work culture.

Loners and resisters can usually be accommodated by groups by designing around them. The special case of the loner who has difficulty in adapting to democratic ways after years of entrenched status differentiations often needs the consultation of the group and management. In extreme examples of sabotage of the group's efforts, management may need to consider horizontal displacement of the individual concerned, or other solutions.

Australia has many examples now of failed democratization due to sabotage. Individuals or minority groups really shouldn't be allowed to sabotage changes for the benefit of the majority. The concept required is that of *Active Sanctioning* which means that top management will move to punish the saboteurs and keep the change on track.

Where explicit cases of resistance to the change of design principle involve core functions of a section, it is of course not feasible to design around the individuals involved. In these cases also, management and unions must intervene on behalf of the majority.

Goal setting. It is essential that the task goals set jointly by management and the groups be compounded of both task (quantity and quality) and human components. Where the goals set are only targets of quantity, the opportunity is opened of subversion of the group into a 'gang'. The incomplete nature of the goal leads directly to intergroup competition, neglect of interdependence, i.e., of group tasks and abuse of individual members — their needs and unique contributions.

What is required is a comprehensive and measurable set of goals, including occupational health and safety, environmental and social responsibility and individual psychological and economic (career path) goals. All of these should fit within the organization's strategic plan — if not, there must be an adaptive adjustment to either the sections' goals or those of the organization.

Leaders and spokespeople. It is unusual for a well functioning group to show a constant pattern of leadership. In the true sense of leaderless group — a group of leaders — the leadership function will move from person to person as the progression of the task demands differing experiences and skills. However, it has often been found useful for the group to nominate a spokesperson to operate intermittently at the boundaries of the group. But this is not necessarily a leadership function, except in the minor sense that communications through the spokesperson are effective to the extent that they are accurate and representative.

The workshop manager. In these workshops it is not necessary that the outsiders are experts in the field of work that is being designed. Their job is to help the assembled workers and management pool their knowledge and use their expertise, wisdom and brains. They are the managers of the learning process and environment. This does entail enough familiarity with the work in question to follow the discussions and sense when bottle-necks are emerging, red herrings being pursued or when pseudo obstacles or conflicts are being generated (it is remarkable to find in any workplace how many things are technically impossible — things that have been done in 'the place next door' for years). But this role is a long way from that of the expert who presents the best solutions. When mirror groups are built into the workshop, they perform the questioning role.

An outsider is relevant simply as *process management and external resource*. A manager can umpire and suggest. As an external resource they can help broaden the workshop's range of experience and deepen their analysis with social scientific concepts.

As well as ensuring the formation of a work group, the behaviour of the manager has indirect learning for the group. Whether or not this is made explicit, the members of the design team now have at least one experience of being a self managing group which has successfully worked towards its task goal. It is useful to point this out to members who become resistant to the idea of groups functioning without constant supervision.

It is rarely that the manager is required to deal directly with technological queries. They may have to enquire on their own initiative at times into the technology, if for some reason work is blocked or analysis shows results which are clearly unrealistic. Often it is useful to be able to cite examples of the same or similar technologies.

The design team may often on their first attempt bring up a design which is incomplete or an example of Herzbergian individual job enrichment rather than democratization. In the case of an incomplete design, it is worthwhile questioning to determine whether it is a simple case of incompleteness or due to such factors as union demarcations.

Summary

It should be restated that these are only a selection of the issues that arise in implementing change from design principle 1 to design principle 2. The discussion given them is drawn from the experiences of those who have worked towards successful implementation, but the reader is reminded that 'credulous imitation' is infrequently a formula for success. The most effective designs are more likely to be achieved by those involved in their own unique variant of people, circumstances and technology.

References

Emery F & M 1976, Part III of *A Choice of Futures — to Enlighten or Inform*, Martinus Nijhoff, Leiden.

Emery F E & Thorsrud E 1964, *Form and Content in Industrial Democracy*, Tavistock, London.

McGregor D 1970, 'The Human Side of Enterprise', in Vroom V & Deci L (eds) 1970, *Management and Motivation, London, Penguin Press*, p.314.

Williams T 1975, *Democracy in Learning*, Centre for Continuing Education, Australian National University, Canberra. See also *Learning to Manage our Futures*, Williams T A 1982, John Wiley & Sons.

Further Learnings about Participative Design
Diversity and flexibility

Merrelyn Emery, 1988, 1993

SINCE THE ADVENT of the little publication *Participative Design*, countless participative design (PD) workshops have been conducted in many highly diverse settings and ways. At one end of the spectrum is the Development of Human Resources Workshop (DHR) which publicly recruited organizations prepared to send teams into a formal learning environment. Then there are the small single organizations learning to redesign themselves in their own, often very informal circumstances and in their own time. Almost every contingency from multi-mirror group structures to different sections of an organization working together to small groups working alone appears to have been required and accommodated. The PD workshop is a highly flexible form.

Nor should it be assumed that PD is appropriate only to places of paid employment. It is as applicable to a group of kids wanting to set up their own local recreational centre as it is to a voluntary organization (Emery M, 1982). Whenever people congregate to plan or act there is also a question of how they can best organize themselves to achieve their goals.

While it is highly adaptable, there are some elements which must be present if it is to be a PD workshop. Basically it is an environment for conceptual and experiential learning about and designing democratic, learning organizations. For maximal learning it must include:

o information about the design principles, the genotypes of bureaucratic and democratic structure;

o an experience of working within a democratic structure; and

o experience of using the concepts and tools for its introduction and long term implementation

The first point probably requires some elaboration. Bureaucracy is a widely used word and to many means waging the paper war. When the concepts of democratic and bureaucratic structure are presented, it is important to make clear that these can be found in any sort of organization; that they lie behind the superficial (phenotypical) features such as impersonality, busyness or poor communication. PD differs from many of its competitors in that it addresses the genotypical core, the design or system principle; the disease if you like, rather than the symptoms. It is possible to spend a lot of time teaching people how to temporarily relieve the organizational aches and pains while the disease merrily metastatizes below the surface.

These elements are non-negotiable. Others are merely good or bad practice and may be judged according to whether they are used with insight as to what is required to bridge an impasse, bring a taboo out of the closet, rationalize a conflict, bolster or restore confidence and integrate new people or sections into the process. Until one gets into a redesign, it is almost impossible to foresee what sorts of forces will be operating and what sorts of resources will need to be brought to bear.

The DHR workshops in their final form were probably as efficient and effective a design to produce first stage learning and cover most contingencies at this stage as any. It was residential hot house, intensive learning and at any point, there was a choice of company, resource people, experience and advice to choose from. Significant and often extensive learning was done after hours. The final design was as follows:

Workshops with Mirror Groups

Figure 1. DHR Workshops Final Design

Plenary. Final briefing, expectations. Collection of data about changes in the extended social field
Small groups work on desirable and probable futures Connections are made to democratic structures
Plenary. Briefing on concepts and tools
Mirror Design Groups. Two disparate groups work together A + B analyse and redesign A's organization. C + D do the same for C's
Plenary presentation and discussion of designs
Reverse mirror groups. A + B redesign B's; C + D redesign D's
Plenary reports as above
Team groups and/or plenary. Next steps. Strategy

Stage 1 followed the normal first stage of the Search Conference (see part IV or Searching, 1982) and was added in the mid seventies when we realized a contextual factor would add to general understanding of the phenomenon of democratization itself. This was at the time when many were perceiving that the sixties and seventies marked a radical change in social climate, mood and value system (e.g., Emery F, 1978). The workshop was begun late afternoon so that the context was part of a welcoming, introductory social atmosphere. These days when democratization is a well established idea integrated into the industrial relations context, the session on the extended social field and its implications is unnecessary.

The briefing on concepts and tools was given next morning followed by the group redesign work. Total workshop duration was three and a half days and nights. It usually finished at lunch or mid afternoon on the third full day.

The use of mirror groups was invaluable we found and we designed for pairs with maximum heterogeneity. Too often when working on their own, natural work groups fail to question their assumptions or 'the way we have always done it'. They tend to be suffused with precedent, unwritten conventions and patterns of interpersonal behaviour, all of which may range from highly conscious to unconscious.

Much of this is observed by the mirror group and they will question its necessity for the work, particularly when it is to be self managed. There were sometimes steamy moments as teams from private and public sectors debated procedures of control and co-ordination. The designs which resulted were much the stronger for this questioning and debate.

This model without the session on the extended social field is still the most effective for an organization consisting of more than four natural sections. In one large Australian statutory authority we ran a series of four team workshops matching up teams of office based staff (predominantly female) with field based teams (predominantly male). This provided maximum learning about the whole organization and reduced the stereotyping of each which had grown in the absence of accurate information about the jobs involved.

Where there are still long assembly lines or separate but closely related functions such as production and maintenance which offer the possibility of integration, mirror groups will be paired to facilitate this purpose. Adjacent sections of a line can be paired to achieve designs incorporating a greater range of tasks and skills. These choices make the point that *there is a process of design at the level of the workshop itself*.

A Larger Mirror Group Unit

For large organizations there is another more extended model of workshop which could speed up the process and aid diffusion. This remains untested but would represent a saving in resources. Instead of a workshop based on four teams, the unit moves to eight teams. The briefings would be given to the eight rather than four. Analyses and redesign work would be done with the mirror groups as above in two sets of four teams. When the four designs of each half are finalized, there would be time for each group of four to prepare for a final plenary of the eight at which shortened presentations could be made.

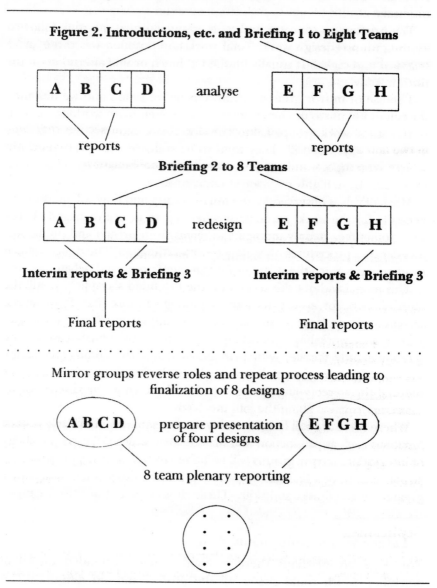

Figure 2. Introductions, etc. and Briefing 1 to Eight Teams

The eight teams begin in plenary with the normal introductions and explanation of the workshop process, followed by the first briefing. Teams then commence work in two streams of four as in the original workshop design. Their analyses of the current organization are reported only in their own group of 4 (A B C D etc.). All eight teams reconvene in a plenary for the second briefing. They return to do the redesign work in their groups of four. The third briefing can be handled within the groups of four as the timing here can be very variable.

At the end of the first two sets of redesigns within each of the groups of four, the mirror groups reverse roles as in the basic workshop and repeat the process without further formal briefings. At the end of this stage when there are four designs for each of the two subworkshops, a final plenary would be held at which presenters from each group of four will report the designs.

This extended workshop design will produce eight section redesigns in two and a half days. If the workshop is not residential and particularly if there is no night work, the process will take three full days.

Workshops without Mirror Groups

Mirror groups serve the purposes of broader organizational learning, the merging of previously separate departments such as production and maintenance and the better handling of interdependencies between sections. While extremely useful, there are situations when it is more efficient and effective to take two or more teams from the one large section into a workshop where they will work in parallel on the design of the whole section. Each of say three teams A, B and C, each of which is a vertical slice containing a mixture of functions and skills, analyses and redesigns the whole. They follow the same process as described above and report to each other after each task. Consolidation and sorting out of discrepancies can be done at each stage so that an accurate and clearly defined redesign gradually comes into being.

This design of workshop is appropriate where only a particular section needs to redesign itself around say a new concept of customer focus, where the size of a section makes it inefficient to send teams as mirror groups with replications and when there are no particular presenting problems with interdependencies between sections.

Replications

In large organizations with large discrete sections there will often be a need for repeated workshops. This applies to workshops both with and without mirror groups. Replications may be by shift team or by other mixed groups across the section. Replication necessarily implies a later integration. Given that not all staff will have been personally involved in the redesign and there must be no imposition of a design, various integrative mechanisms have been tried.

Where people are working in face to face situations it is easy to have the designs further discussed on the job. In these cases, integration of designs after discussion can be done by a group consisting of one or two from each workshop team.

When people spend their working day isolated in vehicles or geographically spread, special events are required to effect both discussion and integration. 'Town meetings' of as many as possible from the section can be organized. The designs can be presented by the workshop teams, compared and the feeling of the meeting ascertained. It is not possible to do detailed design work in a large meeting but specific questions can be asked and those who have special concerns can not only raise them but can also identify targets for further more detailed debate.

Vertical Integration

In organizations with many levels of hierarchy it is often necessary to design in workshops which overlap through the hierarchy. This certainly applies when an organization has made the decision to systematically change from design principle 1 to 2. Such a decision implies that senior management also will change its design principle. Schematically such overlaps occur with middle management.

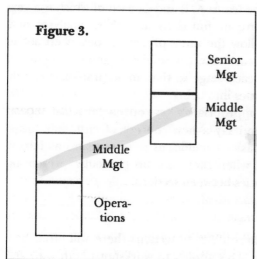

Figure 3.

Senior Mgt

Middle Mgt

Middle Mgt

Operations

Apart from sheer logistics about having many layers in a single workshop, overlapping vertical workshops provide greater choices for middle managers and also reassure the troops that top management is serious about the systemic nature of the change. There is often a lingering suspicion that redesign is seen as something which happens at the bottom of the organization and that management will retain design principle 1. "When is management having its workshop?" is not an uncommon question. It helps if a logical series of workshops has been designed right from the start. This reinforces the fact that there is design work to be done at the macro level of change through the workshops, not merely at the intra- workshop level.

The implication of all this is that systemic organizational change must proceed actively and adaptively as change progresses. On the question of whether change should begin at the bottom or the top, it becomes clear that the answer is both.

Top management must have done its homework before deciding to change the design principle and have made this known. Any work regarding restructuring at the macro organizational level should be at least available as proposals. In terms of the micro intra- section redesigns, it is preferable that this begins at the bottom with manageable redesign focuses. It is important that responsibility for co-ordination and control be handed over and some experience gained with that before people are asked to do redesign work at larger levels such as integration of separate sections. Once the concepts are understood and self managing groups have settled in, they will be confident and competent to redesign at a more complex level.

Workshops Strictly for Education

At the other end of the scale are those workshops which are strictly for the purpose of introducing individuals to the concepts and methods of PD. Sometimes they have been sent as part of an intelligence gathering tour of what is available if the organization decides to move into democratization.

The absolute minimum required in this class of event is a full briefing on the concepts and tools and some idea of how they are applied. However, as in most things the medium is the message and if there is no hands-on experience with the tools themselves, some go away with the idea that a PD workshop is still a top down exercise where the experts design a splendid new organizational form for the client.

Every effort should be made, therefore, for an experiential component. Perhaps the element producing the most learning is the group completion of the six criteria as during this several new perceptions take place, even when the individuals involved are not members of the same organization. Foremost amongst these are the realizations that in bureaucracies, people are often unaware of what other people's jobs are and how they perceive them; that many perceptions of how other people feel about their jobs are stereotypes. Those lower in the pecking order often assume that those at higher levels appreciate their 'good jobs' while the managers see themselves having for example, too much variety and inadequate support.

Above all, the experiential component should be sufficient to convince the most sceptical that the designs will be those of the participants, not the managers of the workshop and not the other vested interests such as top management and union officials. For various reasons, there are often suspicions that the workshop or process managers are only the stooges or front line troops for other parties. And the participants will, therefore, be analysing carefully every statement and move to uncover the professional's subtle manipulative tricks. If the genotypical democratic purpose is not clear, totally transparent and understood at this level there will be continuing scepticism that there will ever be a transfer of responsibility for co-ordination and control to the self managing groups.

P.248 It is critical, therefore, that the workshop manager(s) understand and observe the four principles for effective communication (see Part IV). Inexperienced managers or those wedded to the first paradigm can often convey through their style and/or handling of the process, the opposite of the messages conveyed through their spoken words. It is sometimes difficult for people to realize how subtle human communication really is, how sensitive people are to the many levels of message they receive and just how important it is to establish openness and conversation between peers. It is just as important in a PD workshop as it is in a Search Conference. Needless to say that everybody involved must be absolutely clear that the workshop is strictly for 'learning about' and implies no commitment to change.

Use In Relation to Other Problems

The PD workshop also lends itself as a component of a variety of novel events. Such a one was the series of workshops to explore RSI and preventative strategies. Clearly, work redesign was indicated as a major factor in any preventative strategy but would have been of little use had participants left the workshops without a good understanding of what was actually involved and how it related to the incidence and nature of RSI. This series of workshops gave a glimpse of a further potential for PD which so far hasn't been fully explored (Emery M, 1988).

Importance of Deep Slice

In terms of the technicalities of design, it is necessary to stress the importance of the 'deep slice' or vertically integrated team. In a recent project at the Australian National University the industrial agreement governing the project specified a 'target group' which comprised only the lower levels of the hierarchy, specifically, the lower clerical, administrative and keyboard areas. While the intention was well meaning, it constrained the first phases and in the process, created and/or exaggerated problems way past the extent to which they are normally seen.

The first problem was that in most departments and sections there were not enough staff at these levels to provide any meaningful room to move to more optimal jobs, and certainly little if any opportunity to share the co-ordination and control of the sections. These functions rested primarily with the levels above who were excluded. In a highly specialized division such as Finance and Accounting, the separation of sections meant that some of the target group totally wasted their time in the early stages as they were the only target person and could not share across the internal boundaries. The problem apparently arose because the parties to the agreement did not understand the concept of PD, the central role of co-ordination and control, and had seen the problem as one of more equitable reclassification.

Another serious consequence was the paranoia which developed rapidly amongst the excluded. Although having been briefly briefed, they had no opportunity to experience the concepts and tools and, had therefore, no real idea of the collaborative sharing process which leads to a collectively satisfying design. As would be expected, those who normally have the most to lose in a flattening of the structure; i.e., some within middle management, were most badly affected as were some departmental secretaries. These latter considered they held good jobs apart from the fact that they were inadequately rewarded and could see only that they would be robbed of their job's better features and de-skilled into the bargain. Instead of all levels viewing it as an opportunity, the project became for many an extreme threat. Most of this was unnecessary.

While the centring of democratization within the industrial relations sphere has long been overdue, it is now a responsibility of those involved in drawing up agreements to educate themselves as to what is involved and what will really serve the best interests of their constituents. It would be appear that there is still a long way to go here and that unions themselves must accelerate the process of getting their act together. Another complication at ANU was the fact that different unions signed different agreements leading quite naturally to demarcations, which in turn created complications for any optimal co-operative and productive design.

It is probably worth stressing this point as it highlights the unpre-

with clear objectives decide steps in ? process design

dictabilities which any such long term national process (1969-88 in Australia) throws up. Having long stressed the need for a single channel of representation, unions are now faced with the need to shape up to meet the responsibilities they have demanded and accepted. No longer are there the clear boundaries of the factory gate, the pay check, the heat or the noise. Nor is there the simple adversarial relation. All of this amounts to the need for a learning revolution for both unions and managements and while progress is being made, recent experiences show the gap which remains to be bridged.

Perhaps the reality we saw, as above, is the way it should happen but it seems silly that so many time consuming and self defeating mistakes are caused by a failure of both parties to consult with and take advice from those who have practical experience in the field. If this should sound like a whinge from one of the professionals, it probably is. But the whinge is not towards our greater glory but towards the most efficient and effective human solution.

On the simple issue of whether there is ever any place in a PD process for a lateral group, the answer is yes, but not as a basic design team. Occasionally in the implementation phase there is need for some detailed negotiation between one level, one particular classification group etc, and others. Should this arise, the various separate parties should meet to clarify their position and/or plan their negotiating strategy.

Sometimes a particular sub-group must meet to reassure or deal with one or more of its members. In this respect, the conventions do not differ from those established for any other party to the process. The only real issue is the constitution of the original design team, and this must be in the interests of the whole.

Other Pitfalls

There are two main classes of traps in running PD workshops. The first is turning it or allowing it to degenerate into a personally or relationship oriented, 'communication' or sensitivity, 'group dynamics' event. This is a trap for those who believe that change will only occur if we can change ourselves or the way we behave in relation to certain others. This philosophy has enjoyed a long run, despite the absence of hard data to support it. PD is supported by a large body of evidence that shows if you change the hard realities of the relationships between people; e.g., from the supervisor/supervised to peer or collegial relations, their communications and the general ways in which they treat each other change dramatically. 'Human nature' is not the static, unchanging entity that we have been led to believe.

key learning

132.

Those change programs that have included this sort of exercise have generally been much longer and more expensive in terms of both resource and employee time and energy and many create their own problems during the course, some of which are sufficient to sink the project for once and for all. Don't complicate a simple tool with extraneous purposes and processes. They are dangerous in that people become suspicious as to what management or others are about and often resent what is being done to them in the name of better communication and democracy. Once there are conditions which make it in people's interests to communicate quickly and accurately, they will do so.

Half way houses or immature forms are also dangerous in that they can induce even deeper levels of cynicism. Such innovations as 'quality circles' in the western democracies have a poor track record in the longer term. They are only variations on the old suggestion box and show a similar life expectancy curve. If co-ordination and control are not, to some and an increasing extent, devolved to the people doing the work, any concept or process will fizzle out. This is the learning from history.

A genuine PD process will stress in all its aspects that it is evolutionary. Different groups will choose to start their learning about self management with varying levels of control. From their own chosen starting point, they will evolve at different rates showing irregularities that are analogous to the growth spurts seen in adolescence. These individual differences should be understood and respected by management, unions and workers in associated groups.

Individual versus Group Work

In this work as in all other it is necessary to practise what you preach. This means being open and democratic in all that you do and it also covers the ways in which you ask participants to work.

Several variations have been tried, for example, on filling in the matrix for the six criteria. Individuals have been given the six criteria on a sheet to fill in for themselves before the scores are shared and discussed with the group. Such an individualized approach is used for various reasons; a belief that some people may lack the confidence to put their scores up openly on the wall, will be influenced by others or be ashamed of their high or low scores. Once the individual has scored him/herself, the scores are then discussed. On one occasion, the rule was that an individual did not have to share or discuss their scores if they chose not to.

As this is usually an early part of the process the message it conveys is important. The individualized approach tells participants that it is still OK to behave as in a bureaucratic structure; i.e., work out your position before meeting the group, do not divulge your hand before getting the lay of the land and in the extreme case, claim your right to secrecy, or in other words, refuse to co-operate. These behaviours are the opposite of what is required for democratic working.

Compare the impression conveyed by the alternative practice of everyone sitting around the flip chart making various contributions of their own scores as they see them, their perceptions of other's scores, discussing and negotiating differences in perceptions, changing their scores if necessary and arriving collectively at a picture of how their workplace meets their needs, with an agreed set of relativities built into it. From the beginning the task is defined as a group task and one on which the group must work as group for a successful outcome; i.e., one which will serve as an accurate basis for the design work which follows. This approach features sharing within a context of openness, co-operation towards joint purposes and a positive emotional tone engendered by 'we're all in it together'. The notable characteristics of this include goodwill and good humour with jokes and quick quips designed to break down status barriers and offer an easy entry for those with less confidence. It is fun and group working gets off on the right foot while a great deal of learning about their workplace, about other's jobs and how they see them and about democratic group working, is accomplished.

Sanction, Safeguards and Support

Another lesson from this accumulated experience is what happens when an attempt is made to turn back to bureaucracy an organization which has functioned democratically. A similar set of phenomena are seen when promises to safeguard a democratic structure are broken or when the implementation of it is lacking in commitment or active sanction. There is a cluster of reactions which includes anger, disbelief and hurt, but the process of fighting to maintain what has been gained is conducted with dignity and respect until it becomes clear that the opposition must become implacable. When reasoning fails, the group assumption changes from work to fight/flight (Bion, 1959 and see Part IV) and in the current climate usually takes the form of passive resistance with a breakdown of commitment to the whole.

For some early sites the axe fell quickly and cleanly wielded by new managements brought in as a result of such moves as take-overs or retirements. It was simply announced that the change was to be reversed and 'normality' reinstated. What the boss giveth, the boss also taketh away. For these workers, particularly those in non unionized sites, there was no redress. The consequence of fighting the reversal was likely to be more serious in a time of rising unemployment than resuming bureaucratized work practices. As above, passive resistance and subtle sabotage may provide some short term satisfactions but these are debilitating and ultimately destructive options for most.

We have in our society plenty of people who would wittingly turn back the clock on democratic structures but more common is the failure to understand that the process of implementation requires leadership and active commitment from the beginning. Sanctioning from the top is accepted as a necessary precursor to a change but far too many bosses do not understand what is entailed and appear to really believe that if they issue a statement its substance will happen. Before democratization was centred in industrial relations and government policy, the top management of an individual firm or department was often the place where the buck stopped. Philosophy statements and policies were issued, workers were informed and change programs started. But when resistance to and outright sabotage of the changes began, there was no real action. Management's sanction did not include active intervention to prohibit or deal with the resistance and back the change and the process, therefore, was seen to be just another superficiality or attempt to solve problems without solving the problem. There were so many of those examples in the seventies that for this reason alone, ID got a bad name, lumped in with OD (organizational development or sensitivity training) as another thing to stay away from. But some well organized groups, sections and individuals survived to tell the tale. Many that were successful kept public silence but transmitted in other ways the need for appropriate sanctioning, safeguards and monitoring under the umbrella of an agreement signed in the arbitration and conciliation court. Projects beginning today within this framework are relatively free from the frustrations and disillusionment suffered in the past.

The Implications for Minorities

Most of the following is taken from various discussions of the consequences of democratization for women. This is no more than an historical accident as it is women who have been most organized and active in recent years to improve their status. There is little if any of it which does not apply in full measure to other minorities. The underlying philosophy of democratization is exactly the same as that of liberation or more narrowly EEO (equal employment opportunity) which it should be remembered covers Aborigines, ethnics and the handicapped as well as women.

What is this philosophy and what are its goals? Basically that people can function with and increase their dignity, expanding their range of choice in life and their personal resources to achieve human ends within an organizational environment which is designed by the people to fulfil their collective purposes and live with the consequences. The six psychological requirements are no more than a concrete statement of what is required for human dignity and well being. This includes a capacity to know of alternative ways of working and the environment in which they strive. If these are the aims of liberation and democratization, then there are serious questions to be asked of the means used to achieve them.

Unfortunately, many of the variations on both democratization and the implementation of EEO have and are mechanistic, giving lip service to the principles but denying them in the practice. This applies particularly when recipes or formulas are devised for giving a minorities a fair go but without the recipients having a say in the devising or the receipt. Mechanistic rules, for example, about the amount of time spent keyboarding were intended to prevent RSI and other injuries associated with keyboard and VDU work but as part of a process designed to increase control over one's work, they were counterproductive.

Many of the legislative and other formally imposed means for equality, equity etc have either been subverted by human ingenuity in the service of the status quo or have aroused backlashes even amongst those they were designed to help. But more seriously, the whole question of attitude and behavioural change appears to have been misconstrued. Pure consciousness raising does not appear to be the answer either. While there has been much of it and it has alerted people to possibilities other than their current circumstances, it has often been done without due regard for social environments and the means to change them. When there is a failure to turn humanitarian dreams into reality the dominant elites are alerted to the lack of means and can escalate their oppression. Attitude change by no means guarantees action based change.

Somehow we have to begin the long process of removing, for example, men's fears and hatred of women and white fears and hatred of blacks. History, let alone herstory, shows that these are not going to be achieved simply through legislation or other such direct means. There is a role for legislation but these fundamental changes can only come through processes in which people of all shapes and shades meet and get to know each other as peers around common purposes. Shared co-ordination and control are essential elements in the required structures and processes. And shared co-ordination and control can only be genuinely and constructively exercised in environments which are carefully structured to ensure their development and continuity; i.e., until it is taken for granted that democratic structures and environments are the normal form, that which meets basic human requirements.

As discussed above, there have been many attempts to adapt the basic PD workshop to better cater for groups perceived to be at some disadvantage such as low confidence, springing from their low status or membership in a deprived group. The problem with many of these attempts is that in their execution they only highlight and exacerbate the situation rather than taking a first constructive step towards redressing the balance. In a recent example, it was assumed that women would automatically be disadvantaged in working in a team setting with men. Therefore, the process must be one which secured an equal start. The changes made had the effect of both stratifying and individualizing it to the advantage of none (except the dedicated bureaucrats) while losing the opportunity of ensuring that right from the beginning, people would be learning that there was an alternative and simultaneously developing the qualities that had been stunted by their previous experiences.

Apart from the fact that the more one practises within a discriminatory structure under whatever guise, the more one reinforces that form of structure and its consequences, I wonder today about the wisdom of making the assumption that certain designated minorities will lack confidence, ability to speak up, etc. In the above example it became very clear that many of the 'oppressed' were not only willing to speak up for themselves but did so in no uncertain terms, showing deep insight and sophistication in both their analyses and presentations. They were probably disadvantaged by the changes designed to help them grow out of their lowly status.

Rather than generalize and label, why not try a process which in its very congruence and gentleness allows those who are coming from behind to catch up without being marked as special or different? There has been and is a discriminatory structure built into our society. Nothing less than a wholehearted effort to create structures for learning about the roots of the alternative, how it works and how it feels, will overcome these sources of discrimination. Today, the propensity to form support and action groups of various kinds is one kind of welcome backup for democratization. Another is simply the intuitive realization based on years of exposure, however indirect, that there has to be something else. Planting a small seed is often sufficient to show that this intuition was correct.

And it should always be remembered that while the minorities who are at the bottom of the heap are sometimes badly damaged by living and working within bureaucratic structures, this form of organization damages all it touches, from the bottom to the top. Even if this was not the case, liberation or democratization of a minority will always fail in the long term if it is not the liberation or democratization of all. To paraphrase one of Mao Tse-Tung's most powerful sayings: If you are 90 per cent sure you want to liberate women, you will concentrate your effort on women. If you are 100 per cent sure that you want to liberate women, you will liberate both men and women.

It then becomes clearer why well intentioned strategies such as separating off a particularly at-risk target group such as clerical and keyboard staff will create problems and in many ways deny or devalue the change as one for all people. All are parts of the whole and derive their identities (and stereotypes) from the interdependencies of which the whole is composed. The creation of in-groups and out-groups by any line or purpose of demarcation will continue to haunt a process long after its short term ostensible benefits have been gained. I am using a 1988 example which shows that many, particularly within the women's movement, have not learnt this lesson. Unfortunately we live in times where some, particularly those new to the exercise of power, do not consider it necessary to consult history.

At stake are a set of values and ideals that bureaucratic structures cannot nurture and which separatist movements only further downgrade. If we do really value people and are working towards a sane, humane, ecological (SHE) future (Robertson, 1978) we must provide the settings in which all have the opportunity to gain confidence, not only in their own capabilities and powers but also in those of others. Those at the bottom of the heap obviously have more unlearning to do, of their negative self images and lack of confidence and most to gain. Becoming the new bosses, however, cannot achieve the second objective of bringing together those who were separate. No amount of power and role reversal can achieve its genuine antithesis which is power sharing.

What is commonly not recognized about democratization is the phenomenon of very strong transfer effects from the original experience with participation in and responsibility for co-ordination and control. Because minorities have more room to grow they frequently change very rapidly and once such characteristics as self confidence begin to develop at this rate, there may constellations of changes which appear to others as a personality change.

This inevitably effects the nature of the web of relationships in which a developing individual is embedded. A person treated as and taking responsibility as an adult at work for example is not going to continue to put up with being treated as a child or second class citizen at home or in their community associations. Democratizing a work place may then have the side effect of precipitating a rash of divorces or near misses. This was the experience of the CCE after democratization began in March, 1973 and other organizations have reported similar incidences. Empowerment, the in word at the moment is a direct function of responsibility for co-ordination and control. Thus while the PD workshop is in its structure and process, uni-sex, it is in its effects strongly biased towards women and other minorities.

There are, however, phases and plateaus in every growth process. A common first phase after democratization is developing up to one's first limit or expectation, and then what? Many tend to stop there, satisfied with their achievement which creates a problem for others of their minority group who wish to go further. This limit is often the result of conditioning; a built in barrier to expectations. It is often only a state of rest and consolidation before growth is resumed. But it sometimes hides a deeper reality and one that is rarely discussed. Many women particularly who have had the opportunity to make it to the top have balked at doing it in the old system. To make it would have meant suppressing the system of ideals and values that have shaped their life and to which they steadfastly adhere. To join the rat race in earnest and show how good they are would mean putting others down in a vicious competitive system which is the opposite of everything they believe in and hope to see. At stake here are ends and means. Can people who believe in equality and co-operation achieve them by playing successfully in such a system as a bureaucracy? Many women say 'no'. They opt out, taking only what they materially and psychologically require, without changing their sights; believing that the bigger system will not change and to play it will only damage themselves and others; only further the system.

Others take a paradoxically similar but opposite line (the similarity lies in the fact that they accept that this bit has changed but that the larger system context won't easily). 'Once we're in there, we can change it to serve our value system. Once there is a majority of women in the top echelons, then you will see a change.' That remains a hypothesis. Some go hell bent to win against enormous odds, against the system; some win, some lose. Some do genuinely win and retain their identities, others take on the identity of the oppressor and become the new oppressors.

These consequences contain several lessons. The first is simply that if you wish to redress the power balance between the sexes or other oppressor/oppressed groups, going to the heart of the problem does work and has flow-ons which some may not consider desirable, but which do indicate, perhaps more powerfully than at the original site, that the problem is one of bureaucratized power.

The second lesson is that women and other minorities have rarely been so badly damaged by their learning in bureaucratic structures that they need specialized training in assertiveness, stress management, effective communication or democratic behaviour. In short, they do not need activities divorced from their normal flow of life activities to learn that they are human beings and how to behave as such. All they need is a fair opportunity. But if oppressed minorities are to remain in bureaucratized structures, then of course they will require these sorts of boosts to enable them to survive.

If we were really serious about a democratic society then our strategy would be to change the structures in all our institutions, particularly the 'educational' ones. A combination of the second educational paradigm plus PD at all levels would be a powerful preventative of the human and organizational realities that keep social scientists in work today.

References

Bion W 1959, *Experiences in Groups*, Tavistock, London. Emery F 1978, 'Youth - Vanguard, Victims or the New Vandals?', *Limits to Choice*, pp.4-32, Centre for Continuing Education, Australian National University, Canberra.

Emery F 1978, 'Youth—Vanguard, Victims or the New Vandals?' pp.4-32, *Limits to Choice*. Centre for Continuing Education, Australian National University, Canberra.

Emery M 1982, *Searching*, Centre for Continuing Education, Australian National University, Canberra.

Emery M 1988, 'Learning about the Unpredicted: The Case of Repetition Strain Injury (RSI)', *Studies in Continuing Education*, 10 1 pp.30-45.

Robertson James 1978, *The Sane Alternative*, River Basin Publishing Co, Minnesota, USA.

The Differences Between STS and Participative Design (PD)

Merrelyn Emery

THERE ARE TWO major competing methods for changing an organization from one designed on the first principle, redundancy of parts, to one designed on the second principle, redundancy of functions. Both of these methods as they are practised today are offspring of the original theory and method of sociotechnical systems (STS), analysis and design. (Emery F, 1959, 1978)

While both are offspring, STS looks very like its parent. Participative Design is an adaptive mutation, adapted to today's environment.

A Sociotechnical System (STS) is Simply That.

There is today a confusion about what 'socio-technical' means. The name was coined in 1949 to describe a new unit of analysis. Rather than separate analyses of the social structure and the technology, the new approach examined both and the relationships between them as a system in its own right.

A section of one of our old production lines with a person with a narrow, unskilled set of actions at every station and a section supervisor carrying responsibility for control and coordination of the section is a sociotechnical entity. It is a sociotechnical system built on the first design principle. 'STS' does not imply any particular form of organization.

Therefore, 'STS' as it is sometimes used today to imply a design principle 2 or democratic structure only causes confusion. It destroys the concept of a unit of analysis by specifing a type, thereby removing a useful tool for the analysis of organizations. Worse than that, it avoids identification of the basic determinants, the genotypical characteristics, of a particular sociotechnical system, namely, the design principles.

Source of the Confusion

The confusion arises because as the study of sociotechnical systems progressed, it became apparent that if the enterprise goals were to include high productivity and quality, low wastage, sickness and absenteeism etc, there had to be a form of work organization suitable for human beings. (Trist and Bamforth, 1959) Psychological and physical health in and commitment to the workplace were found to flow from a congruence between the social and technological systems. The principle was joint optimization of social and technological. (Emery F as above)

When the principle of joint optimization is applied to a sociotechnical system, it becomes necessary to take into account not only the traditional economic and technological criteria for measuring organizational well being but also a third set, the human criteria. The example given above of a Design Principle 1 sociotechnical system is one in which the principle of joint optimization does not apply. When this type of sociotechnical system is analysed in terms of the six human criteria, as they are in a PD workshop, they are usually found lacking.

The History of STS in the USA

Lou Davis is the father of STS in the USA. He was apprenticed to the Tavistock team in the early days when a great mass of experimentation with different forms of work was occuring and the method was itself was evolving. It was the long detailed, expert performed and experimental method that Davis took back to UCLA.

All of that was necessary in the experimental phase so that there could be high confidence in the scientific reliability and validity of the results. But the experimental phase finished with the Norwegian National Industrial Democracy Project.

Over time in the USA, that old method has been somewhat refined. It is however, basically the same arduous, expert based procedure as it was in the 50s and 60s. The experts have changed. Rather than the social scientists of the 60s, they are now an organizational or divisional 'design team' trained up to collect the data, do the analyses and provide the redesigns for the organization or division. The process is still heavily dependent on consulting academics and practitioners.

A brief history of sociotechnical systems analysis and redesign in the context of the shift in Australia to Participative Design is given in the 1989 introduction. The confusion today about what 'sociotechnical' means is a result of not knowing the history.

Critical Methodological Differences Between STS and PD

The table (opposite) summarizes the key differences between STS as it practised in the USA today and PD.

1. **Two Meanings of Expert.** The first two points describe the expert dimension of STS as opposed to the participative nature of PD. THE

Critical Methodological Differences Between Sociotechnical System and Participative Design

STS

PD

Two Meanings of Expert

STS	PD
Design team selected for whole division, etc.	Each small section designs itself.
Therefore, design imposed on many	No imposition. Designs incorporate individual wishes

Conscious Knowledge

STS	PD
Design team not given simple visual concepts of design principles based on responsibility for co-ordination and control	All are given these conceptual tools and their consequences. Presentation takes 30 mins
Therefore, design principles never consciously understood	Design principles consciously understood, used and available for future change
Therefore, can end up with an unworkable mixture of principles, such as TLC	End up with clean, lean structure of responsibility

Process

STS	PD
Design team trained in long series of steps, including matrix of variances; can take months	All given 2 simple tools (6 criteria and skills matrix) to analyse current organization; takes 90 mins
Process of analysis and redesign takes months or years	Analysis and redesign takes a day

Frank Heckman – A. Anderson redesigned unit in 3 days

Diffusion and Cost

STS	PD
Supervisors not necessarily involved in redesigning their futures	Supervisors involved with workers and management from beginning
Therefore, sometimes less than optimum solution and bad feeling	Most optimum solution for all
Total process of years	Total process of weeks
Very little diffusion	Enthusiastic, extensive diffusion

design team in STS plays the same role as did the outside experts. Part of the design team's role, because they are separate from the rest, is to attempt to sell their redesigns. Even if they are bought, they are seen as imposed with all the problems of subtle resistance this raises. In PD however, all of the workers are the experts as nobody from the outside can have the same intimate and detailed knowledge of a given workplace. The process results in a collectively agreed solution which is less likely to generate resistance.

2. Concepts / Design Principles.

The next two points address the central role of conscious understanding of the design principles. An Australian manager whose factory was currently going through STS said that the design team couldn't explain what they were doing. They had no basic concepts, only a superficial and hazy impression of what the steps were supposed to do. They were frustrated with having to follow the detailed process because they knew all about the variances anyway. In addition, they could not see a clear relation between the process, the rationale and the goals.

In the PD workshop, the design principles are given upfront with their associated structural building blocks. There is never any doubt about the choices involved or what they mean. The tools provided relate explicitly to the design principles.

There is a danger for those who even successfully complete the STS process in that although they may end up with a design principle 2 organization, they won't really recognize it or know why. This imparts a degree of vulnerability to their redesign. If they can't explain it clearly and simply in terms of its motivation and rationale, they will be subject to the changing whims and fortunes of others who can use conceptual arguments and who are more powerful and articulate than themselves.

More immediately, however, they are likely to compromise with a resulting mixture of design principles, a solution that simply will not work in practice. At the moment, we have a rash of such designs utilizing the concept of TLC—a supervisor behaving as trainer, leader and coach. (see paper herein)

3. Process.

The STS design team must firstly be trained in the method. It involves a long process of detailed and precise steps drawn from industrial engineering and social science. It is an elaborate research task.

When the research is complete, the design team must then use the results to carefully balance (jointly optimize) the social or human resources with the technology towards the enterprise goals. It is a demanding task and one for which most workers have little training or patience, given all the above. A lot of STS projects fail before completion.

The evolution of PD has shown that once people understand the design principles and their consequences, and are shown some quick and simple tools of analysis, they just get on with it because they want to. Most Australian workers jump at the chance of resdesigning for a structure in which they can work as responsible adults. Detailed quantitative phenotypical analyses and matrices of variances are irrelevant when the essentials of design are grasped. The essences, the design principles and their associated structural building blocks are so simple that a collectively optimum and adaptive design can be done in a day.

4. Diffusion and Cost.

In terms of short term economics, STS compares badly with PD. It is long and chews up time off the job. In the long term it compares even less well, particularly when the frustrations and probability of failure are taken into account. What is the cost of coming up with a design that will not work in practice? What is the cost of offering redundancy packages to supervisors without adequately exploring other solutions? There are a host of such questions.

What is the cost of the uncertainty engendered by workers not knowing how the process will finally affect their jobs? Of them not being directly involved in the design process? Uncertainty, insecurity and alienation are frequently and inversely correlated with productivity. Staff with these characteristics do not comprise a solid foundation for confidence in the future of the enterprise.

And what of the multiplier effect? Diffusion requires two things, a conscious knowledge of the substance, the concepts and methods and a strong affectual or emotional component. Excitement and joy are the drivers of diffusion. (Emery M, 1986) Workers who are not enthusiastically involved in making change and who cannot articulate what its about are not going to diffuse the concepts or the process.

The following comments come from North Americans who attended the 1991 STS Roundtable meeting in San Fransisco.

Reflecting on more than ten years STS consulting I feel that while it is an excellent tool for new plant design it is actually an impediment to organizational change...We achieved no permanent fundamental structural change as a result of STS, even though some corporations entered into prolonged and detailed STS.

They (managers) soon came to the conclusion that the time needed was so expensive that it seriously threatened their short term goals.

As a consultant who has witnessed groups get bogged down in variance analysis, I want to learn about Participative Design.

The Adaptive Dimension

STS and PD share the goal of genotypical structural change. They differ in some critical methodological ways which amount to different relationships with the environment.

In almost all industrialized countries now, the race to change is on. Amongst populations at large, the degree of awareness of what that change means and entails varies. Many are aware that it involves significant value shifts and extensive structural change, macro and micro. Many are aware that the future of our national economic health depends on it and that time is short.

There is a deeper level of environmental trend however, and that entails people demanding greater control of their lives. They are demanding both knowledge and the right to make decisions about the different aspects of their lives, including their futures in the workplace. In brief they are demanding participative democracy following the logic of design principle 2.

While the proponents of STS and PD agree that the ends embody design principle 2, the means they advocate are differently related to the ends they pursue. There is an incongruence in the relationship of STS means and ends. The STS process involves a representative selection process (Design Principle 1) with consequent problems reminiscent of the political process.

PD set its sails on total congruence from the beginning. Every stage of the process follows design principle 2. Given the nature of a Type IV environment which is characterized by relevant uncertainty, only a method which locates responsibility for design with those who have to make it work will meet the demand for participative democracy and thereby reduce the uncertainty. A disjunction between means and ends can only foster uncertainty and symptoms of maladaption such as cynicism and dissociation.

In today's world with its much greater awareness of and desire for human dignity through decision making, conscious knowledge of the design principles and the six criteria which are consequent upon applying design principle 2, take centre stage. Once these are grasped and under the control of those doing the design, we have a totally open method, the basis for commitment and responsibility to improve the economic and technological subsystems leading to systemic change of the entire enterprise.

STS with its reliance on a representative process, quasi-experts and 'consultation' is an appropriate method for a Type III environment. It is a Type III method is a Type IV world.

It is this overriding characteristic which helps to produce the more negative results of STS, its slowness, costs and its doubtful ability to produce spontaneous diffusion. These are signs that it is not maximizing commitment, productivity and conscious, available and conceptual knowledge of the fundamental nature of the change.

On all these counts, STS is yesterday's method. Today we don't need a hangover from the experimental past, we need action and change on the ground with a commitment to it from an educated population.

References

Emery F E. 'Characteristics of Socio-technical Systems'. 1959. Reading Four (pp 38- 86) of Emery Fred. *The Emergence of a New Paradigm of Work*. 1978. Centre for Continuing Education Australian National University.

Emery M. 1986. 'Towards an Heuristic Theory of Diffusion'. *Human Relations* 39.5. 411-432.

Trist E L and K W Bamforth. 1951. 'Social and Psychological Consequences of the Longwall Method of Coal Getting'. *Human Relations*. IV 1 3-38.

The Concept of TLC—Trainer, Leader, Coach

Merrelyn Emery, July 1992

ONE OF THE DISTURBING features of the new wave is the increasing trend towards trying to change the role of supervisor to that of 'trainer, leader and coach'. It is easy to see the superficial attractions of this approach as it appears to offer the learning organization and increased productivity without having to change the bureaucratic structure.

What it really shows is that understanding of the design principles has not kept pace with the rush to make change. Once the design principles and their implications are understood, the idea of a TLC makes no sense whatsoever. The design principles cannot be mixed.

If an organization is structured according to the second principle, redundancy of functions, and a group responsible for its own management decides in some situations to delegate responsibility for control or co-ordination to one of its members, then that is their own legitimate concern. It shows that design principle 2 may at times include a design principle 1 operational structure. But as this power of delegation of responsibility is still held by the group, the organization remains one of redundancy of functions.

When an organization is structured according to the first design principle, redundancy of parts, with roles and responsibilities enshrined in individual duty statements and job specifications, then these are the legal and binding agreements. Regardless of informal arrangements, communications and other training of supervizors and changing their name and role to TLC, their binding responsibilities for coordination and control of the level of operation below them remain intact.

The logic of this is simply that while a design principle 2 structure may contain elements of design principle 1, the reverse cannot hold. (Herbst, 1990) The concept of TLC is, therefore, a nonsense. It sounds pretty but does nothing to change the structure to one in which people are genuinely working as responsible, self managing adults. It is only by changing the design principle that the conditions for continuing learning and the productivity accruing from dignity, respect and creativity can be instituted and sustained.

Let me illustrate this with a recent example.

A large company has devoted significant resources to explicitly securing a 'learning organization'. One of the approaches tried was a corruption of the Participative Design Workshop involving the concept of the transition of the supervizor (S1) to Trainer, Leader and Coach. (TLC)

The initial motivation of the Steering Committee overlooking organizational development sprang from a belief that the workforce was not 'ready' to move to self managing groups and that there must be a way of bringing them up to scratch and easing them into it gently.

While some sections of the organization were clearly told that the transition of S1 to TLC was merely a step along the way to self management, others developed the idea that the one and only transition to be effected was that of S1 → TLC. The resulting confusion of course caused problems of its own. This was not helped by the overheads developed by some of the internal change agents. These showed the traditional diagrams of Design Principle 1 and 2 organizational modules but with the self managing group having a position above. The only difference shown then by the Design Principle 1 and 2 modules was that in the first, people were drawn as individuals with an S1 while in the second, they were drawn as a group with a TLC.

Because this is recommended by some prestigious consultants, no thought had been given to the practical consequences of introducing such a distortion. Nor did those advocating this approach warn of any of the quite predictable contradictions and problems involved. Much time and money had been spent on training to turn the S1s into TLCs.

The practical problems appeared immediately after implementation began. During a meeting of managers from one part of the organization, one after another of the managers reported various forms of standoff and disaffection between the so called self managing groups and their TLCs. Even the managers who were in favour of retaining the concept of TLCs reported increasing problems.

I also attended a meeting of a so called self managing group whose implementation began on 6 April. I met with them in the afternoon of 18 June after they had spent most of the day evaluating their experience and judging the situation to be untenable. All of the problems were documented and they bore no ill against their TLC, wishing instead to protect her from having to expose and report on the unworkability of the design.

Just a few moments analysis shows that the notion of TLC involves two problems:

Problem 1

The roles of leaders and trainers or teachers are quite different, to say nothing about the role of a 'coach'. The skills and behaviours required of them are quite different and in some instances would be in conflict. To have all of these rolled into the one person at the same time is clearly a source of confusion and unfulfilled expectations.

Problem 2

The concept of TLC induces a crisis of responsibility. A self managing group is clearly told that it is responsible for its own coordination, control and outputs. But the ex- S1, TLC placed as either 'team leader', coach or trainer, is just as clearly still in a higher level of the hierarchy or placed in a position of responsibility *for the team*. **Who then is responsible?**

These problems were perceived by those put into the position of this pseudo self management. Different managers had variously communicated to either TLCs or the groups creating further confusion and generally getting people's backs up. Workers who believed they had been constituted as responsible self managing groups felt betrayed when managers communicated only with TLCs. Despite all the training and encouragement to be warm fuzzies, some TLCs realized they still had responsibility for the groups and continued behaving like S1s. Communications handed down to TLCs were selectively not being passed on just as happens in a usual bureaucratic structure. They and their like minded managers worked to discourage further moves towards self management.

In the Participative Design workshop we ran for this organization with four teams, the workers and TLCs had as usual, no problems dealing with clear, accurate explanations of Design Principle 1 and 2. Not did they have any problems designing workable Design Principle 2 solutions. Recognizing the experience carried by TLCs, they designed structures using genuinely self managing groups with self managing groups of previous TLCs as resources.

They thus created group to group relationships of symmetrical dependence between different levels of a functional hierarchy rather than continuing the one to one relation of asymmetrical dominance of an S1 to subordinate or the utter confusion of a TLC to a so called self managing group.

This example highlights one of the critical differences between introducing change through the PD workshop and other more diffuse methods. The PD workshop specifically includes a third part in which the groups go back over their skills matrix to determine and make explicit the training required to make their design work. These requirements may range from nil to a few needing only informal training on the job to some involving external formal courses.

This sequence of arriving at the best design followed by spelling out their various training requirements leaves the group in control of future training. Training on the job which in many cases is no more than experienced members providing greater experience of some tasks for other members makes it clear that no one person in the group or section has all the experience, knowledge or expertise in training to be the 'trainer'.

If education or training off the job is required, the group simply goes to management with its analysis and negotiates the schedule for that.

Without these steps, it is easy to look at a design and simply say that training is required, particularly so if the design process has been under the control of a manager or a consultant. This automatically leads to the conclusion that 'the workers are not ready for self management' which further leads to the need for a 'trainer', leader or coach. Such externally based designs and perceptions, and even PD workshops which finish with the design rather than the third stage of working through the requirements raised by the design, leave the loophole into which the the concept of TLC may be plugged.

When the full working through of the design and its implications remain under the control of the group, such a concept never arises.

In reporting my experiences and discussing these issues with managers and the Steering Committee, I recommended that in pursuing their vision and values they should not attempt to introduce TLCs into other parts of the organization. I explained that what I had seen in other sections was a workforce who was more than ready and willing to be responsibly self managing. It then became clear that the concept of TLC had been seen by some as a way of avoiding the hard work of genuine democratization towards a 'learning organization'. Some admitted they could not even conceive of an organization without supervizors. This is, of course, a result of the belief that oneself is the only responsible human in the world. In management circles it translates into the belief that workers are by definition irresponsible and must come under constant supervision.

But as workers know themselves to be responsible, we have here the foundation of the 'them and us' syndrome. This is accentuated when workers have been fully trained and many in this organization had been. Today's workforce is increasingly well educated and sophisticated in analysis of social systems. It is common for them to express their perception of the discrepancy between being treated as responsible adults in their family and community life and as children at work. Renaming S1s as TLCs does nothing to bridge this gap.

The concept of TLC is nothing more than a modern version of the old *Human Relations* theory. It does not address the fundamental structural changes which bring learning, responsible adult behaviour and productivity. It is a con because it pretends to be something which it is not and to deliver something which it can't.

This is certainly not the first time the concept of TLC has been criticized or found not to work. It is fashionable today to advocate or at least turn a blind eye to advocacy of the concept of TLCs. But those who do this should be aware that such behaviour is detrimental to the people involved, the organization and the community which hopes for the most efficient and effective path to productive workplaces in which people can learn and grow.

Reference

Herbst David P. 'The Battle of Design Principles'. pp258-268 of Felix Frei and Invars Udris (Eds). *Das Bild der Arbeit*. 1990. Verlag Hans Huber.

Human Resources Management

Fred Emery, July 1990

Much more efficient use must be made of this country's resources—above all its human resources, which up to now, as everyone knows, have been scandalously underemployed.

It will be the task of any modern Government to ensure that the human plant available is thoroughly modernized, by :

   (i)   introducing more competition into the people market.

   (ii)   insisting that human beings are operated on a strict cost efficiency basis.

   (iii)   getting the maximum output from each unit, consistent with proper servicing and repairs.

   (iv)   making provision for early scrapping and replacement as new models come into production.

Mankind represents an enormous reservoir of potential wealth, which has never been fully exploited up to now.

IF YOU THOUGHT that this statement on human resources emanated from one of today's hard headed gurus of Human Resources Management you could be forgiven. If you sensed that it was a put down you would be quite correct. The words were penned by the arch English satirist, Michael Frayn, in his column in the Guardian, 20th March 1966. Frayn was satirizing the systems theorists who were planning for a man on the moon and believed that their techniques would solve the social problems of efficiently mobilizing human resources. To fit human resources into their mathematical models, the planners had to reduce the qualities of those resources to a common dollar measure. Thus human resources entered their models as costs for recruitment from the market, training, maintenance and replacement. Their morale, creativity and co-operativeness were not representable in the models except possibly as estimated costs of labour turnover, absenteeism, time and materials wasted on the job.

As we enter the 1990's we seem to have come full circle to once again thinking of human resources as we would think of mineral, financial or technical resources. I suggest that we are misguided if we accept this appearance at face value. Over a period that reaches back to well before the 1960's managers have come to realize that human resources are mere potential unless those humans accept some personal commitment to the achievement of the objectives of their employer. It has also been recognized that contractual deals relating pay, perks and promotion to level of commitment are next to worthless when it gets down to the day to day realities of working life. It is at that day to day level where people form judgments about whether their contribution is valued and their efforts respected.

The history of bureaucracy and traditional labour management proves that 'reliable systems can be made from unreliable parts'. Well, fairly reliable, and only if the parts are so cheap and easily replaceable that high levels of wastage are tolerable.

If an enterprise for its purposes, needs human resources that are expensive and not easily replaceable then it needs reliable people, and such an organization cannot afford to go down the traditional track of people management. Reliable people in this context are people who can be relied upon not just because of the skills and knowledge that they can bring to bear but because of their personal commitment to seeing that jobs get done properly and efficiently. This principle is simple and straight forward. Translation of this principle into organizational practice requires two steps (at least):

° personal commitment has to be created,

° the person has to know what jobs are important, at what times.

I think we know some of the solutions to making the first step.

However, we should perhaps first review our hard earned knowledge of 'solutions' that have proven useless. When we are talking about the sort of personal commitment that carries over to the daily activity in the workplace then we can place into the waste basket such things as exhortations and glossy communications from on high, profit sharing and advisory bodies such as joint consultative committees and Works Councils. Schemes for worker representatives on corporate boards deserve a special place near the bottom of the waste basket. These things might all serve to convey messages about togetherness or mutual distrust but they neither create nor sustain personal commitment on the job.

In ordinary circumstances people will take responsibility for seeing through to completion courses of action that they have chosen, or have had a significant say in choosing. If pressured to pursue a course of action of someone else's choosing they will seek the easiest way of appearing to meet the other's demands, or some excuse for not being able to do so. The obvious solution to creating committed employees is to involve them,as far as is possible, in the setting of task goals and in deciding the courses of action. This is quite a radical way in which to approach the design of jobs. It is diametrically opposed to the principle of locating goal setting and decision making at least one level above that of the 'doers' (which must be done to make a 'reliable system from unreliable parts').

The second step bridges the gap between theory (principles) and the concrete organization. This step places the principles in the context of the enterprise that maintains special forms of interdependence with particular parts of its environment by organizing the activity of particular kinds of people around particular material means and inputs. Only 'open sociotechnical systems' theory provides a systematic way of defining this sort of context and hence of placing 'human resources management' into a practical context. Sociotechnical systems can be studied from their economic and political aspects but such studies cannot encompass the concrete realities of substantive sociotechnical systems. The social and technical systems can be considered separately if our prime concern is with some or other of their subsystems, e.g. a grievance procedure or a boiler house. It is, however, only in consideration of how we can achieve joint optimization of the directively correlated sociotechnical system that we can decide what tasks have to be carried out, in what order and with what priorities.

What I am saying is that 'human resources management' is a subclass of the problem of co-ordinating social and technical systems to yield viable productive enterprises (or, as the military prefer, 'viable destructive enterprises'). By implication 'human resources management' cannot be subsumed as 'just economics', 'just politics' or 'just psychology'.

The Management of Self-Managing Groups

Fred Emery, November 1989

THIS TITLE IS NOT MEANT as an oxymoronic play on words to disparage either the notion of management or of self managing work groups. The title is meant to remind us that even if responsibility for co-ordination and control of workface activities is largely vested in the workface operators there are still the problems of managing the support and renewal of these groups and their relation to corporate objectives. In this context 'corporate objectives' should not be thought of as simply goals devised by top management to suit their whims. Corporate objectives reflect the multiple external relations that must be sustained if the corporate body is to survive, let alone grow.

It might be thought that existing management structures and practices can readily cope with the management of a workforce that is organized as self managing groups. An argument along these lines would be that each group could be regarded as equivalent to an individual in the traditional bureaucratic organization. If that were so then all that would be needed is close observance, by managers, of good 'Human Relations/Human Resources' practices. I will argue that that is not so.

First, the shift to SMGs (self managing groups) radically changes the content of the management task and the *amount* of managing that is required.

Second, the relation between a manager and an SMG cannot be properly described as being a superordinate -subordinate relation.

Third, the tasks of management cannot be effectively conducted in superordinate- subordinate relations between managers. *"leodership"*

I will expand on each of these three points.

The change in management's tasks can best be appreciated by comparing these with those required by the modern bureaucratic form of organization. (The traditional bureaucracies were typically civil services. The administrative systems they evolved were less visible than the practices of secured tenure and organizational loyalty by which they sought to insulate themselves from external influences. However, the so called management sciences are no more than the systematization of the bureaucratic administrative principles.)

The 'system principle' of bureaucratic organization is that 'decisions about co-ordination are made at least one level above that at which the tasks are carried out'. Only by following this principle is it possible to isolate, for overseeing and evaluation, the work of each and every individual and thus control the work performance of the individual. At each level in the bureaucratic organization including the managerial levels, the same principle is followed. At each level there is always some individual with designated responsibility for supervising what is actually being done by subordinates. This work of supervision is the necessary work of bureaucratic management, and for a great many managers, their main work.

In government departments and in statutory bodies, it is easy to live with the demands of supervisory work because they live in a relatively slowly changing environment defined by law and official regulations. In a very real sense, the only work they can find to justify their jobs is that of turning inwards to check what their subordinates are up to. The only external matters that they have to watch are the influences on their political masters and the top civil servants make sure that this is no concern of their subordinates.

In private enterprises on the other hand, there is constant tension between the demands of the supervisory task and the demands of the 'boundary riding' task. This latter task is that of watching the changing relations between the organization and its environment and planning for the maintenance or adaptation of those relations. Private enterprises are, by comparison, highly exposed by their competitive environments. If these environments start to change rapidly and in unexpected ways, then it becomes harder to justify the costs and sluggishness of the bureaucratic form of organization. As private enterprises grew to corporate size at the turn of the century they adopted bureaucratic forms of organization (Chandler,1977). These private bureaucracies burgeoned with the emergence of increasing numbers of staff functions and then the move to divisional forms, with each division wanting its own staff.

Middle management in the corporations could sometimes almost, but not quite, achieve the remoteness from external realities that was built into civil service roles. By the middle of the nineteen sixties it was obvious that the corporate environment was becoming increasingly turbulent and corporate management started to live with almost constant organizational restructuring.(By the mid seventies 'organizational restructuring' had become a standard managerial response to any problem). It became obvious that the primary task of senior management was boundary management. Having to manage internal problems was a diversion from their primary task. Even middle managers found that their primary service to their departments was in watching both the organizational environments and their seniors so that they could anticipate the next restructuring. But at all levels the managers had to find time to co-ordinate the activities of their subordinates in order to maintain internal control. Typically this work absorbs more of their time than does their primary task.

With the shift to self managing groups, depending on the conceptual demands of the work, the amount of work to be performed by middle managers is radically reduced and their remaining tasks become more demanding. Effective management probably requires only a third to one half the number of middle management positions required by the bureaucratic system.

The demands on the remaining middle managers also change. They have to be able to plan their own department's work for a much larger time span, and they have to be able to contribute to fire fighting or troubleshooting in many departments other than their own.

The time span of middle management must increase with the extension of the time span of planning at the workface. With the introduction of group working the latter typically increases from a few hours to a weekly span. Operational plans have also to be more explicit and more detailed with respect to all of the parameters that effect group working e.g. supplies, maintenance, storage, feedback of results, staff levels. So long as middle management could work through experienced supervisors it was often enough to give the senior supervisor a general idea of targets and guidelines and let them get on with the job. This is far too sloppy when negotiating agreements to explicit and detailed plans is the major tool for relating group work to corporate goals.

The 'trouble shooting' requirement arises from the fact that the amount of work required for even this more demanding planning will rarely warrant the appointment of one middle manager for each department. To justify middle management appointments the appointees must be deployable to assist with temporary management crises wherever they occur in the enterprise. Their spare time, when pooled, becomes a valuable reserve force for higher management.

The second change noted above, is that the relation between management and workers is no longer properly described as a super- subordinate relation. The relation is more complemental in the very real sense that both parties accept that the sufficient conditions for changes in organizational goals or procedures may proceed from either party, depending on the particular circumstances. The key to this change is that middle managers cannot, with the aid of their supervisors, narrow challenges to their judgement down to individuals. They are confronted by the considered judgement of groups whose members have practical, up to date experience of what they are talking about. Individuals may not be consistently strong on logic but a process of challenge and discussion within a group means that the group can arrive at a consensus on the correct logical deduction. Managers will ignore this at their peril. Taken as a complement to management's analysis of the situation it greatly enhances the chances for adaptive action.

Management of this complemental relation requires leadership on the part of the middle managers. It is not enough to hand down orders and instructions as if 'to the manner born'. It is not enough to try to blind the workforce with science and figures. Middle management must negotiate targets and plans with the work groups and re-negotiate them when unforeseen contingencies disrupt those plans. In all of these negotiations the middle managers have to give credence to the greater knowledge that the work groups have of the ongoing work but must, when necessary, be able to lead those groups to see the logic of the over riding plans and objectives of management. Middle managers must exercise this leadership in a face to face context if the corporate objectives are to prevail over the run of negotiated agreements with the work groups.

Introducing a term like 'leadership' is almost an open invitation to slack thinking because it defies strict definition. However, when a situation demands leadership we can be painfully aware of its absence. Thus, analysis of World War II records makes it very clear that the American Army was painfully deficient in leadership at the lower officer levels compared with the Wehrmacht (van Creveldt,1982). What calls for leadership in the new work situation is the necessity to keep the complemental aspect of the management worker relation to the fore whilst ensuring that corporate objectives are attained. A middle manager displays a lack of leadership if he sacrifices the latter in order to avoid arguments. Equally, a lack of leadership is indicated if a middle manager thinks that every argument has to be won, not just that in the run of arguments the corporate objectives must prevail (even if the corporation, not the middle manager, has to change its objectives!).

Lack of leadership would also be indicated if the manager failed to provide support e.g. supplies, maintenance, training, personnel help, when the need could have been foreseen. Finally, we would expect to find a lack of leadership if a group that was on a learning curve plateaued out for no good technical reason. As we have indicated, leadership is like justice, hard to define positively but very easy to identify in its absence.

In the case of leadership it may be because leadership comes in so many different shapes and sizes. Only a couple of features seem to show up all the time (almost all !) in leadership behaviour. The leader is credited with having a bigger picture that makes sense of the picture the group are working to, the leader is credited with more than average commitment to a mission they subscribe to and that the leader accepts that their relation is one of mutual dependency.

We are not concerned here with charismatic leadership nor with the selection of people 'born to lead'. Our concerns are much more down to earth. When a work group is locked into their immediate tasks, managers in their leadership role, have to remind them of the broader context within which their efforts will be judged. Safety is one such matter, as in group working individuals are known to voluntarily take risks that they would not take if they were working on their own. Whilst the work group may relax a bit and take things easy after achieving some immediate goal, the managers must be planning the resources and targets for the next stages.

If some individual seems to be exploiting the goodwill and tolerance of the group or, conversely, the group seems to be unfairly dealing with some individual, then the managers must find some way of reminding the group of their mutual dependency and the standards of conduct that that demands. If managers shrug it off, let slip or turn a blind eye in these kinds of situations there is a failure of leadership, the managers are failing in their duty to actively represent to the work group the constraints and requirements of their broader organizational context. If managers fail in these matters one can expect a work group to quickly perceive that fact and then to withdraw its own commitment to pursuit of organizational goals. In my experience, work group in this situation do not regress but tend to freeze at the levels of performance that they have attained and ignore opportunities for further improvement.

Where and how are organizations to find or create such leadership qualities ? MBA programs do not produce these qualities and standard managerial selection procedures do not select for them. Some Japanese corporations have innovative procedures for selecting managers with leadership qualities but the Bushido code that they conform to is incompatible with the challenges we are discussing.

Modern armies have come to realize that they need to select, train and promote officers for their leadership qualities. Industry now confronts the same demands. Unfortunately, most armies have been so hidebound by traditions and social statuses that they have solved few of the problems.

The British Army was confronted with this problem after its losses at Dunkirk and the need to vastly expand its forces. The 'leaderless group' selection procedure and 'regimental nomination' were devised to meet their need. (Wilson, 1951) The former procedure was subsequently adopted by the British Civil Service for entry into its general administrator grade.

These measures do not seem to go far enough.

It seems more likely that we will have to consider the practice of the Wehrmacht and the Norwegian Merchant Marine, selection through initial service at the workface. This is not to suggest that future managers should first wear a hair shirt or undergo the humiliating and demeaning experiences usually dished out to potential officers of navies and armies. Initial participation at the workface will do little unless it is participation in self managing work groups. In such work settings we are able to see how an individual meets the conceptual challenges involved in multiskilling which includes the tasks of co-ordination usually associated with first line supervision. It also enables us to see if the person is able to effectively exercise personal leadership in the group. The persons themselves can get a feel for whether they are cut out for managerial roles all with financial gain, not cost, to the individual or the organization ! When an organization then commits itself to financially support education for the transition to management, it knows that it is putting its money on a likely winner.

Special entry paths will always be necessary for some specialists but this seem the way in which we can best identify people who can contribute to managing in a way that will itself become more collegiate in form.

References

Chandler A D 1977. The Visible Hand: *The Managerial Revolution in American Business*. Belknap, Cambridge, Mass.

Creveldt M. van. 1982. *Fighting Power: German and US Army Performance, 1939-45*. Greenwood, Westport, CT.

Wilson A T M 1951 (Nov) "Some aspects of social process". *J of Social Issues*.

Management by Objectives

Fred Emery, October 1990

IN THE NOTE on 'management of self managing groups' I stressed the central role of 'management by objectives'. To those who have followed the history of theories of management this must have seemed a conclusion arrived at in ignorance or despair.

When Peter Drucker spelt out the concept of management by objectives in 1954 it was widely acclaimed. It was an obviously sensible idea .It provided the much needed contrast of the different levels co-operating in the 'management of things' to the traditional, supervisory centred, notions of the 'management of people'. Drucker's notion suggested ways in which the value of a manager to a corporation could be judged in fairly objective ways instead of being judged by how he or she played up to and appeared in the eyes of their boss. It was a proposal that offered a considerable increase in the self control of managers.

MBO (Management by Objectives) was enthusiastically adopted by the major corporations. By 1970 it was being seen as a waning fad (Levinson, 1970). Critics were not denying that it was a splendid way to run a business but they were pointing out that it was incompatible with the bureaucratic form of organization. Attempts to graft MBO onto bureaucracies either failed outright or evolved into a personnel control mechanism for rewarding or punishing managers- a sort of Taylorism for managers.

The reason is simple and fundamental. Objectives can be meaningfully formulated only at the level to which activities are co-ordinated and controlled. The 'system principle' of bureaucracy is that co-ordination and control are located. as far as possible, at least one level above that at which the work is done. Thus, in a well organized bureaucracy, the only objectives a manager can be personally responsible for are those relating to the activities of his or her subordinates. The objectives of the activity of that manager are in turn the responsibility of his or her superior, not the managers. How the superior decides to co-ordinate that manager's work with that of the other managers similarly reporting is the superior's business, not the managers. It is also the superior's prerogative to decide what the subordinates do, how much, by when and to what standards. In this setting MBO simply means that each manager has to be more explicit about the work he or she plans to get from subordinates. The superior then resets the plans as an explicit statement of the controls under which the subordinate manager will perform. The superior goes through the same process with his or her superior.

When a bureaucracy has completed the process of installing MBO the basic dynamics are unchanged. Each individual's activity is a pawn in some superior's objectives. Individual managers have objectives for getting work from subordinates but only job specifications for themselves. What has changed is the harshness of the climate as MBO naturally gives greater weight to the 'bottom line' and other such measurable outcomes.

This increase in harshness might be justified if the introduction of MBO could be relied upon to yield something of the increase in efficiency that Drucker wrote about. It should be remembered that Drucker based his case on the assumption that the objectives would be appropriate and timely for the business the organization is in. It is difficult if not impossible for a bureaucracy to determine objectives that were 'appropriate and timely'. MBO assumes that those engaged in the daily operations will identity the measures most relevant to those operations. The higher levels of management supposedly relate this information to that coming from other managers and to the corporate mission.

In practice, at every level up to and including the CEO in his relation to the corporate Board, the prime motivation of each person is to look good to their superior(s). Their concern is to be judged by objectives that they know they can easily manage. If tough measurable objectives are imposed on them then they will seek to get the numbers by cheating. If all else fails, shift the blame. All such tactics invite counter tactics and the organizational focus becomes on MBO as a mechanism for controlling individuals instead of being a co-ordinating mechanism for better pursuit of organizational objectives.

If organizations are first de-bureaucratized then MBO is both necessary and possible. (Of course, if MBO was not then possible the only alternatives to bureaucracy would be anarchy or arbitrary autocracy.)

There are still practical problems with introducing MBO to organizations that have moved to self managing workface groups. Something can be learnt from earlier efforts even though they failed to overcome the bureaucratic barriers.

First, it is always inadequate to set only one objective. Any work or service system takes many inputs and transforms them into one or more outputs, creating waste in the process. No one figure, ratio or index is going to capture all manageable aspects of that transformation. On the other hand, we cannot expect people to try to manage every theoretically relevant dimension of the process. In practice many dimensions can be treated as if 'constant' or can be made such by automation. In practice we are probably looking at three to seven objectives for self managing work groups. Three seems to be the least number that can give a person a hands on feeling for an operating system and seven is the most that people can keep in mind at one time. A mnemonic device for an agreed upon set of objectives might make it easier for people to routinely operate with the higher levels of six or seven objectives. At the higher levels of management more objectives may need to be spelt out but if they are organized in levels, e.g. with respect to time span, there need be no more than seven at any level. In any case it seems wiser to aim for fewer objectives and negotiate more frequently about what those objectives ought to be. A large number of objectives encourages people to 'duck and weave' about what has actually been accomplished.

Second, because objectives have to be negotiated between parties with separate interests, even though complemental, those objectives need to be ones that can be explicitly defined and objectively assessed. This does not warrant the assumption that the best objectives are those that are most easily measured. Relevant objectives cannot even be formulated unless an organization sorts out what business it is in and that is a qualitative statement. Given a mission statement that defines the business one is in, then one can get on with defining objectives and selecting measures that are sensitive enough to measure real changes but not so sensitive as to spark off false alarms or raise false hopes. As a guideline to selecting measures they should be checked to see that they are appropriate to:

○ the business one is engaged in;

○ the environment in which that business is being conducted;

○ speed of feedback needed for the organisation's decision cycle time;

○ the range of responses available to the organisation.

Third, it is desirable to explicitly identify on a grid all of the sections of the organisation that share each of the objectives. This may indicate the need for different co-ordinating and information procedures. At least this procedure should lessen the chances of important responsibilities just 'falling through the cracks'.

Fourth, there is an important distinction to be made between maintenance objectives and change objectives. The former establish responsibilities to maintain standards whilst the latter usually entail the development of new ways of working. To enable people to get on with the former it is common practice to set up special temporary project teams or task forces to implement the change objectives. The understanding behind this is that once established, responsibility for those objectives will be passed over to those sections currently charged with the maintenance objectives. This may be a quick way to develop new ideas about organization and procedures but it almost guarantees a prolonged and messy 'passing over' period,with a high risk of failure. Initial progress probably will be slower if responsibility for the change objectives is given to the same sections as have responsibility for the maintenance objectives. However, it locks the conflicts into individuals and groups, with them responsible for resolving the conflicts, and prevents the conflicts being turned into inter-group conflicts, with all that that means for personal relations, blocking and sabotage.

Fifth, a distinction needs to be made between operational, managerial and corporate objectives. This distinction reflects the natural hierarchy of *functions*. The distinction does not imply any necessary hierarchy of statuses. Managerial and operational objectives must remain within corporate objectives only so long as they are sustainable. When they are not, those responsible for formulating corporate objectives must respond to the experiences of the managerial and operational levels. Similarly for the relation of managerial and operational levels. Further, it in no way follows that those capable of exercising the authority of competence at one level has any such authority at other levels. The hierarchy of functions dictates complementarity but not subordination.

Sixth and last, it is necessary to come back to what was implicit in the introduction. At that stage I pointed to the fact that it had proven next to impossible to implement MBO in bureaucratized structures. The clear implication is that if organizations are to define objectives appropriate to the management of self managing groups then those organizations need to be organized in non bureaucratic ways.

This point was made clearly many years ago by Ralph Kingdon in his study of matrix organizations. He studied R&D teams in the US defence industries. Those teams tended to be organized as self managing groups but were constantly frustrated and in conflict with their organisations which were bureaucratically organized, despite the fact that these R&D groups were the leading edge for the corporations' profit making. Kingdon noted that the conflicts seemed inevitable. One can go further and state that no organization can maintain its integrity if its workforce is organized according to one system principle and its management to another.

If an organization decides to advantage itself by introducing self managing principles into its workforce then it would seem that they should reorganize their management structure according to the same principles. As the table of differences between the two system principles shows, the differences are not trivial.

Fig. 1. Characteristics of the New and Old Organizational Paradigm

Basic Design Principle	Redundancy of Parts	Redundancy of Functions
Unit of Analysis	maximum task breakdown, narrow skills; building block is one person–one task	multiskilling, 'whole task' grouping; building block is a self managing group
Organizational rules	technological imperative – people added on. Aim to design people out of the system	design for 'man-machine' complementarity and hence for optimal staffing levels
	co-ordination and control decisions located at levels above the workers	co-ordination and control located, as far as possible, with those doing the work
	aim at total specification of responsibilities and author-ities	aim at minimum critical specification of respons-ibilities and authorities

Typical Outcomes:

Sociotechnical	fragmented sociotechnical system resistant to change	dynamic process of joint optimization of the socio-technical system
Cultural	autocratic	democratic
Psychological	alienation	involvement and commitment

References

Drucker P F. 1954. *The Practice of Management*. Harper, New York.

Howell R A. 1967 (Fall) "A fresh look at management by objectives". *Business Horizons*. pp51-58.

Kingdon D R. 1973. *Matrix Organization*. Tavistock, London.

Levinson H. 1970 (July-August) "Management by whose objectives?" *Harvard Business Review*. pp125-135.

Sherwin D S. 1976 (May-June) "Management of objectives". *Harvard Business Review*. pp149-160.

Matching Effectivities to Affordances in the Design of Jobs

Fred Emery, 1985

IN AN OPEN SYSTEMS framework or in other words, a framework for ecological learning, system and environment are interdependent, mutually defining the other and imposing limits on each other. Affordances are what the environment offers to the system at any point in time. An environment containing a hungry tiger does not afford the opportunity for a relaxed picnic. It does afford the conditions for a rush of adrenalin, a quiet retreat to the four wheel drive or a bit of target practice. Each of these latter are effectivities, the actions the system can make on the environment.

These new ways of conceptualizing the relations between system and environment allow us to be more precise in our analyses of organizational structures. The following is, therefore, a more powerful elaboration of the six psychological requirements for human activity [Ed].

° People's actions do not arise as mere responses to external stimuli, neither do they arise as responses to internal stimuli such as images, thoughts and memories. Their actions arise in response to the situation defined by the relations between their effectivities and the environmental *affordances*. Such meanings as the situation may have for the person are in these relations and not in the person or in the environment taken separately. Environmental affordances can only be specified with respect to the effectivities of some organism; effectivities can be specified only with respect to what some environment affords.

° Any model of communication that attempts to explain human action must deal explicitly with the interrelation of affordances and effectivities.

° Extended organized activity is facilitated by communications as they enable co-actors to match their joint effectivities to affordances presenting in different places at the same time or at the same place at different times.

° Organizations are nothing other than the controlled and co-ordinated effectivities of the co-actors where these effectivities include their abilities to detect affordances and to communicate with each other.

Decision making

When conditions have been designed for operation via a self managing group the question must be faced as to whether the group has within it sufficient knowledge to make wise operating decisions. They can of course not just refer questions to an experienced supervisor. If they have enough knowledge they can make quicker and many more precise decisions than could any single supervisor who has to try and supervise the whole operation.

For the operators it will not be enough that they know one specific job. If they are to make the most of the flexibility built into the design they must know what is going on at any of the posts they may find themselves at any time.

To be effectively multiskilled they need to know the logic or science that governs the whole operation in their sections, not just the isolated bits that are traditionally associated with one or more of the jobs in the section. In the staffing of the new Porsgrun Fertiliser plant, 1965, this necessitated over 200 hours of formal training in industrial chemistry, instrumentation etc.

In the staffing of the Woodlawn Mine and Treatment Process, 1974, this required up to 800 hours of formal training (although most of this was skills training rather than knowledge creating). Increasingly self managing groups will need to have knowledge of the statistical and other computer aided techniques used for control over quality and system analysis. Decisions that an experienced supervisor might make by 'the seat of his pants' will, in a self managing group, often need to be grounded in facts. A debatable area is whether members of self managing groups need educating in the managing of themselves. There are those who recommend training in Group Relations. This is justified on the grounds that work experience will have given people very little positive experience of cooperation.

However, because the authoritarian organization of work does not afford opportunities for overt cooperation we should not overlook the covert cooperation that is a feature of worklife and the extensive experience of teamwork that most people get in sport and other nonwork activities. We should probably accept that if people are able to carry on a conversation they can cooperate. To treat them otherwise verges on an insult.

Opportunities to learn and go on learning/Capacity to learn

A properly designed self managing operation will afford opportunities for the two essential objective conditions for learning, namely that the groups can negotiate for variation in their goals so that they be confronted with an optimal level of challenge and they get timely and adequate feed-back on their performance. Without the latter there can be no experimentation to find better ways of working and goal achievement is simply a matter of luck.

Whether the possibilities for learning are realized depends upon whether the people of the self managing groups are capable and desirous of making the most of them.

Not everyone in a self managing group needs to be fully multiskilled or an expert in all of the operations of the group. It is possible to operate efficiently if there is a core of people who can cover each other in the event of absences for sickness, holidays etc.

The existence of such a core depends upon prior selection and the existence of procedures whereby the group can dispense with members who are unable or unwilling to learn. We are referring here to an essential core. Where a core exists it is easier for such a self managing group to find a useful and meaningful place for a handicapped person than it is for a traditionally organized section.

Optimal variety/'Programs for action' (Planning)

We can design for a self managing group so that it allows the members to achieve reasonably optimal levels of variety.

However, we often cannot design out some routine work that could be sub-optimal if engaged in for long stretches of time. Also, we sometimes cannot design out the need for a number of highly demanding tasks that, if they cropped up at the same time could cause overload.

There is thus a challenge to the workers to plan their work so that no one gets too much of the routine and no one is too long stressed by overload. More importantly the work needs to be planned so that the routine tasks are embedded in the completion of significant tasks and that, where there are a number of significant tasks that could compete for attention they should be prioritized.

Just as the capacity to learn is enhanced by improving the knowledge base of the members of a self managing group then so their ability to optimize task variety should be enhanced by their knowledge of what is important and their ability to learn better ways of working. A 'job enrichment' plan imposed from without is hardly every going to be as good as the plans they evolve to meet their particular circumstances and their personal needs.

In extreme cases prior selection for ability to tolerate boredom or stress might be justified. Generally speaking they would not be. Given the freedom of movement that is designed in for self managing groups even minimal planning should reduce the stress found in the traditional one person-one station jobs. Also, the social climate allowed for in self managing groups should help most people to live with degrees of boredom and levels of stress that they would not tolerate on their own.

Mutual support and respect/'Co-orientation'

The crucial feature of the design of self managing groups is that it does not afford support for individuals to pursue egocentric or competitive work goals. It affords support only for cooperative efforts.

The critical question would appear to be whether people whose working life has been spent in 'looking after number one' in competitive settings are able to adjust to such a radically different style of working.

Note, however, that the job design requires only that people relate to each others efforts so as to fulfil the objective requirements for completion of the tasks. It is to be expected that, with a little experience, they will develop an appropriate level of respect for what the other brings to the joint task and a willingness to support others, as they expect others to support them. If friendships should develop in the process then so be it, but there is no way that the design presupposes or requires friendship.

What a self managing group affords or does not afford in the way of mutual support and respect is very obvious to any participant. They can see it for themselves and do not require fancy concepts or special courses in sensitization in order to detect it. Whether they are prepared to work in this way can be determined only by self selection processes.

Meaningfulness of job and product/Relevance

In self managing work groups there is no room (at least no necessity) for donkey jobs. It is possible for all members to contribute to the significant tasks of the section. There is, however, little that job design can do with respect to the social value of the section's end product except to enhance the quality of that output.

Whether the group members feel that their job has relevance may depend a good deal on how well they are informed of who their ultimate customers are and how well their product is respected.

Desirable future/'Expectations' (level of aspiration)

How far can design of jobs afford objectively better future opportunities beyond the organization?

Perhaps self managing groups should consist only of people whose career aspirations do not extend to the top level of multiskilling? That is not too realistic. There will be many whose level of aspiration will be raised when they discover how easily they can master new skills and how well they can contribute to the management of their group. Those who have expectations of achieving managerial levels might be encouraged to enter via this path rather than via an MBA.

Overall observations

There is a long tradition of trying to scientifically match people to jobs (effectivities to affordances).

The problem is radically transformed with the introduction of self managing work groups. They are able, within limits, to constantly vary the way they work to find a better match. Nevertheless they require resources of education, skilling and task related information that are not found necessary in the traditional workplace. They also require rights in the selection process that are not normally extended to employees. When we are dealing with the staffing of a new 'greenfields' site then the way the jobs are advertised and explained usually works very efficiently to attract those who welcome what self managing groups afford. When an old workplace is being transformed there are always many serious problems with individuals who stand to lose what was a privileged niche. Often the niche is no more than a privileged relation with the supervisor, job ownership of a particularly efficient bit of equipment or a cushy task.

These are not questions of potential effectiveness but of willingness. They are no more open to 'decision by rule' than are divorce proceedings. The only guidelines emerging from past experience of unionized plants and offices is that the easiest way out is to buy out the opposition (as it is for displaced supervisors); if that is not possible use peer pressure before using the Personnel Department.

Laissez-Faire vs Democratic Groups

Fred Emery, May 1988

THE FOLLOWING IS an edited covering note and letter from Emery to Fiorelli after the publication of his 1988 paper.

There are many social scientists, usually those seeing themselves in OD (Organizational Development) who believe that laissez-faire, consensual groups are a half-way house in moving from autocracy to democratic work groups. Therefore, they argue, it makes good practical sense to change one step at a time. Furthermore, most managers are happier to just ease up on the traditional autocratic patterns a little at a time, with the reassurance that they can readily revert to those familiar ways if the going gets tough.

This is not what Lewin found in his series of social climate experiments but that was in the late thirties. Few subsequent empirical studies have provided a direct, simultaneous comparison of the three forms. Such a comparison is provided by Fiorelli, 1988.

Fiorelli saw that his evidence challenged the popular notion that "the interdisciplinary team approach is equivalent with shared decision making and broad-based participation." Re-analysis of his data suggests a much stronger case for his views (and Lewin's and mine) than Fiorelli is able to make using conventional methods of analysis.

Dear Dr. Fiorelli,

I share your concern that much of what is passed off as teamwork in inter-disciplinary work settings is just so much eyewash, and your beautiful research design has produced, naturally, a beautiful set of data.

My concern is that in following the generally accepted forms of analysis you have done justice neither to your data nor your theoretical and practical concerns. I have re-worked your matrix of correlations and will outline what I think your data tells us, then outline the method of analysis I have used.

1. The correlations you observed between the three social climates are rather puzzling (p.9) in the light of the confident statements made by Rostow and others about teamwork and consensus. However, the

following little graph is the only logically consistent statement that can be made on the basis of your data:

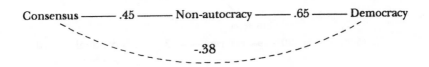

Consensus ——— .45 ——— Non-autocracy ——— .65 ——— Democracy

-.38

You have reaffirmed what Kurt Lewin discovered in 1937-8. You may recall that Lewin helped Ron Lippitt to set up his experimental studies of autocratic and democratic social climates and was then horrified to find that the 'democratic' groups were chaotic, unparticipative and unproductive. He then discovered that Lippitt's idea of democracy was consensus, 'laissez-faire'.

So Lewin, Lippitt and White ran the next series of studies that included autocratic, laissez-faire and democratic social climates (thank heavens). They then found what you have found. Namely, that for all the fine sentiments associated with that sort of team building it is disruptive of genuine self determination. Consensus and a wide range of tolerance for each doing their own thing has damn all to do with democratization of the workplace.

The critical thing in the latter is that those who contribute to group performance make the decisions about how they coordinate their work; not some superviser. If some individuals insist on a consensus that permits them to do their own thing, in their own way and at their own pace, then they are in the wrong work group.

2. We can graphically represent the data in the matrix of correlations to see what they tell us about what the 'management styles' mean for populations like your sample. The results are presented below.

The dynamics can be read off these graphs as you would read a road map. Simply ask 'what processes do we have to go through, instead of towns, to get from one point in the graph to another?'; e.g., social climate to productivity. If I make a few comments it may help orient you to this way of dealing with the data.

Autocracy

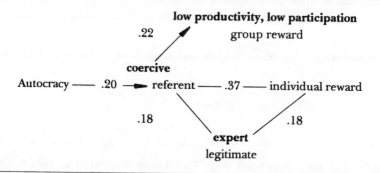

Thus, in the case of autocracy the critical mediating variable (system principle) is 'coercive/referent'. In this sort of setting individuals in your sample show a significant tendency to 'crawl' (referents) or cover their backsides with qualifications and/or knowledge of the bureaucratic rules (expert/legitimate). The only significant contribution to productivity/participation is the ability of the authoritarians to exercise coercion and demand respect (loyalty?). The data indicate that the individuals are watching the boss, not productivity; also that rewards go to supporting the authoritarian status quo, not productivity, nor participation.

Consensus

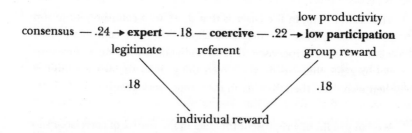

Consensus differs primarily in that expertise and legitimation are up front instead of coercion and 'reference'. It results in a closer identification of personal and group rewards, but within the same context that treats productivity and participation as irrelevant. In the last analysis, coercion and 'reference' remain as the direct determinants of productivity and participation, and are still having negative effects.

Democracy

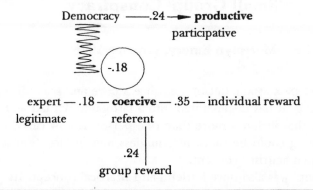

Democracy ——.24 —► **productive**
　　　　　　　　　　　　participative

expert — .18 — **coercive** — .35 — individual reward
　legitimate　　　　　referent

　　　　　　　　.24
　　　　　group reward

Democracy reveals a radically different pattern. It is the only 'social climate' that is related to higher productivity and participation. And this relation is direct and unmediated. In this sample, however, we note that it coexists and is negatively correlated with (constrained by) the typical bureaucratic pattern that ties personal and group rewards to coercion and formal statuses.

Do I read too much into these graphs?

Quite possibly. I can certainly read much more from these graphs than anyone who has not got comparable knowledge of the previously observed relations between these variables in other studies. But even if this is fallible, the main concerns here are the kinds of judgements I try to make about the premisses yielded up by this form of logical analysis of the data. Unlike the Blalock type of 'causal path analysis' the method used here is not contaminated by prior judgements about which of a thousand and one models should be put to the test. The weight of my judgement obviously depends on the validity and reliability of the data but the data can only assert what is in the graphs. If the data is accepted and replication of the analytic procedures reveals no error, then any debate has to be about the explicit judgements I have made. The essence of the method I have used to rework your matrix of correlations is given in Emery F, 1981, Vol.1.

References

Emery F 1981, 'Causal Path Analysis', *Systems Thinking*, Volume 1, pp.293-298, Penguin.

Fiorelli J 1988, 'Power in Work Groups: team member's perspectives', *Human Relations*, 41. pp.1-12.

Getting to Grips with the Great 'Small Group' Conspiracy

Merrelyn Emery, January 1978

THE CONCEPT OF A SMALL GROUP was once a pure and scientific concept with a meaning. It has degenerated into a fashion and a fad and almost any situation that includes more than one person is now called a 'small group'. Nothing could be more meaningless and in fact destructive of what was once a heuristic concept.

'Small group' was also once a useful and practical concept. Its proven usefulness arose from two streams of practical theorizing; from those whose job it was to help the sick and socially inadequate, and from those who realized that it is the structure of society which is sick and needs restructuring. These were not mutually exclusive streams but simply varieties of purpose within a learning network of action researchers.

What is a group—really? It is a group of people who are commonly engaged on a task, sharing without status distinction the responsibility for:

○ completing the task to some agreed level of satisfaction; and

○ their own control and coordination. If anyone of these elements is lacking, the aggregate of people gathered together in the one place is not a group.

'Small' is variously interpreted as somewhere between four and 15 people. The most misunderstood and misnamed situation is that where there is a gathering of people with a leader. This is by definition not a small group. This situation was originally designed by the therapeutic stream where the goal was to restore to the sick their capacity to function fully as human beings in society. The aggregate and their leader only became a group when the sick had become strong enough to negate the status distinction between themselves and the leader, either by throwing her or him out, or by making it quite clear that the leader could be a member of the group on strictly equal terms; i.e., cease to be the leader.

This paper was originally delivered to a conference of 'small group trainers'. The author was once a member of this tribe but left its ranks after becoming aware of some of the manipulations involved, the elitist purposes for which they were often practised and not least the fact that there were genuinely democratic alternatives. Minor changes have been made to the original.

Bion's classic studies of the development and dynamics of groups make quite clear the fact that people wish to be members of self managing groups but in the early stages of coming together are no more than an immature form or prototype. In fact, Bion's work was as a therapist with war casualties and his job as the leader or therapist was to bring his immature groups out of the grips of the 'group assumptions' into a consistent stage of mature group function; self management. The 'group assumptions' of Dependency, Fight/flight and Pairing are the assumptions an immature group makes about its relationship with its leader before they have the confidence to become a well functioning and independent group. This Bion called the Work Group because it could and wanted to purposefully do a task important to all its members. These group assumptions or emotions are consequences of structure (Bion, 1952, 1959; Emery M, 1982, 1986).

Today we rarely see in the fashionable form of 'small group' work, the case of a leader being deposed. There are several good reasons for this. One is that most leaders enjoy the status and power of being the leader and consciously or unconsciously manipulate the situation so that the hierarchical distinction is maintained. The second is that the leader who is genuinely intending to use the situation for therapeutic or democratic learning purposes must have exceptional skills, knowledge and personal abilities. This is a rare combination and a lot of people who 'run' groups these days wouldn't know what I'm talking about. The groups they are 'running' have nothing to do with democracy. They do have a lot to do with subtle autocracy, laissez-faire and the group assumptions.

The genuine therapist's task is made even more difficult when they operate in a society whose members have been socialized from birth to accept and revere status distinctions and the concept of a 'higher authority'. A leader in such a situation who is themselves infected with the spirit of a 'higher authority' or who does not have the requisite skills to decontaminate their clients, is doing no more than reinforcing the sickness of authoritarianism which exists in the structure of the society at large.

This very simple fact appears to have been lost in the great rush to 'go into groups'—for every conceivable purpose, many of which do not in fact constitute tasks; e.g.,at conferences, to have a discussion. No wonder many normal healthy people come out of this feeling angry and frustrated. Many walk out of sensitivity or team-building 'groups' feeling the same way and for the same good reasons. They are suffering from the group assumption of fight/flight brought on by being denied the right to exercise some control over a situation in which they find themselves and/or being asked to perform a non-task in the same circumstances. They practice the assumption in the flight mode because the situation contains nothing worth fighting for. But they won't put up with being treated as less than human and exercise their right to leave.

Why has there been this phenomenal stampede into the fad of 'groups'? First, because most people survive the bureaucratized society relatively undamaged but very aware that there must be something better: they search and they end up in 'small groups'. Second, because those reared to believe that some are more equal than others see in the 'small group scene' opportunities for maintaining the status quo and procuring a top spot in it for them, by the manipulation described above. The phenomenon bears all the hallmarks of a profession bent on imperialism. The motto could well be 'keep them busy and involved' (but keep them infected with respect for the leader).

This aspect though covers only the experiential, high visibility side of the strategy. The other nine tenths of the iceberg, the culture of silence, is widely shared. Almost nowhere in our Western culture is there any opportunity to learn conceptually and cognitively about structure. Yet it has been learnt and known for centuries that for knowledge to become 'understood' and therefore usable, it must be conscious and conceptual as well as experienced. If the 'small group' practicians were to start arming their clients with the conceptual tools to analyse and understand the structures of the 'small groups' they are running, they would quickly do themselves out of a job.

Let's do away with all the mythology and trappings of the great 'small group conspiracy' and start being honest with ourselves. If we really want a society where people can exercise their so-called democratic rights to take responsibility for themselves and start functioning as full scale human beings, then we have to do two things. We have to:

○ start helping people learn about the concept of structure and it will involve the direct transmission of some information (a no-no for some 'group trainers' dedicated to learning experientially);

○ provide situations where they can practice with the genuine article, the genuine small group.

Perhaps we are worried that self managing small groups won't fulfil the claims made for them, or that perhaps people don't want to take responsibility for themselves and share the decision making about control and coordination with their mates. Be reassured, they do and they do. Anybody who has ever seen a group take the bit between its teeth when they were given the chance to start making these decisions in the interests of the whole, and the ways in which they react if they suspect later that the exercise was not genuine, won't need my reassurance.

Mind you, if a group suspects from the start that a project is a con and if it does not have sufficient sanctions to safeguard their whole hearted participation, they will practice fight/flight, usually the second half. While this is actually a rational response, it can be taken or interpreted as a refusal to accept responsibility. But once a group or organization does have the bit between its teeth, it is a brave or foolhardy manager who will attempt to turn back the clock. As was said above in the introduction, it is hard to put down ideas which really fit with people's expectations and nature.

There is also more to the concept of structure than what a genuine small group looks like and what happens inside it. Organizations, institutions and societies also are and contain large systems, and small and large systems are systematically related. We must also teach structure on this scale. To do less is once again misleading and can be downright destructive.

To turn a small number of people into a genuine small self managing group through experience but without any conceptual understanding, and send them into a hostile and ruthless environment, which is what a large bureaucratic organization becomes when it is challenged or senses a threat, is courting defeat and damage to the people and leaves the bureaucratic organization unchanged. It is even worse to take an individual and send them back alone. But that is exactly what is happening and what many 'small group' practitioners are promoting as in the interests of democratic learning for democracy.

If we are really going to change this society we must embark on a strategic educational campaign reaching eventually all its members, of all ages and at all levels in the current pecking order. And we must provide them with an education which is both conceptual and experiential. It is possible.

References

Bion W R 1952, 'Group Dynamics: a review', *International Journal of Psychoanalysis*, 33, pp.235-247.

Bion W R 1959, *Experiences in Groups*, Tavistock.

Emery M 1986, 'Toward an Heuristic Theory of Diffusion', *Human Relations*, 39, 5 pp.411-432.

PART III

DEMOCRACY THROUGHOUT THE SYSTEM

THIS PART CONTAINS the three original documents in Emery (F's) thinking about extending democratization, design principle 2, from the small group or work section level to the integrated enterprise, whole system and governmental level. The first paper is extracted from his most recent thinking published as Towards Real Democracy, 1989. In his introduction to this new volume Emery writes:

> Twenty and more years of experience with worker participation in industry has radically changed the perspective both for democracy and for the role of adult education. The change in the first perspective is immensely more important—a change that suggests that the democratic process of 'government by the people' might actually become a true 'university of life'. This is not a theoretical paper. It is concerned with extrapolating to politics from practical experiences in the democratization of work. (p.iv)

Thus the nexus of adult education and participative democratic structures is highlighted. If adult educators are not concerned about promoting organizational environments which automatically produce learning, they will have to be content with knowing that they are aiming only for second best, always attempting to fill in the gaps and redress the damage done by structures inimical to learning.

The 'Adaptive Systems' paper marked the high point of a trip to India at the request of Professor Nitish De, sponsored by the National Labour Institute, New Delhi. In typical style, all the critical questions and issues raised and the first answers provided appear to have stood the test of time.

Following its presentation, we visited several sites in India only to find that India had its own indigenous examples of the jury system being applied to management in industry. It was clearly an idea whose time had come and demonstrated once again the spontaneous and simultaneous springing up of initiatives around the globe, as intuitive adaptive responses to needs created by a changing environment.

The third paper was a submission to the Minister for Industry and Commerce following the report of the Jackson Committee on manufacturing industry. It addresses the actual structure and operation of an industry council as a participative rather than representative democratic body. As such it serves as an example or analogue for other purposes. In the fourth, the principles, rules and logistics of the jury system are elaborated as they would need to be in the political or governance arena. Together, they form a set of basic guidelines for the extension of participative democracy from the single organization to the total societal infrastructure—the need for which was outlined in the first paper of this volume.

Towards Real Democracy

Fred Emery, 1989

IT SEEMS AS IF each major election in a Western democracy brings forth another spate of serious public discussions of the weaknesses of the democratic forms of government. If it is not the quality of the candidates that is being deplored it is the quality of the electoral campaigns or the cynicism of the electorate. Between elections the media appear to be constantly preoccupied with the recurrent scandals of political corruption and deception.

Some of this can be dismissed as 'media hype'. A great deal of this cannot be so dismissed.

What is absent is any sense of our learning from the seemingly endlessly repetitious analysis of the faults in the system. It is not quite fair to say that. There has been, over the past couple of decades, a number of promising ideas; e.g., for Ombudspeople, Freedom of Information and more effective electoral registration and redistribution. However, even when these ideas have been adopted, the expected improvements in our self governance have failed to appear or, if they did appear, were quickly and seriously attenuated. The only real learning appears to be that nothing can be done.

I have suggested that this debate is bogged down because we cannot think in terms of anything but representative democratic systems. Furthermore, I have suggested that those systems have a powerful and compelling logic of their own. Locked into that logic we finish up with Churchill in deploring 'democracy' but deploring the known alternatives even more. It has been my contention that, behind the backs of political scientists and others concerned with political democracy, practical democratic alternatives to the representative systems have already emerged. These are alternatives that enable us to move closer to the ideal of democracy; i.e., toward participative democracy in the conditions of the modern industrial society.

I have not been discussing participative democracy just as a theoretical possibility—there was quite enough of such empty speculation in the late sixties. I have been discussing implications of enduring practical experiments in the harshly practical world of work. In the world of work those ideas of participation have gone from being interesting possibilities to serious probabilities that have to be considered in the design of any work organization. All that I have done in the world of politics is to claim that this experience has transformed the idea of participation from a mere theoretical possibility into a real, practical possibility. Not much of an advance—but then people will only take seriously those things that are real possibilities in the world in which they are living. If we fail to recognize that real democratic alternatives to representative systems are possible, then we remain condemned to continue on the flight path of the fabled ooloo bird who flew in ever decreasing circles.

Life, Liberty and Property could well have served as a title for this document (Towards Real Democracy). That title was, however, pre-empted by Alfred Winslow Jones in 1941 to cover in his own way the same social dilemmas of modern democracies. These dilemmas are the provision of social support to the needy without creating dependency, maintaining civil peace and good order without creating servility in the face of 'the majesty of the law', allowing for the property rights that are a condition for people entering the market as free people whilst guarding against those extremes of power that make a joke of the economic freedom of the majority.

These dilemmas have confronted all democratic societies. There is nothing surprising in this. Whilst some market oriented societies have not been democracies, all known democratic societies have been market oriented. One can expect that when people experience the freedom that comes with participation in markets (as propertied persons, not slaves) there will emerge social pressures to exercise similar choice of preferences in their governance. If it is accepted that they are competent to do the one, they will not readily accept arguments that they are incompetent to do the other. However, reliance on the market instead of administered exchange fairly, inevitably means that many will be 'needy', that many will emerge with great wealth and that those with great wealth will unduly influence the law makers and the enforcement of the laws.

The dilemmas have been greatly intensified by the emergence on the one side, of the massive bureaucracies of corporations and public administration, and on the other of a highly educated electorate freed, for the most part, from the mind dulling drudgery of labouring and menial service. It is the new level of these dilemmas that has been addressed by people like Dahl and Lindblom. But in 1977, Lindblom could still conclude that "boldly conceived major new democratic alternatives have not yet been designed. They may never be... "(p.344)

After analysing the interlocking roles of modern markets and modern politics, Lindblom observed that we have still failed to appreciate adequately the probability that "more than class, the major specific institutional barrier to fuller democracy may, therefore, be the autonomy of the private corporation "(p.356). It is this failure that appears to lead to his conclusion that without boldly conceived major new democratic alternatives "it may follow, then, that it is impossible for democracy to develop significantly beyond what is found in crippled form in existing polyarchy "(p.353). Without apparently knowing what had been emerging in the world of work since 1951, Lindblom felt that "the most fertile field for a more participatory democracy appears to be in industry...an arena in which authoritarianism has been for so long universally practised and little questioned "(p.334).

I have argued for a "bold major new democratic alternative". I have argued for this on the basis of lessons learnt from the emergence of participatory democracy in industry. Whatever the shortcomings, I hope that I have established that Lindblom's expectations about the most fruitful starting point for finding a bold new alternative have been justified (Extracted from *Towards Real Democracy*, 1989, Ontario QWL Centre, Ministry of Labour, Toronto, pp.119-120 and pp.211-213).

Reference

Lindblom C E 1977, *Politics and Markets*, Basic Books, NY.

Adaptive Systems for our Future Governance

Fred E Emery

First Rafi Ahmed Kidwai Memorial Lecture delivered on
14 April 1974 at the Indian Institute of Public Administration,
New Delhi

THERE ARE TWO PATHS which we can take in our basic social designs. I am concerned only with that which bases itself upon the multiple capabilities of the human being. I am not concerned with improving on designs that start from assuming that the individual is a redundant part, a cog. We have shown in our work that efficient large scale production does not necessitate that people be designed into the systems as readily disposable parts (Emery & Thorsrud, 1975).

Similarly, I think it has been demonstrated that mass education does not have to proceed on that assumption (Williams, 1975). More than that. The practical demonstrations have shown that productive systems and learning systems are far more efficient when they are designed to utilise the multiple capabilities of workers and students.

In the process of making these practical demonstrations over the past two decades we were in effect demonstrating that participative democracy could become a reality, even in the hostile autocratic climate of industry. This would appear to be so regardless of technology; there appears to be no form of work requiring the coordination and control of human effort that could not be better done by creating some degree of self management. After many years of experience it became clear to us that this was true also of management work and the work of research and development teams.

But, all of that is to my mind as a scientist, just about past history. The basic theoretical problems of democratising work have been confronted and have been solved.

The problem I now wish to direct myself to, in honour of the cause for which Rafi Ahmed Kidwai worked himself to death is, how can the ideas that successfully led to participative democracy in the workplace, be projected in the higher and more remote areas of management and government, to replace or at least supplement the Westminster model of elected representatives?

It was one thing to have demonstrated what can be done at the workface, the coalface, bench, desk and drafting table. At that level it was practically always possible to allocate responsibility to groups that were small enough to participate in helping each other to manage their tasks. How, however, does an operator or even a middle manager participate in the decisions that affect him when 5,000 others in a town of only 100,000 participate? How does a citizen in a nation of even 3,000,000 participate meaningfully in national decisions on things like economic policy or defence one has only to pose the problem in these terms to see the apparently insuperable difficulties.

A large number of premodern societies based on small self sufficient communities have used participative forms of democracy. However, even meetings in the village place or town square have their marked limitations - to be easily swayed by orators, by rabble-rousers and by unscrupulous chairpeople; too little time to allow but a few to speak; too little 'round-table' discussion to explore differences or test out whether agreements are based on common understandings; too little preparatory work by most to permit effective participation; too little shared knowledge to permit complex and technical matters to be discussed.

The difficulties in the large and complex modern societies are so great at first sight that only last year, when I confronted the problem, I felt compelled to conclude that "it is not possible to democratise those arrangements (of social power) in any form of (modern) society of which we know." (Emery & Emery, 1975, p.172) The best I thought that might come to pass was "that they (the power-holders) so arrange their exercise of power that it is consonant with a democratised society." (p.172 ibid)

It would seem the crassest form of hubris for one to tackle this problem with any expectation of success. I will nevertheless make the effort because;

(a) I think it is a hurdle we must sometime, some place, succeed in jumping, or else our hopes of adaptive large scale human societies are foredoomed;

(b) new ways of effective participation have been evolving (and I am not referring to telecommunications technology); and

(c) I do not set myself the target of succeeding. I set my sights much lower, namely to convince others, if they also try, that one day this service for humankind will be successfully performed.

If the problem is so difficult why do we not just settle for using representative democracy to cope with the extended forms of social cooperation and control? After all, when we set course to devise participative forms of industrial democracy in Norway, in the early 1960s, we accepted the possibility that they could put flesh and blood on the formal representative schemes such as Works Councils and thus enable them to function fruitfully (Emery & Thorsrud, 1969, p.97). Participative democracy was subsequently brought into many workplaces but the representative structures did not come to life. Worse than that. When a new labour law in Norway (1973) required elections for Works Councils the workers in the already democratised plans showed a very significant lack of interest.

I think we have to look below the surface similarities of representative and participative democracy. The system characteristics of representative democracies are not quite what we have been led to believe by the so-called Westminster tradition. First, at the interface of politician and electorate everything possible will be done to turn it into a 'safe seat', a 'blue-ribbon electorate'. This means actively working to create a captive and non participative electorate, one that does not pressurize the representatives about the changing requirements of their community. Second, the interface with the executive apparatus of the state, or city, will be as tightly centralized by the politicians as is possible.

Thus, even the majority of elected politicians must be non-participants in the work of Government. Third, the tiny minority of representatives who become Minister, or the equivalent at the local government levels, find that they must accommodate to other sources of social power, sources of power that do not operate via the electoral machine.

In defining these characteristics of this system, I have drawn on experience with representative democratic systems at the social level; i.e., community, region and nation. When the forms of representative democracy are brought into organisations there is one pervasive difference— the owners and managers retain prerogatives of power that are equivalent to those retained by monarchs and lords in the early days of the Westminster model. Those were the days before the Cabinet system became so prominent. And so we find it with the representative forms of industrial democracy: the first and third characteristics are clearly displayed but the second is in an embryonic form.

There has not yet evolved a 'cabinet' system whereby some are elected from amongst the workers' representatives to exercise on their behalf the power they collectively represent. Instead we find individuals trying to curry favour so as to appear more influential with the bosses. It does seem to me that representative systems of democracy in society and in industry are all members of the same class of systems. They differ in maturity and power but they have the same inherent dynamics. In effect, they are systems that inherently act to minimise participation. In fact one might say they thrive on the apathy and anomie of the great majority. However, they induce many who have social power without standing for elections to engage in the fine art of politicking to 'fix' which minority of politicians will exercise the decision-making functions, and about what. This lobbying is admittedly a form of participation but it has more to do with corruption of the body politic than with democratic ideals.

These tendencies of representative systems to generate mass apathy, elitism and corruption are my reasons for believing that we cannot stop with what we are already doing with democratisation of work. In some way or another we must find a way to redesign our larger scale systems of government so that they are truly based on the multiple capabilities of all the people. Only thus will these systems be adaptive enough to cope with the social turbulence we face.

Before suggesting some new adaptive designs, let me first point out that the problem is not quite as insuperable as it originally seemed to me. Elsewhere, I have shown that replacing a bureaucratic structure in a large organisation with self managing groups at the grassroots reduces the amount of up-and-down communication by about ninety per cent (Emery & Emery, 1975).

More than that. The them-us context of communication in a bureaucracy distorts all communication and stimulates the insatiable need for ever more communication. This is transformed. The very emergence of self managing groups defines an area of common interests and a context of 'we-ness' which encourages open and truthful communication. More mutual understanding between managers and workers is achieved with a mere fraction of the old amounts of talking and formal reporting.

I have been talking here about effective communication in large *organisations*. Whether a similar change would take place with a grassroots transformation of an extended aggregate, like a city or a sector of industry, has not, to my knowledge, been demonstrated. I suspect it would. In fact I find it hard to even imagine anything that contributes less to mutual understanding in a community than the current vast expenditure on one-way communications to the masses via television.

Let us now take a close look, in turn, at the possibilities for new participative forms for the management of very large enterprises, and for the governing of large populations. Remember that we are looking only for points where a start may be made; we are not expecting any final theoretical solutions.

Alternatives to Management arising from the grassroots participation of the workers

Let me sum up the situation, as I see it, in three points:

○ When worker self management is established, we find that the Managing Director works much more on serving the whole range of concerns of the board, not just internal management and the immediate interfaces with customers, suppliers, regulators and others. He lets his management team look after a great many of the matters of internal management that were formerly centred in his role; that is, coordinating and controlling their efforts so that the operating teams know what is being asked of them and are supplied with what they need to get on with the pursuit of those objectives.

○ I do not think that our experience with democratisation at the workface has suggested that no one should be in the management unless he or she has a proven capability to carry the managerial responsibilities, or has been selected because they are judged able to learn to do so. There seems to be no role for a workers' representative, as a departmental or divisional head. This is because there are still many areas of difficult decision making for which experience at the workface is not an adequate training. Something like management training is required, because the need for managers is still there in all the larger organisations.

○ What meaning can participating democracy have at this level? I think that participation in management has at least three necessary features:

 • that the work of the managerial employees be itself democratised;

 • that the interface of management with the work teams be participative. Therefore, the translation of management objectives into team objectives and of team performance into release of more company resources needs to be conducted at regular and frequent meetings of a 'core group' of workers and management (Emery & Thorsrud, 1975; McWhinney, 1975);

 • that the interface between management and the board be transformed by: (i) clearly defining their shared values by a statement of organisational purposes and philosophy, one that recognizes the principle of trusteeship (Hill, 1971); and (ii) that conscious efforts be made to ensure that the mental models of the organisation and its environment held by management and the board be more closely matched, although in the first instance those models should be arrived at as *independently* as possible.

Alternative to the Company Board

I do not think that the functions of the board are best served by increasing management participation on the board. That sort of participation, even though it is democratic in form, threatens too many other wider and longer term social interests. I see no viable alternatives to the company board, and that applies equally to private enterprises and nationalised enterprises (Emery & Thorsrud, 1969). No other body can perform the function that they serve; i.e., overseeing the allocation of generalised capital to particular investments so as to maximise the growth of that capital.

A board is hindered in serving this function if it includes *representatives* of outside parties, be they customers' representatives, workers' representatives, representatives of regulatory bodies or the like. All such representatives will be biased toward their special interest regardless of the overall company picture. Negotiation about such special interests must be postponed until there is at least some overall picture arrived at by the board.

Then what does participative democracy mean at this level? I can see four steps that will at least help a board to keep the exercise of its power 'consonant with a democratised society':

○ the board explicitly recognises the essentially social ownership of the resources they use. If they can induce their shareholders to accept this proposition of trusteeship then they are in a position to instruct their management to make their decisions in this socially responsible way;

○ the board produces an explicit statement for their management of the philosophy that must be observed in the management of human resources;

○ the board works with the appropriate regional and industry sector organisations to determine in more concrete ways the objectives they can and should pursue in the society; and

○ the board itself works as a group having joint responsibility for all of its actions; not each acting as if they had their own private domain.

Now let us review what has been spelt out as the necessary limitations on participative democracy.

The model I have presented leaves us with three different levels of function—board, management and operators.

The boundaries between these functions should not stay where they are now, but it does seem that in large organisations these functions are at any one time best performed by different people. It also seems that these functions wouldn't be better carried out if those responsible for policy making had to be joined in the first stage of their work by representatives of those who would be subsequently influenced by their decisions.

What I am saying is that if someone is an operator, even a very good one, this is not evidence that that person could act as a good manager; being a very good manager is not in itself evidence that that person is what a board is looking for as a member. The reverse also holds. Also being good at management is no qualification for an operator's job.

Do the reservations I have spelt out about management and the board mean that participative democracy in large-scale organisations is a lame duck; won't fly far or high; representative democracy is a dead duck? I think not.

But, if there is to be participation it must mean something other than being personally present at all decision making or always being represented by an elected peer.

With the introduction of self managing work groups the operators have effective *organisational power* and hence the relations between the three parties need not take the hierarchical form that is inevitable when the operators are powerless. The control of each other, the workers, the management and the board, can be mutual, and directed at some shared objectives. The model for their relationship should be the model which we have already successfully tested for teams in which multiskilling is not feasible or feasible only to a minor degree; e.g., R & D project teams, teams of craftsmen in heavy engineering and management teams (Emery & Emery, 1974; Herbst, 1976; McWhinney, 1975). That is, for the purpose of getting the work of the organisation done, we recognise three broad classes of workers whose skills are not interchangeable to any marked degree; i.e., at management, at the board and operations.

For a large organisation to function in this non hierarchical democratic way there needs to be:

○ sharing of inputs so that coordination is possible;

○ mutual awareness of each other's role of what each is best fitted for and in a position to best do or decide;

° an explicitly agreed hierarchy of objectives (not a hierarchy of statuses) as a basis for allocating tasks and responsibilities.

The minimum set of mechanisms adequate to bring about and maintain these conditions has been outlined above in discussing the roles of management and the board. Many more and varied ways can be expected to evolve. However, two principles need to be observed in the functioning of the core groups: linking management and operator teams.

° What might be called the *jury system*, whereby every employee can expect to be called on to serve in the *core group* at some time; whilst serving he or she is expected, like the jury person, to make their own contribution, not to act as if they represented anyone else. The fact that some individuals may not be able to make much of an obvious contribution is not a real drawback if the able ones are prepared to give a bit extra.

° The principle of *reafference or search*. Expecting that learning is necessary, the effort should be made to learn by doing and constantly searching out and trying out new ways. If the people in the core group relapse into just pooling existing knowledge a pattern of dependence on the experts will certainly assert itself, and personal statuses, personal praise and blame, will displace the task orientation required for successful search.

Toward Matrix Organizations

Let us now turn to the other class of problems. How can participative selfmanagement emerge in the governing of such extended populations as cities, regions, nations or sectors of industry? There is an advantage in being as concrete as possible, so I will concentrate on the most developed practical solution that I know of from personal involvement - the development of participative self governing machinery for the Australian manufacturing industry.

There has been a long history of efforts throughout this century to enhance the self government of industry. Robert A Brady has given us the most detailed analysis of the efforts up to the 1940s. Remarkably similar mechanisms emerged in USA, Germany, Italy, etc, all pointing toward the corporate state model. The essential characteristics identified by Brady were:

...hierarchical implementation of patrimonial class domination by monopolistically oriented and compactly organised vested interest groups. (Beer, 1972, p.58)

I think these features are easily recognisable. The state lends its authority to the highest councils of industry and they lay down the law for the lower levels of councils in the branches and the regions. Within this framework the largest and most monopolistically organised firms can claim the right to be on the highest councils and then proceed to shape things to suit themselves. Nonbusiness interests are excluded from the inner councils although the councils are enjoined to extend to the workers fair and just treatment, as a father would to his children. They are also typically enjoined to eschew sharp business practices and to ensure that the customers get good quality at fair prices.

It is just too easy to recognise that these forms of self government are not consonant with a democratic form of society.

The so-called Jackson Committee for the future of manufacturing industry set its face against such a form of selfgovernment. It deliberately sought to design a matrix organisation such that:

∘ Councils would exist for national, regional and industry branches but they would be non-hierarchically arranged, because, "networks work better than hierarchies" (p.216). There would be no assumption that national interests necessarily override regional ones or that branch interests naturally override the interests of a manufacturer, even a small one. The underlying theoretical model is that of the 'self managing group based on minimal multiskilling'—the model we have just been discussing.

∘ Representation on the councils would not be based on similarity of business interest but on the principle of common concern for the resources of the society that are drawn into the manufacturing process. The workers, consumers, government officials and other interests are naturally drawn into the deliberations of the councils; not excluded as in the corporate model. Membership of the councils would naturally overlap.

∘ The overriding task of all councils is to strive for common understanding of what is happening in the social ecosystem that they share, and what are the ideals they share, and what it is that they commonly value. It is only within the framework of such mutually shared understandings that they seek to identify the changes they need in existing policies and regulations or they seek to innovate in new directions. This is a reversal of the typical joint stock operation or gambling syndicate. The first step for the latter is to decide what each wants to get from the venture and only then to consider the social ecosystem. They consider that, only in the narrow sense of what the market will bear, or what the society will wear.

○ These councils will not seek to do their primary business of searching out common values and what is happening 'out there' by operating in the traditional mode of committees meeting or papers-and-discussion in conference. Their processes will require a new tradition in which the searching is conducted without reference to the relative statuses of the participants and stringent efforts are made to ensure that the fight-flight emotions of horse trading are given no chance to emerge before a framework of mutual understanding exists. This will not be achieved by sitting around in meeting rooms with the usual paraphernalia of chairperson and agenda; nor by passing on business from one meeting to the next. To search successfully they will have to be prepared from time to time to take themselves off to some secluded place for several days and nights of continuous working (the committee expected that members would be so occupied three to five times per year).

In this connection, I will recall the Council of the National Farmers' Union (UK) trying to conduct a search operation through a series of fourteen half day meetings. Only after all of this effort did they admit that they were getting nowhere and in fact were making matters worse as confusion, misapprehension and dissension deepened. They finally in despair took the whole fifty of themselves out into a country retreat and in two days and nights produced a radically new perspective for the agricultural industry. That perspective was so well worked out that it guided them through a whole series of successful decisions for at least seven years (my knowledge of NFU affairs ended then).

To judge from just the four points I have mentioned, it should be clear that the design brought forward by the Jackson Committee stands in diametrical opposition to the corporate model and it does imply some break with the Westminster traditions. It is firmly based on the principle that "integration (of policies) is better done by those involved, in the light of understood and accepted principles, rather than by imposition of a superior authority." (p.225 ibid). Is this a workable design?

Provided that the Councils can learn to work in the style of a genuine 'search conference' I see no real obstacles. The existing bureaucracies will bitterly resent having their noses put out of joint but they can hardly claim that their way has been successful.

To return to my overall theme. Now that we have had so much success in solving the problems of grassroots participation, we should take up the question of more participative forms at the higher levels. I have tried to indicate some ways in which participation can be increased. We are certainly not in sight of the end of the road but the work of the Jackson Committee demonstrates that even the few theoretical tools we have are practical working tools. The encouraging lesson to emerge from this exploration is that the same basic principles of participative design that guided us in redesigning the work of skilled craftsmen, scientists, engineers and managers at grassroots level are fruitful guides to redesigning at the higher levels at which we seek to govern ourselves.

Now I think I must confront the question of whether these directions are appropriate ones for the less developed countries.

The organizational forms for industry, commerce and administration in these countries are not very different from those in the western countries or for that matter in the Soviet Union. Hence our discussion of how we might democratise total organizations is of relevance for the less developed countries.

The principles of the extended matrix organization were illustrated by reference to the introduction of democratic non hierarchical forms of self management to the Australian manufacturing sector. The principles are certainly not limited to this. In fact the first consciously evolved matrix organization started to emerge in the British agricultural search conference to which I have just referred. Also from my preliminary studies this seems to be the most fruitful direction we can go in our present efforts in Australia to evolve democratic, non hierarchical forms of regional self government.

I cannot see any general reason why the matrix type organization would not be equally appropriate in any of the less developed countries that are genuinely striving for participative democracy.

However, I can see a practical difficulty that looms larger in the less developed countries. To work effectively the participative bodies and the government administration at every span of concern, from the village to the nation, most have mutually shared understandings about the tasks they both face and the values and ideals that guide them. We think it is a hard enough problem in Australia to create this mutual understanding between civil servants and farmers, labourers, businessmen, pensioners, young unmarried mothers and the like. We are taking the problem seriously enough to consider discarding some of our civil service traditions. The gaps we are disturbed by are infinitesimal concerned with those that exist in the less developed countries. In these countries even the minimal education which will let a person into the lowest clerical grade of the civil service is enough to turn a person right away from village life and indeed from any form of manual labour, even skilled labour. When the vast majority live by physical labour in towns and villages this is a very serious barrier to participative bodies ever effectively commanding the services of their civil services.

I think that the crux of the problem is at the narrowest span of interest; e.g., where the village development officer is face to face with the villagers, the police constable face to face with the local citizens. If, at this point, there is no effective communication leading to shared understanding there is not likely to be much shared understanding when broader spans of interest are involved.

It is possible to do something about this critical interface without waiting decades for the educational level of the villages to be raised or a hundred years for their style of life to be transformed. In the Northern Territory of Australia, the interface between the Department of Aboriginal Affairs and the nomad and camp aboriginals have traditionally been the district patrol officers and camp superintendents. Each district officer had his own territory and I think we have to conclude that the majority of officers gave up the struggle to understand the viewpoint of the other officers. The aboriginals had no chance to understand the policies of the Department. All that they could see were the individual officers, some young and eager to help, some lazy and indifferent, some bossy and angry. As a first step to remedy this, groups of four to five officers were given group responsibility for the whole of the four to five districts that were previously their individual territories. We found, as expected, that these groups of officers enforced amongst themselves a consistent interpretation of departmental policy and insured that, regardless of change of personnel through promotion, transfers, etc, this consistency could be maintained over some time. Working this way the officers were able to deepen their understanding of the situation of the aboriginals and support each other to the extent that each could go on learning. The old pattern of personal enthusiasm giving way to cynicism and then to drunken neglect of the aboriginals has, as far as can be detected, disappeared.

We found it possible to go a step further when Papua New Guinea decided to evolve an administrative structure that would serve their traditions of village self government and not the colonial traditions of centralised paternalistic controls. The step further was to develop in the civil service a new type of civil servant at the interface with the villages. This is now being done in two test regions, so far successfully. The set of ideas underlying these practical trials were fairly complex and hence the briefest way of communicating them is to present the original design document. It outlines both the new ways in which these 'barefoot' civil servants were to be selected and trained and the way they would work.

'Toward a Village Development Service' – 3 Basic Principles

1. teamwork at grassroots interface—four or five officers responsible together for an area;

2. learning not teaching, not a didactic training of officers;

3. the where and when of learning to be decided by 'student' requirements; i.e., down near the grassroots, in their best time. Not some sort of 'one academic year' in the physical context of an urban teaching institute.

Basically a plan for learning that starts from the villages and is contrary to the present organisation for teaching in educational institutions, and contrary to the usual modus operandi of their staffs.

Principle 1

○ 'Teamwork' not just 'team spirit'. Team spirit is only going to be persistent and significant if it arises from teamwork; from the people who are supposed to constitute a team actually accepting joint responsibility for carrying out together some significant work and joint responsibility for its outcome.

○ The interface at the village level (grassroots 'interface') must literally be a team; e.g., four to five officers responsible for four to five villages.

  • Ideally the officers would be fully multiskilled but in practice we would have to accept that each would have strong points and weak points. It would be up to the team to help out as much as they could in which every village needed this help at any one time. In this process we would expect a growth in personal skills. We would also expect such a team to cover each other for absences due to holidays, sickness, continued education.

  • To start with, the 'officers' would be no more than the people recommended by the village for a slight upgrading of skills of use to the village. The intervillage teams would start from such selected people learning together at some district centre for a week or two, then subsequently by helping each other out in joint projects.

- As an intervillage team started to emerge, the team would be given opportunities to improve their operation as a team and, in particular, to develop a social mechanism whereby they could set periodic goals together with the local council and the district coordination committee of departmental representatives.

Principle 2

○ The educationalists should accept that teams chosen for an area should design their curricula, decide what resources they will use and how, and decide when and where they do their learning. If some educationalists feel that they cannot go along with these decisions then they can stand aside.

○ The extension officers should be encouraged to do as much of their learning as possible on the job or at least in the villages they are going to serve. If in the villages, then as many villagers as possible should be included in each particular learning session.

○ In keeping with the way they are going to work, learning should be organised around self managing learning cells. Co-operation between teams should be practised between those having contiguous territories.

Principle 3

This invokes the broader principle of preserving the identity of the extension officer with his locality. Insofar as their work will concern agriculture, transportation, communication, commerce, medicine, as well as social organisation, they should be less prone to politicalisation than the North American 'community development officers'. Their career structures must allow for officers to advance by the process of broadening their skills (as a Boy Scout adds on his badges). This would mean continuous education for these people.

Establishing such a general purpose extension service requires, at least:

○ Getting it strongly sanctioned by national leaders—political and public service;

○ Mobilising PNG teaching institutions—possibly overcoming their rivalries through establishing a joint venture with a fair degree of independence. A search conference would probably be needed to achieve this and to firmly tie such a joint venture into the three principles enunciated above;

o After the first three teams have been tentatively brought into being, the middle structure of district management should be tackled;

o The scheme should not have its sights locked on the young, educated male.

What I have described in the Northern Territory and in Papua New Guinea are only small steps but it is a good place at which to conclude. Most of the designs I have mentioned are first steps or small steps. I know of no other way of advancing other than this step-by-step process of carrying ideas into practice. Elaborate theoretical or mathematical models of adaptive human systems are only a barrier to anyone putting ideas into practice,

References

Beer, Stafford 1972, Brain of the Firm, London, Professional Library.

Brady R A 1943, Business as a System of Power, New York, Columbia University Press.

De Nitish R 1976, 'Training Strategy for Required Attitudinal Change', New Delhi, National Labour Institute Bulletin, January. (This reports on the development of self-managing teams in Bharat Heavy Electricals Ltd., Hardware)

Duke C 1975, 'Bachelor Camp Papers 1973-75', Centre for Continuing Education, Australian National University, Canberra (These papers report on the reorganisation of the district administration in the Northern Territory).

Emery F E and E Thorsrud 1969, Form and Content in Industrial Democracy, London, Tavistock Publications.

Emery F E and M Emery 1973, Hope Within Walls, Centre for Continuing Education, Australian National University, Canberra.

Emery F E and M Emery Participative Design: Work and Community Life, Centre for Continuing Education, Australian National University, Canberra.

Emery F E and E Thorsrud 1975, Democracy at Work, Martinus Nijhoff, Leiden.

Emery F E and M Emery 1975, Choice of Futures, Martinus Nijhoff, Leiden.

Herbst P F 1976, Alternative to Hierarchies, Martinus Nijhoff, S'Gravenshage.

Hill P 1971, Towards a New Philosophy of Management, Epping, Gower Press.

Jackson R G, R H Carnegi.e., R J L Hawke, B W Brogan, N S Curri.e., E L Wheelwright 1975, Policies for Development of Manufacturing Industry: A Green Paper, AGPS, Canberra.

McWhinney W 1975, Dual Hierarchies, Los Angeles Graduate School of Management, UCLA.

Rice A K 1958, Productivity and Social Organisation, the Ahmenabad Experiment, London, Tavistock Publications.

Sommerhoff G 1975, Logic of the Living Brain, London, John Wiley & Sons.

Williams T 1975, Democracy in Learning, Centre for Continuing Education, Australian National University, Canberra.

Industry Councils:

Comments on one aspect of the Jackson Report

Fred Emery, 1976

THE JACKSON REPORT attached great importance to the Industrial Councils but did not attempt to give a blue print of how they might be staffed, their reporting channels and their modus operandi.

At the Sun City workshop* one of the three syndicates devoted itself to these questions and debated its views in two plenary sessions. This note is one person's perception of what was worked out.

Staffing of the Councils

We found it easiest to start with identifying what would not be satisfactory. A council made up of Ministerial appointees seemed too likely to be a tool or front for the Department and to be seen as such. An elected body seemed more likely to be independent and to be seen as more truly representative of the various interests in an industry. However, and quite apart from the messy problem of defining the electorates, we had some doubts about how long such bodies would remain 'truly representative'. International experience (Brady, 1944) suggests that very soon the big organizations would push for and win the commanding heights. No doubt they would welcome some continuing token representation of the small organizations and minority interests in order to maintain the facade.

These token representatives are likely to be seen as Uncle Tom's by small business people etc, and encourage their apathy toward, and rejection to the Councils. The behaviour of these token representatives is likely to re-reinforce these trends. They will tend to regard themselves as a cut above their electorate by the mere fact of being elected to such auspicious bodies.

The candidates backed by the big organizations would soon occupy the key roles and probably, because of the patronage, they would act as a Shell representative, a Mobil representative, an AMWU representative or what have you, not as an industry representative. The implied risk is that

*Workshop on the human and social aspects of the Jackson Report. Sponsored by Faculty of Commerce, University of WA, Sun City, Yanchip, 15-18 June 1976.

the business of the Councils would be confined to horse trading and posturing, and much of the real business of the industry would still be conducted by back door lobbying.

We sought very hard for some other way in which the Councils could be manned so that:

○ they could command the *respect* of Australian parliaments and the people because of their collective experience, knowledge and representation of the major interests directly involved in the industry;

○ they could command the trust of parliaments and the people because they were patently villain-proof.

I personally feel that unless both respect and trust could be ensured the Industrial Councils should *not* be set up. Councils that do not meet these conditions would be a misdirection of resources and a nuisance.

A promising alternative emerged. The principle involved is that which underlies our Anglo Saxon system for selecting juries and which has found other applications both ancient and modern (see next paper). It is the same principle that is used in probability mathematics to draw a random stratified sample that will represent a large and varied population. In order to get to grips with the practicalities, the syndicate at Sun City set itself the task of formulating guidelines that would help the oil industry set up an Oil Industry Council (three members of the syndicate had a good deal of experience with that particular industry). It seemed that:

○ some of the key parties in the industry can be readily identified; e.g, the 9+ oil companies, their employees, unions, service station owners, NRMA and other consumer organizations, local governments in refinery areas, industry and government users;

○ representatives of these parties would have the responsibility of drawing up a list of directly interested parties (it was assumed that governmental processes would be responsible for looking after those less directly interested). This list would have to be acceptable to parliament and the people;

○ much of the parties would have the responsibility of creating an electoral roll of people in their strata of interests, and providing a publicly defensible explanation of their basis of choice. For very numerous strata, like users of heating oil, the list need not be more than a few hundred;

○ posts on the ICs to represent a particular strata are drawn by a random sampling technique, not by nomination and not by voting.

There are problems of details here, but let us first see what flows from the application of the principle.

One negative implication seems apparent—the outstanding individual cannot be selected out for special service and the incompetent passed over. This is inevitable. If selection from the lists is by a genuine random process then the dullest person on the list has the same chances of appointment as the most brilliant. In the systems of appointment and election it is possible that the best would be chosen more often than chance would have it. Possible, but not usual. In appointments, loyalty and such factors are generally of more importance than proven competence. In elections, popularity and strength of backing are critical and neither of these factors favour the tall poppies. For these reasons we were not over impressed by this objection.

On the positive side the 'jury system' appeared to have several things going for it:

○ the selected representatives know that they are on the council just because they are on the industry-strata list, A random selection procedure got them there so they have no grounds for self-delusion; they are still 'one of the old network' and can be expected to be treated as such. More than that, they are beholden to no one for their appointment or potential re-appointment. They have no patron; no party debts to pay off. He or she may not be the brightest person in the strata but at least they can participate in the work of the Council without having to follow outside instructions;

○ The Council will be more likely to be seen by Parliament and people as being their own selves. Their advice may be judged to be erratic, ill informed etc but there will be less of the suspicion that hidden hands have drafted the advice;

○ If such Councils exist to give public advice, then private lobbying channels are likely to dry up. Even if a parliament felt a Council's first advice was incompetent, it would probably feel happier about referring the matter back to the Council with guidelines as to what evidence it needed, rather than turn to lobbying channels that are ipso facto biased sources of information.

With these points in mind, one negative and three potentially positive, let us consider some of the obvious practical problems.

Initiatives and Reporting

Our feeling seemed to be that the Councils should, like statutory bodies, have the privilege of tabling their advisory reports in Parliament. It seemed quite undesirable that they report only to a department, or only to a minister, or to a cabinet. Only in this way did it seem possible that the Councils could avoid the suspicion of going into collusion with department parties or ministers' behind-the-scenes pressure on the legislature. The manner in which a Council arrived at its advice could be kept fairly private, but its advice should be open to public scrutiny in the parliament and the media. The government of the day would determine how the advice was acted on, but only in the knowledge that it was publicly known what advice they had received. If for some reason the Government needs private advice they have many other channels for getting it. We are simply suggesting that if the ICs are used for this purpose it would undermine their role.

It seemed to us desirable that any approved IC, be it regional, sectorial, state or national, should have equal right to table its advisory reports in any Australian Parliament, state or federal. This would require Federal-State agreement, but we did not feel that should be too difficult to achieve. Any parliament could ignore a tabled submission if it so desired. We felt that this was important because some matters that could arise in a regional council could have national significance, some matters of national importance might be particularly significant to several of the states.

We felt also that this was one way in which a network of councils could be established instead of the traditional hierarchies. It seemed to us that it could be only in the national interest if a regional - industry sector council could directly advise at state or federal level without being filtered through a next higher level council which would not necessarily appreciate their concerns.

Within this network of councils we would expect that initiatives could arise at any point. A parliament might refer a request for advice to any council that they thought appropriate. Ditto between councils. Councils might also in some way, query a parliament as to whether it would appreciate advice on some matter. (A thought: it occurs to me in writing the above, that we were in effect trying to turn the councils into creatures of the parliaments, not of departments, ministers, powerful manufacturing enterprises or powerful unions. This bothers me not.)

Reports that are tabled in our parliaments can easily finish up in limbo. Mr Fraser's recent innovation of the back bench committees suggests a way in which at least the major ICs might avoid that fate. Such a back bench committee that assumed a responsibility for an IC would be a fair assurance that parliament, the minister or the cabinet did not walk away from serious, though controversial advice. The press would be a back-stop.

Resources

To gain and hold respect, the ICs would have to mobilize resources that enable them to give advice that cannot easily be put down by Government departments or non-government interest groups.

The first question concerns their internal resources: what the council members themselves possess in terms of experience, knowledge and competence. This brings us back to the objection to random selection we outlined earlier. The first answer is just this: if the strata lists are built up on the system of the reference-jury list (see next paper) we can reasonably expect from probability theory, that any dozen will be pretty well as good as any other dozen that will emerge from random selection. To ensure the operation of this mathematical principle we must be prepared for councils of 20-40 members, so that at any one time each of the major stratas of interest has four to six members. This is still a workable number for the purposes the ICs are expected to achieve. We will discuss this below. Such numbers also allow for the overlap of service, and hence continuity, that we have in our Senate system.

The second question concerns 'owned resources'. We felt that each council should have a staff of resource people to service the council's meeting arrangements, its briefs for its own meetings and its briefs to other bodies. We felt, however, that the staff should:

° be minimal so that the cart should not direct the horse;

° be composed of people on secondment from the various strata of interest including governments for about two year periods, so that they could identify with the purpose of the council.

Arrangements would have to be made to ensure that satisfactory service on secondment counted for more, in terms of promotion, than a similar length of service in the 'home' organization. Hence that 'field service' would be eagerly sought.

The third question concerns 'accessible resources'. If the ICs are to be discouraged from building up their own staff empires they must have access to capable and publicly creditable sources of research. Our thoughts centred on the Jackson Committee's idea of a Bureau of Manufacturing studies and the Crisp committee's recommendation of an independent Australian statistician. We felt that all approved ICs should have the power to make reasonable demands on such bodies for collection and analysis of data. Beyond this, we felt that the ICs should for most practical purposes be regarded as 'standing Royal Commissions'; i.e., able to receive submissions.

If the ICs develop the standing with Parliament and the people that we expect, then they would not need to be endowed with the legal powers of Royal Commissions. Independent missions of enquiry into an industry would be needed only in the very rare instances where powerful groups in an industry were seen to be subverting an IC.

If a parliament is uneasy about the advice it gets from an IC it is still able to refer to other independent sources; e.g., the IAC.

Modus Operandi

To be representative in the way we envisaged, the ICs would need to be of 20-40 in number. Only thus could we be assured of a reasonable quality of representation for each strata, and be reasonably assured that the representatives had not been seduced by special interests.

This ceiling number of 40 can work effectively, in my experience, at the primary task of identifying common interests, just so long as they do not try to operate via the traditional media of chairs, agendas, motions and voting on motions. To be effective the ICs would need to meet in a more open mode, probably less frequently than the existing Industry Panels, for a couple of days and nights at a time to thoroughly search out the emerging matters of importance in their industry, and frame their advice within the longer term common interests that they can identify. This might mean coming together once every nine to twelve months. It might mean more frequent gatherings if the particular industry is in a state of turmoil.

An IC will probably need an executive committee to carry on its work between its workshops/conferences. Again, to prevent the building in of biases, we felt that the executive committee should be selected by random selection processes, not elected or appointed. Thus each person knows that when their name is on an industry-strata list, they have a social obligation to serve a stretch on council if their number is called, and a further obligation to serve on the steering committee, if so rostered.

It seems unnecessary and undesirable to appoint an independent Chair from outside the industry. Such appointments would create a bias toward formality so that the Chair could exercise its assumed authority.

Conclusion

It was generally agreed in the syndicate that it was not fruitful for them to try and go much further along the lines indicated above. The next useful step seemed like that suggested in the Green Paper (p.221): appoint a working party in a couple of sectors and let them get down to work out concrete proposals suitable for their sector. It seemed to us that a lot of their learning could be carried over to the benefit of other sectors.

Reference

Brady R A 1944, *Business as a System of Power*, University of Columbia Press, NY.

The Jury System and Participative Democracy

Fred Emery 1976

THE JURY SYSTEM is expected to yield a valid representation of what the community feels and thinks or wants in terms of justice, fair play and decency.

Their decisions can ruin a person's life career, inflict long periods of incarceration or even lead to the abrupt ending of a life. These matters have long been regarded as too serious to allow jury selection by voting and too serious to allow decision making in the jury by a majority vote.

If a jury fails to achieve consensus it is a 'hung jury' and it is dissolved, to be replaced by the original selection procedure. This selections procedure has at least the following essential elements:

○ all adults have a duty to serve;

○ they are not selected by popular vote but by turns;

○ they cannot be lobbied as they are not viewed as representatives;

○ they must seek consensus.

The use of this procedure for determining government service would write off elitist assumptions. Such elitist assumptions are implicit in elected representative systems; eg, the evolution of the Westminster system. Some people assume that they are better fitted to rule by reason of birth, property, education etc. The elected regard themselves as a cut above others.

Notes on 'Jury System in politics'

1. As with the legal jury system, some people are ineligible for the lists because of age (immaturity), insanity or criminal record.

2. Once nominated by ballot there must be a 'posting of bans' (as with weddings). If challenged an open public hearing must be held. If a majority at that meeting vote for or against the nominee it is open to either nominee or challengers to demand a secret ballot by their community. This may seem expensive but it seems improbable that more than a small minority of nominations would be challenged. Thus the total cost should be very much less than holding general elections. Even the cost question is not critical. The overriding

consideration is to prevent stacking of public meetings to manipulate the appointments by special interests favouring or prejudicing the chances of service of a nominee for their own ends, not community ends.

3. It is an important feature of this procedure that it weakens the role of political parties. The majority of the candidates would be beholden to no party for their election, nor for their future. The parties might for a while campaign for challenged members but that would bring them little credit.

4. As compensation for service and an aid to readjust to private careers persons would have the right to as many years of education at state expense as their years of service.

5. The levels of government might be:

   ° collective (urban or rural, 300-500 adult voters)
     or some 1,000 persons);
   ° region;
   ° state.

Sampling frame

		Sampling ratio	N
Federal/State	all who have held regional office		
Regional 200,000	all who have held town-district office		
Town-District 10,000	all who have held town-district office		
Local (500)	complete electoral roll of the locality	1:100	5

Note: Using this sampling method for representation should ensure that women are properly represented right to the highest level; ditto for all minorities.

Nomination to higher office should be restricted to those who have served in lower officer. If their service was not well done they could be challenged.

Two-up, one-down

Election to Local level should mean one year as assistant at regional, then back to local service. Ditto for other levels.

The 'two-up, one-down' principle: The purpose of this is to bridge broad gaps in extent or span of concern. By participating in a meaningful way in the policy formulation at the broader level (without the responsibility of making the decisions) people can get a greater understanding of the context in which they will subserviently be contributing to decisions at the borrower level.

Thus, for example, by understanding the limitations to the powers of Federal and State governments, and additional demands on them, the regional 'public servants' can be more reasonable in their requests of those bodies.

In effect it helps create a shared psychological field between bodies whose prime concerns are different. They should realize that the different and potentially conflictful ends are being pursued by people at least as honourable as themselves.

Note: the interpenetration of levels will also occur because after service at any of the broader (higher) levels a person is still likely for subsequent selection for the lower levels. These people may not be numerous but would be valuable resources for any governing body. At the narrower levels of locality and town-district, people should be so familiar with both levels that this mechanism may not be required. This familiarity is not likely, however, when a person moves to the regional level and has to deal with region-state and region-federal interfaces.

Precedents

This notion was inspired by George Collier's account of the traditional system widespread among the Indians of Mesoamerica:

> The positions (of public service) are ranked into levels, service in all but the first level presupposing earlier services et the level below. Every mature male is expected to provide ritual service for the community at some point in his life by occupying a ritual position as the lowest level. During his year of service, the man will leave his hamlet to live in the township center to perform ritual at great personal expense. The heavy cost of this ritual requires years of careful

savings of the meager excess earnings of farm production above subsistence needs. Yet the spiritual and social rewards of service are such that many seek subsequent service at additional heavy cost in positions at higher levels of the hierarchy later in life. Indeed, those men who succeed in performing at all of the hierarchy's levels have proved themselves worthy of the greatest respect. *(Fields of the Tzotzil*, 1974 University of Texas Press, p.13)

Among the Pathans there is another variant of participative, non Westminster democracy:

The *jirga* is probably the most interesting of all the Pathans' institutions. It can best be described as an assembly or council, and it serves the functions of both. The word can be applied to half a dozen men sitting down together to discuss what they should say to the political agent who is coming to object to their sons shooting off the porcelain insulators from the nearby telegraph line.

More properly a *jirga* is a group of members of a particular sub group of Pathans considering a matter of common interest. There is seldom any formal selection of representatives. Among the tribes virtually every adult male may attend. Among others tradition clearly indicates those who are entitled to participate. In any event there is no making of motions, and no voting. Decisions are unanimous and are arrived at by taking the 'sense of the meeting'. (Some of them would chill the blood of the peaceful Friends who coined the term.) The traditional penalty for anyone who defies the decision of a jirga is the burning of the culprit's house. Since the tribesmen do not lay aside their arms while deliberating, punishment can be executed promptly.

Apart from enforcing its own penalty for contempt, there is little of the judicial or police function in the jirga's role in the community, It does not ordinarily determine guilt or inflict punishment but seeks to achieve a settlement. (Spain J W 1962, *The Way of the Pathans*, Karachi, Oxford Uni Press, p.50)

Other examples could be drawn upon, and I hope to write about these in the near future. My point here is to emphasise that democracy did not begin with Westminster. Further, they were models that sought for participatory democracy.

The evolution of the Westminster model, however, has been a history of giving way to popular demand but seeking to hold participation to minimum.

Misrepresentativeness

My concern about the utility of the Westminster system of representative government is twofold: (1) It always leads to a misrepresentative elected body. More men than women, more rich than poor, more lawyers than business people, more farmers or workers etc; and (2) it inevitably acts to dampen down participation (See first paper in Part III).

The kind of representativeness that we could find in the 'jury system' type of government is clearly explained by a US Supreme Court judgement of 1957:

> The American tradition of trial by jury... necessarily contemplates an impartial jury drawn from a cross section of the community. This does not mean, of course, that every jury must contain representatives of all the economic, social, religious, racial, political and geographical groups of the community... it does mean that prospective jurors shall be selected by court officials without systematic intentional exclusion of any of these groups. (Bloomstein M J 1968, *Verdict: the jury system*, pp.54-5, NY Dodd, Mead & Coy.)

I think I have indicated my preference for a random sampling procedure from an up-to-date list of all eligible adults. However, in many circumstances this may not be the best solution. The cost of creating and maintaining such a list of citizens can be exorbitant in an underdeveloped country; it may be too much trouble to contact and gain the cooperation of a randomly selected sample even in matters of life and death in a highly developed country, with cars, telephones, etc.

This problem has been faced by the US Federal Courts. The methods of federal selection includes recommendations by leading citizens of the community, known to court officials for their good character.

The social reference system is one we have used for three community and one university Search Conference. On each occasion it yielded a sample of citizens that could not be faulted because of misrepresentativeness.

An Idea of the Sorts of Magnitudes That Would Be Involved in Australia

A.

Size of Unit	Size of 'Electorate'	Number of Sub-Units Included			Rate of Sampling at Each Unit	Number of Reps per Level in Nation	Approx. No. of Level Reps Committed	Time Committed
		States	Regions	Towns/Districts	Localities			
Federal 16,000,000	8,000,000	7	64	1,600	16,000	1 in 120,000	142	142	Full
State* 3,000,000	1,500,000	-	12	300	3,000	1 in 30,000	50	350	Full
Region 250,000	125,000.	-	-	25	250	1 in 2,500	50	3,200	-
Town/District 10,000	5,000	-	-	10	10	1 in 250	20	32,000	-
Locality 1,000	500	-	-	-	1	1 in 50	10	160,000	-
								196,000	

(*Median Sized)

i.e. 2.4% of 'electorate'

B.

	Initial Rate of Sampling per Electorate (Voters)		'2 up* 1 down'	Length of Tenure
Federal	142 / 350	1 in 2.5 ⎫	x	4 years
		⎬ 1 in 6		
State	350 / 3,200	1 in 11 ⎭	x	4 years
Region		1 in 10	x	3 years
Town/District	38 / 140	1 in 5		2 years
Locality		1 in 50		-2 years

C.

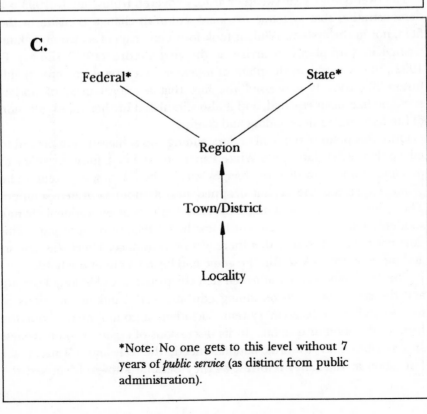

*Note: No one gets to this level without 7 years of *public service* (as distinct from public administration).

PART IV

IN EDUCATION

THE YEARS FROM 1989 to 1993 have seen a wave of activity and further diffusion in the world of work. It is also in this period that we have finally begun to see the transfer or flow-on effects from twenty years of learning about changing design principle in the workplace to the education system.

The education system has always been a target for change in people's minds, but it has for many proven a disappointing or illusory one. But change is now accelerating on many fronts, and in what has become the heartland of the first design principle, and the first educational paradigm, the universities, the lords of the educational manor. They are perhaps still more feudal than bureaucratic, despite some moves towards economic rationalist managerialism. Simultaneously goes the change in the behaviour of the lord's handmaiden, the secondary system.

The twenty-four year sweep of history covered from 1969 to 1993 is a demonstration that systemic (national, cultural) change is made in the field, not in the system. While it took fourteen years of focus on making change in workplaces to arrive at the first Accord (1983) (Emery F, 1992), this Accord was the point of inflexion in a typical learning or diffusion-(S)-curve. It expressed the fact that a critical mass of understanding had been reached, and it also stimulated further rapid diffusion of fundamental understanding and change.

Once this point of national understanding was achieved, it appeared to take only the Dawkins 1988 White Paper on Higher Education Policy to precipitate a rash of diverse changes within the education system. The White Paper was the crystal dropped into a super-saturated solution. The many small and seemingly unrelated efforts at educational change suddenly fell into a pattern which few had difficulty recognizing. This does not mean, of course, that there was no resistance. There was, and is; and more on this below. But the genie had been let out of the bottle.

The 1988 White Paper affirmed that the principle of life-long learning and the sector of adult/continuing education are fundamental parts of the Australian education system, including a commitment from the higher education institutions. In its discussions of equity, responsiveness and responsibility towards national need, the Dawkins (Minister for Education at the time) reforms, as they became known, identified the universities as *open systems*. This was the immediate point of recognition and paradigmatic confrontation.

Needless to say, although I heard many a debate, I never heard one about whether universities should be open or closed systems. The debates came closest to this core issue around questions of 'academic freedom' and university autonomy versus governmental control, directed and regulated research. Most emotional, however, were those debates which focused on a lower conceptual level of 'standards' and those which implicitly appealed to status and prestige.

For those higher education institutions which had a history of vocational relevance, an understanding of the principles of adult learning and a commitment to adaptive change, the White Paper was a bright green light. The example of this I have chosen is that of the University of New England, Northern Rivers (Lismore, NSW). It is the best documented development (Treyvaud and Davies, 1991) which includes a detailed study of the resistance to that development plus an outline of the strategy implemented to overcome the resistance and simultaneously accelerate the development of a radically new concept of a university. It should come as no surprise that the co-author Davies (above) is the same Alan Davies who features in this Part IV.

Before we come that that story, however, we should note that the government followed up its White Paper with a series of moves to support the thrust towards open systems and those institutions which were changing in order to produce learning and a democratically organized, multiskilled citizenry and workforce.

Government steps included instituting:

○ The Training Guarantee Levy (now 1.5% of payroll) which gives organizations a choice between training their employees or paying an equivalent tax penalty.

○ A Senate Committee investigation of Adult/Community Education (ACE). As the fourth but largest educational sector, ACE has now been recognized, and financially and otherwise formally takes its place in the dynamic merger of work and education. As *Come in Cinderella* makes clear, ACEs have been showing the way for years and "the time has come for us to back a winner" (p.xvi). Recommendations from this Committee have been or are being implemented.

○ A series of reports culminating so far with the Carmichael report (1992) recommended a move to proven (practical) competency- based training and life-long learning.

Establishing competencies is now underway through a wide range of industries. The establishment of competencies for academics is being resisted by the universities. A competency is a measure not only of 'know' or 'know how', but of 'can do'. Competencies are outcome-oriented. The Australian Vocational Certificate (AVC) training system will develop competencies in:

○ key areas needed for employment (key competencies);

○ vocational competencies specified by industry or enterprise.

Key competencies are specified as language and communication, mathematics, scientific and technological understanding, cultural understanding, problem solving, personal and interpersonal relations.

There will be four levels of certificate, training is open to all Australians, not just school students or leavers, and will be delivered by any mixture of schools, TAFE (Technical and Further Education) colleges, industry, community organizations, etc., and previous or current work or life experience. If competency can be demonstrated it will be recognized regardless of method of acquisition.

Open learning and self managed learning will be the norm, with 'teachers' who *manage the learning process*.

These changes which have been accepted by the government, amount to a wholesale change to design principle 2 and educational paradigm 2. In integrating theoretical (academic) work and experience acquired from any source, the 'education system' becomes a truly lifelong and nation-wide apprenticeship. It has the effects of:

○ destroying the stratification of students (people) into academics and others;

○ blurring the boundaries between educational institutions and all other parts of life.

In some universities also, totally new forms of provision in terms of content, process and access are adding to the transformation of the educational landscape.

University of New England. Northern Rivers

The University of New England, Northern Rivers (UNE.NR) has been a leader in this transformation with its pioneering of Centres for Professional Development (CPDs), and now a proliferation of Open Learning Centres.

> The introduction of the Unified National System of Higher Education in 1988 and the consolidation of all NSW institutions into a university system provided the trigger for extremely rapid growth in CPDs at Northern Rivers. (Treyvaud and Davies, 1991, p.vii)

In particular, they mention the requirement for universities to be more responsive to Australia's economic imperatives and to break down the rigidities of conventional modes of educational delivery.

The CPD model is as follows:

- A *partnership* ('co-ownership') between UNE.NR and one or more employing organizations. Design and delivery of course material is a shared responsibility among mutually recognized staff. (CPDs use a mixture of university and 'adjunct' staff—those from industry with appropriate qualifications and experience.)

- CPD learning material is co-ordinated with, and accredited by, the relevant faculty and credit is accrued through a modular system. Partnership ensures industry relevance and university theoretical requirements.

- Right to assessment is retained by UNE.NR. *Advanced standing* or recognition of prior learning (RPL) is given (up to 75% of a degree, 1992) where a student can prove competence in a course.

- CPDs are financially self-sufficient and income-generating after a maximum of three years. All have non-disadvantaging sunset clauses.

- There is no central administrative structure to control CPDs. Co-ordination is managed between the relevant faculty and partners.

- Partner organizations use their own delivery systems and networks for delivery. This breaks the nexus between being on campus and university accreditation.

- Evaluation is independent and reported to both partners. It covers the objectives, the process and the product—whether "Participants have performed more effectively in the work system" (p.34). "The concept of the CPD is incompatible with the notion of the university as exclusively a scholarly, cloistered retreat" (p.54).

At the time of the evaluation report (1991), there were CPDs in Education, Health Sciences, Community and Human Resource Development,

Corrective Services and Telecom Integrated Management Development Program. Growth projections indicated that CPD enrolments in 1993 will approach the traditional type enrolments.

In addition to the original concept of CPD, UNE.NR is rapidly expanding its resourcing of Open Learning Centres which *facilitate* the provision of post-secondary education to meet the needs of a whole regional community (p.66). These centres cut across all institutional boundaries by providing access for independent learners to all learning support systems. Integrated theoretical and practical (experiential) learning is now an accepted part of daily life and work.

> Attitudes and value systems about the role and nature of universities become crucial issues at this point. A university which is not comfortable with a mission that seeks to provide more relevant learning for students, develop a greater appreciation of vocational skills and make contributions to national productivity will be unlikely to provide a fertile environment for the sort of co-operation required by a CPD. To do so calls for a readiness to acknowledge that universities are, in these times, not necessarily the major repositories of specialist knowledge and that change to their traditional nature may not only be embraceable without detriment to their role as society's intellectual cutting edge, but essential if they are not to be passed over as anachronistic and irrelevant. (Treyvaud and Davies 1991 p.55)

Resistance at UNE.NR

It was clear at UNE.NR that there was substantial resistance to the changes taking place which focused on the CPDs. A careful empirical study was made of both the resistance and support, in order that UNE.NR could devise strategies for co-operative relations towards further development (Emery and Emery 1991).

At the time of the study there were five CPDs in operation, but 55% of the sample knew little or nothing about them. This did not prevent them having strong attitudes towards them. There were two clusters of attitudes within those who actually knew little or nothing, one of which represented a solid rejection of the idea that the ivory tower was connected in any way to the outside world and a similarly solid rejection of the second educational paradigm (Part I).

In a further refinement of the data we found that:

○ attitude or paradigmatic belief systems are nearly three times as powerful as knowledge;

- knowledge is less relevant when the attitude is positive, i.e., when the second paradigm is accepted;

- when there is knowledge, there is a strengthening of the paradigmatic systems or arguments which widens the gap;

- when there is knowledge of CPDs and a strong paradigmatic belief system, the argument centres on the need to respond to social change by replacing the traditional concept of a university with more democratic arrangements.

This last point, and some of the very strong, dogmatic responses to the questionnaire, reinforce the centrality of the White Paper's message— that universities are open systems. The hard core of resistance denied this and hence could argue that there was no need for change.

As these points make clear, a direct strategy of attempting to increase knowledge about CPDs would have increased conflict.

The strategy adopted by UNE.NR, therefore, was an *indirect* one, involving traditional and CPD staff with industry partners in a series of Search Conferences to set strategic goals for the university in what they themselves perceived to be a type IV, turbulent environment. By pooling their perceptions of changes in the external field, making meaning of these and then taking responsibility for the future adaptations of their university to this field, Davies claimed (personal communication 1992) that the ratio of 40% support for, 60% opposition to, change and CPDs had been reversed.

This strategy and indeed the move to innovative and flexible alternatives which were borne of Search Conferences bear out Emery's (F. 1991 p.8) contention that beyond individual organizational strategic planning lies the need to control their shared environment and agree on the values that should guide such control.

This UNE.NR example illustrates the major theme of this Part. The theory presented in 'Educational Paradigms' is eminently translatable into a range of educational practices, particularly when it is integrated with the tools and methods developed for participative democracy. It is, of course, no accident that the reports mentioned above speak of 'life-long learning'.

We can now see clearly the integration of adult learning principles, the design principles and new internally consistent methods themselves integrating sectors such as work, education and community. Australia is now moving seriously towards a more coherent design principle 2 culture, the need for which was outlined in 'Agenda for the Next Wave' (Part I).

Much of the previous discussion has concerned the strictly adult realm. But the new integrations and methods apply just as well to the turbulent phase which encompasses adolescence, as Carmichael has recognized. As the last training ground for the academic tertiary sector, the high school or junior college has already proven a weak link in the entrenched, bureaucratic system.

It is here, perhaps, that we can take the required debate about 'structure', based on some experience and free from conceptual confusion. Much of the previous debate about alternatives in education has floundered on 'the inadequate dichotomy' of structured and unstructured learning. This paper is included to prevent some of the sterile debates about essentially laissez-faire or autocracy which ignore the structural alternative of design principle 2. And even now there is the ever-present danger that democracy in learning will be interpreted as laissez-faire.

The paper of 'Training Search Conference Managers' has been elaborated to provide a better guide and also, as was done with the PD workshop, to attempt to prevent confusion.

The workshop described is designed to be only a first step in the learning process for those who wish to become effective process and structure managers. It covers the minimal specification of the interdependencies of concepts, design and management and alerts the apprentice to their practical, human and organizational consequences. Those who wish to learn more will actually have to do it in practice, become apprentices and learn on the job. Much care must be taken if people are to experience a positive and constructive example of democratic working. Managers of these complex learning events carry the responsibility for transmitting the democratic virus. It reinforces the message that participative democracy is as structured as—and in fact requires more planning and understanding than—bureaucracy.

A word of warning here:

The Search Conference is a tool for the democratic learningful way of planning. It is not an appropriate method for changing organizational structures from design principle 1 to 2. It can certainly be used by organizations to plan their futures, including their goals and strategies for democratic working. But at this point the Search is replacing by the Participative Design workshop where the actual design work takes place.

Those who care to read both Participative Design (Part II) and Part IV will note the commonalities and differences between PD and the SC. Organizations which have confused the two methods have become frustrated and bogged down. The Search Conference does not include the concepts and tools required for design, and the people appropriate to do organizational planning are not the appropriate people to do the designs. These must be done by the people who work in the individual sections.

Davies documents his broad-ranging experiences with introducing participation and self management into previously traditionally *taught* educational events. The result of this body of experience is a set of unsurpassed, practical guidelines. There is nothing quite so traumatic as a failure on one of these major events, but many risk this experience by trying to re-invent the wheel. We may be able to prevent some of this if there is a well established and understood conscious knowledge of reliable methods translated from good theory.

Because Davies has pioneered participative methods in areas which were previously the province of the first design principle, we realize again how silly it is to continue with teaching in the bureaucratically structured classroom. The practical wisdom covered in his paper makes it clear that the second principle is applicable in all our educational systems and efforts. Apart from all these conceptual and practical understandings, all that is required is a little faith in the intrinsic motivation and ability to learn and purposefulness of our species ('People aren't stupid, you know').

References

Carmichael L, Employment and Skills Formation Council, 1992. *Australian Vocational Training Certificate System*, National Board of Employment, Education & Training, Canberra.

Dawkins J S, 1988. *Higher Education: A Policy Statement*, AGPS, Canberra.

Emery M and Emery F, 1991. *Attitudes towards Centres for Professional Development at the University of New England*, Office of the Deputy Vice Chancellor, UNE.NR, Lismore.

Emery F E, 1992. The Australian Experience. Paper presented to Tusiad Symposium 'National Participation and Consensus', April, Istanbul.

Senate Standing Committee on Employment, Education and Training. *Come in Cinderella: The Emergence of Adult and Community Education*, Commonwealth of Australia.

Treyvaud E R and Davies A T (1991). *Co-operative Education for Professional Development in Regional Areas*. Department of Employment, Education and Training, Canberra.

An Inadequate Dichotomy:
'structured' vs 'unstructured' learning

Fred Emery, February 1978

A GOOD DEAL of debate continues to go on about the relative value of structured and unstructured learning. The former tends to be identified with the traditional classrooms modes and the latter with modern forms of person-centred learning. The debate has not been very fruitful. One side becomes fashionable and then something like Sputnik happens, or youth unemployment and the other side becomes fashionable.

I suggest that some of the troubles in the debate stem from the very use of the term structure. We assume that when we use the term structure to describe properties of social groups and events we are using it in the same way as when we describe the structure of a building, an anatomical structure or the structure of a molecule. Pressed hard we might admit that it is only an analogy, but then insist that it is close enough to permit us to make rigourous statements about social structures. This is far from being the case. When we are describing the structural properties of physical systems we can and do refer to geometric, kinematic, mechanical, physical or morphological properties (Ackoff and Emery, 1972, p.18). (Note that 'morphological properties' refer to "a set of physical properties—each the same function of the same geometric, kinematic, and basic mechanical properties" (ibid, p.17). In this usage, structure is the opposition of function. When we describe *social* structures we are not describing something that is contradictory of function, and nor can we ever hope to do so because "Organizational structure is a *functional* concept describing the allocation of choice... determination who is to be responsible for what...determination of which parameters of choice should be influenced by whom (such as staff functions)" (ibid, p.222).

If we use the term structure in a way which is appropriate to social structures then there is a clear sense in which a learning process can be described as 'structure-less', namely, when there is no attempt to develop or maintain a division of labour. This we would normally describe as a laissez-faire setting.

Ambiguities emerge when we look at the other end of the implied scale, structure. People usually tacitly assume that there is only one possible form of structure, one kind of division of labour, in learning processes. Elsewhere I have shown that there are at least two basic designs for social structures. Thus degree of structuring can be measured on either of two dimensions, not just on one. If this is not recognized in debates about the structuredness of learning settings then misunderstandings are inevitable.

As an example we can take our Centre for Continuing Education experience with both the DHRs (Development of Human Resources) workshops and Search Conferences. It is not unusual for people, experiencing these learning events for the first time to express a desire for a little more structure. This usually means that the person has been so accustomed to the transfer of knowledge being done according to the first basic design, teacher setting pupils their tasks, that they have some craving for this sort of protective dependence. The same requests could have a very different meaning when the person accepts learning in a type 2 design, within which DHRs and searches are construed. (When social scientists or management consultants start by taking 'social structures' as the given it is quite clear that they have ruled out of order any question about whether a better form of division of labour might be considered.)

Let us consider what structuring means in this latter context. It is clearly not the sort of structuring involved in a university course or a consultant's package. It is not a predetermined set of lectures, exercises, individual reports and assessments. Less detailed structure is imposed but there has to be some structure imposed to ensure the best division of labour between the time that is spent on the necessary phases of the work and the time spent in plenary, in parallel groups, specialist groups or in receiving expert individual inputs. To a much greater degree than the ordinary teacher, the managers of DHRs and Search Conferences have to monitor and revise their initial proposals for structure (division of labour). To a much greater extent they must seek to alert participants to 'what is involved and what is to be expected'. Without this, expectations about what the group will choose to work on and how quickly they can get to grips with the task are likely to be much awry.

Problems of achieving optimal structures are to be found regardless of whether learning settings are designed according to the first or second design.

In the first design there are always problems of how much to leave to the student and of allowing for differences between students.

In the second design there are no standard modules of individual curriculum-task. At best, there are some benchmarks derived from experience of what some kinds of groups can and cannot do. This kind of generalization can be dangerous; e.g., the 1976 Search Conference where a quite unique group were brought together about an unprecedented task (M Emery, 1982). The allocation of tasks to individuals is the structuring that must be left to the plenary or working subgroup; and is usually no more formal than allowing or drawing individuals into making a contribution.

The managers of a search conference have the difficult task of advising the group how they can best divide up their shared time; when they have arrived at a point where they need to test out apparent subgroups; i.e., subgroups working independently from premises formulated in plenary; when they are secure enough in their shared premises to separate into special interest or skill groups and use their special knowledge for the furtherance of the overall concern; when they could be best served by a presentation from an expert individual; when the subgroups should come back into plenary; when all should take a break from formal work to relax or engage in informal discussion; when they should work into the night. These are all structuring decisions, and the list is by no means exhaustive. Many of these decisions can be embodied in the original design, but only tentatively.

The conference managers cannot avoid taking major responsibility for these decisions and for ongoing revision of the initial design. Coming back to the point raised at the beginning of this chapter, it will be seen that the successful design and management of a search conference derives primarily from achieving optimal structuring not from trying to maintain a state of minimal structure.

If we probe a little deeper we find that contrary to superficial impressions the most likely error of search conference managers is to overstructure. The reason is quite simple. If the conference is allowed to idle along in a particular phase, because the manager has not sensed the need for restructuring, this may be an irrecoverable loss of time. (The commitment of people to a search conference practically always entails a non negotiable end point in time.) On the other hand if the conference is too quickly taken through a particular phase it is always open to the suggestion that they recycle through that phase until they have done the work properly. To ensure a good outcome it will always be tempting to err on this side; i.e., to overstructure. Note that this is not at all the direction of overstructuring that a teacher is tempted toward in the design 1, teacher-pupil learning setting.

In both designs 1 and 2 the error of over structuring generates a student or participant reaction. In the first design this may not be apparent until there is a student mutiny. In the second design there is usually early warning, before too much alienation has occurred, because the group and the subgroups already have legitimation in the learning process and it is not mutinous of them to assert a group view.

Addendum—on definitions

It might be thought that the ambiguities in the word 'structure' arise simply from the particular definitions that Ackoff and Emery chose to put forward in 1972. If the rest of the text, and in particular, the discussion of 'division of labour' (pp.222-27) have not dispelled this doubt, then it is worthwhile consulting the dictionaries to appraise the diverse and changing meanings of the word. The use of structure to refer to function is clearly made in Websters Unabridged, 1890.

> **Structure**... (L. *structura*, from *struere*, *structum*, to arrange, build, construct...)...1. The act of building...

Definitions 2-5 refer to structure as we have defined physical structures.

In 1970, SOED, we find that the first meaning is then "Now rare or Obs." However, they proffer a sixth meaning, illustrated by "The general law of organization...is that distinct duties entail distinct structures. Spencer." Obviously the functional meaning lingers on, although the illustration is rather dated. Websters Unabridged, 1961, found they needed 57 lines to define structures as against 21 in 1890. There was no added space given to the first usage "the action of building"; the expansion was in the scientific usage. However, a new 19 line entry occurs for structure as in "structured, structuring". It is devoted to usages of the word 'structure' where allocation of functions describes the structural relations between people. There is no parallel development in SOED.

In Britain the scientific usage has gone further in displacing the meaning of structure as social function. This probably does no more than reflect the extent to which different social functions have been frozen into structures in that country—at least in the language the educated Britons prefer to use. The entries in the 1961 Websters for the new term show a clear bias to recognizing what is behind the structure of interpersonal relations.

References

Ackoff R L and F E Emery 1972, *On Purposeful Systems*, Aldine-Atherton, New York.

Emery M 1982, *Searching*, Centre for Continuing Education, Australian National University, Canberra.

Emery F E 1977, 'Two basic organizational designs', in *Futures We Are In*, pp.91-100, Leiden, Martinus Nijhoff.

Training Search Conference Managers

Merrelyn Emery, 1987, 1993

·AS A PURE Design Principle 2 method of planning, the Search Conference has been taken very much for granted. There hasn't really been a debate about the training or appropriate learning needs of Search Conference managers. There are several reasons for this.

First, adult/continuing educators have traditionally preferred to stay away from notions of accreditation, believing amongst other things that such a move would inhibit access and run counter to our purposes of serving the general community and particularly the disadvantaged. The ethos has been profoundly democratic.

Secondly, it has been correctly assumed by experienced managers that the best way to educate new managers is by apprenticeship, learning on the job. Most managers have trained up several recruits in the last thirty years (the first Search Conference was in 1958), each in their own idiosyncratic way, using a different selection of conceptual and practical emphases and rules of thumb.

Third, but not least, good experienced managers make it look easy and hardly worthy of consideration as a separate body of conceptual and practical knowing and skills.

While few would rush in to do brain surgery or mental illness therapy without some training, many have rushed into running Search Conferences (SCs) without any awareness of the theory and 'know-how' required. In many ways, these analogies are sharp as the purposes of SCs encompass cultural and individual mental health.

The following diagram (Fig. 1, see over) illustrates the spiralling consequences of bureaucratic structures taken from much research over the years. The consequences of 'expert' planning are the same.

One result of this feverish activity showed up in the late seventies. We began to hear reports from disgruntled participants about these things called SCs. It soon became apparent that enthusiasts had been running things called SCs, but which weren't. Some had included activities such as requiring participants to fill in questionnaires at stages throughout the process, cutting across the momentum of work and breaking such basic rules as attempting to *increase* the participants' control of the outcome.

Others removed what they saw as 'irrelevant elements'(e.g., the environmental or L22 scanning) or modified bits so drastically that they be-

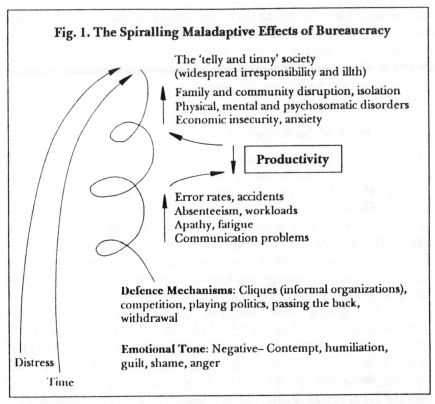

Fig. 1. The Spiralling Maladaptive Effects of Bureaucracy

The 'telly and tinny' society
(widespread irresponsibility and illth)

Family and community disruption, isolation
Physical, mental and psychosomatic disorders
Economic insecurity, anxiety

Productivity

Error rates, accidents
Absenteeism, workloads
Apathy, fatigue
Communication problems

Defence Mechanisms: Cliques (informal organizations), competition, playing politics, passing the buck, withdrawal

Emotional Tone: Negative– Contempt, humiliation, guilt, shame, anger

Distress

Time

came inimical to the progress and value of the whole. Another tack was to run through the stages as efficiently and mechanically as possible, leaving participants to go home and wonder what had hit them. But by far the most common occurrence was to scatter 'speakers' through the process—on the unspoken grounds that ordinary people wouldn't be able to use their experience, come up with ideas or work together to arrive at workable plans or solutions. This more than anything else tells you something about the parlous state of our culture or humanity. Calling in the 'experts', while cynical about them, is called 'synoptic idealism'. It expresses both dependency and lack of faith in people's purposefulness, wish to learn and control their own destinies.

Clearly, what had gone missing in the rush to use new, more effective methods for social change through learning was a basic understanding of their foundations. For a while there, SCs were treated with contempt as just another fad which had failed to deliver the promised goods.

Early objections to these distortions were met by comments that we were being anti-democratic and should 'let a hundred flowers bloom'. These comments confirmed that the revolutionary mood of the times was strongly laissez-faire, and the best we could do was to continue practising the real thing in competition with the other flowers. This we did and in its own good time the culture settled down again. Finally we began to design and pilot workshops for introductory training purposes and to alert others who may find themselves as participants, to the nature of the genuine article.

Another Wave of Confusion

Unfortunately, today there is again accumulating evidence in Australia of another wave of miscellaneous participative events—and some not so participative—parading as SCs. Efforts to maintain and restore the method and its good name have once again resulted in its being a name 'in good currency' with the consequent effect of it being vulnerable to abuse. This may be a cycle which will continue until there is a critical mass of understanding. Until those responsible for choosing and/or approving methods for change and learning can discriminate the SC as a discrete, defined method from the infinite range of other participative social technologies, it would appear that the problem will remain.

Noting could have accelerated the confusion faster internationally than *Discovering Common Ground* (Weisbord, 1992). Under the name of Future Search Conferences Weisbord has lumped together a widely diverse set of participative activities. The Search Conference has disappeared again into the fog of participation.

An earlier and simplified version of this paper is included in *Discovering Common Ground* and comments here will be confined to the debate in the book engendered by that paper. Just a couple of points will suffice to demonstrate how confusion is generated and diffused to the point where any sense of genotypical design principles and clarity of definition of methods is lost.

In his introduction to my paper on training SC managers, Weisbord states that what I mean by the 'mixed mode' is "mixing task- focused searching with experiential learning exercises, training modules, 'icebreakers', expert lectures, question and answer sessions, or any group activity that takes people away from the central tasks they have come to do" (p.325).

My paper actually defines (on p.328) the mixed mode as "the alternation of contrasting *design principles*". The mixed mode since *Searching* 1982 has always meant the mixing of design principles 1 and 2 in one event. After Weisbord's interpretation *we are one step removed from the original concept and the design principles.*

Weisbord then points the reader to reflections of his interpretation of my concept of the mixed mode by Fambrough (1992) in the context of her first attempt to run a so-called Future Search Conference (FSC).

Fambrough begins by expressing her sensitivity to 'my' distinctions between *"the two modes, searching and training"* (p.351. We are now two steps removed from the concept of the mixed mode and the design principles. Weisbord's interpretation plus Fambrough's interpretation of his interpretation and my discussion of the training course as a mixed mode have led to the critical distinction now being between searching and training.

Fambrough leaves no doubt that this is the core issue as she sees it. On page 357 she asks as a central point "Is an activity- encouraging use of a generally foreign medium for non-verbal symbolic expression of ideas a training technique? I don't think so." She wonders "where to draw the line between the two modes: training and searching" (p.357). She speculates about the key issue in defining what is and isn't training. On page 360 she speculates about doing her conference again, to what extent she would consider using "training activities".

At this stage all conceptual distinctions have disappeared and total confusion reigns.

The second major point made by this little confined debate, which is basically about the value of training courses for SC managers, involves what Fambrough actually did in her conference. The diagram (Fig. 2, following page) is her design reproduced from p.354:

Comparing it with the classical schematic design of a SC (Fig.12) shows the very real lack of correspondence between the two, even at this level of external structural design.

Third, we learn from page 353 that one of the outcomes was to generate "lots of data...to use in the analysis phase of strategic planning". Page 359 similarly tells us that one of the goals of the presentations was "to communicate a sense of how the data would be used". Clearly, this was a participative event to generate material for a strategic plan. It was *not* a SC in which the participants created a strategic plan for themselves, a plan which they would be responsible for implementing and the consequences of which they would have to live with.

At the level of internal structure and elements of the process, Fambrough deviated significantly from design principle 2, from Asch's four conditions for effective communication and for preventing outbreaks of the basic group assumptions. There are many other points which could be made.

She was lucky to get away without some disaffection, and one major reason that she did is simply that the participants were not there to plan

---

Fig. 2. ICOM Future Search Design

Domino Survival Exercise

The Past: Individuals, Company, Industry and Society

Best Job/Worst Job

Best/Worst Companies to do Business With

Values Exchange

Personal Vision and Values

Stepping into the Future

An Exercise in Imagination and Creativity

The Present

Strategic Thinking and Strategy Formulation

ICOM's Strengths and Weaknesses

Opportunities and Threats

Mapping the External Environment

Possibilities and Options

Next Steps

---

their own long-term future. They could happily co-operate in playing games, discussing their personal values and providing data—knowing that the responsibility for the ultimate result lay elsewhere.

The second major reason for her success is that participation on this scale is genuinely new to a lot of USA citizens, a point Fambrough makes herself (p.352). I get the impression from working in the US that even a step towards design principle 2 planning, such as Fambrough's, is grasped enthusiastically. Many in the US are as fed up with design principle 1 as are people in other cultures, but they have little to use as gold standards. The mixed mode, that is, the mixing of the design principles, will probably be tolerated and used to capture as much ground as possible in the US, until an appreciation of pure design principle 2 planning is widely shared.

Fambrough obviously designed and managed an enjoyable, basically *participative event*. That it is called a Search Conference or FSC is a bit sad and a step backwards in the process of creating, defining and diffusing social methods which are reliably effective when applied to the appropriate purposes and tasks.

Rather than debase the value of training SC managers, this little debate highlights its value and the great need for more of it.

The Introductory Workshop

It is from this history and its recurrence today that the introductory workshop emerges. In no sense is it designed to replace an apprenticeship which is essential. It serves merely as an introduction and a first opportunity to discover whether one is really cut out to be a SC manager. Some people are naturals, others will never make it. Others again will become good managers, but only with sufficient experience to overcome the many barriers they have internalized from previous socialization, educational and otherwise.

The workshop is designed to provide a basic appreciation of both the theoretical and practical dimensions of the Search Conference. It includes, therefore, conceptual presentations and some experience with the process. I have run variations of it from a half to two days. After the experiential components the reasons for the manager's comments, questions and moves are debriefed to give a broader base of understanding of the approach as a whole and as a lead into deeper questions and discussion. In the short half day versions, only the first stage can be experienced, but as much understanding is made of this as possible.

It is always difficult to fully integrate conceptual and experiential sections, and their quite different dynamics, within a single exercise. This problem is that of the 'mixed mode', the mixing of the two design principles, as debated above. Too long a top-down presentation at the beginning will induce dependency which subsequently interferes with the growth of the working mode demanded by the experiential component and the longer and more powerful the working phase, the less participants can be bothered with subsequent theoretical discussion. Therefore, one of the skills required for a successful workshop of this type is to keep each component short, concise and with many leads and pointers backwards and forwards into other section, creating both continuities and 'zeigarniks' (bits of unfinished business). Another is that required in the management of the Search Conference itself, namely, to hear the operating dynamic, the 'music' or second level message of the group and manage it towards the most creative learning.

Above all, it is necessary to stress the difference between the workshop and the Search itself and that the workshop cannot model the coherent dynamic of the Search Conference. There *is* a paradox here and it is not resolved until those who wish to learn more take the next step of becoming an apprentice.

While some of the components must be conceptual, they must also be presented in ways which encourage interest and learning, with such aids as overheads, illustrative butcher's paper and invitations for participation through questions to clarify statements made. Extended question and answer sessions must be avoided, as these reinforce any emerging assumption or dynamic of dependency on the 'expert'. Above all, these top-down components need to radiate the *excitement* the presenter feels about the Search Conference itself. This cannot be simulated and if it is lacking, such a workshop—and certainly the management of a Search Conference—should not be attempted. As will be clearer below, the method is predicated on people as whole systems living within bigger whole systems, within even larger whole systems. Participative methods in general, and the Search Conference in particular, cannot be approached with a view of people as uneasy amalgams of cognitive, affective and conative subsystems. The method is designed on and illustrates the efficacy of Open Systems (Emery F, 1981) (Fig.5).

It is also necessary to stress as above that these workshops can be no more than an introduction to the Search Conference, as learning to run a successful Search necessitates

° gaining an adequate working knowledge of the theoretical substratum of the method through reading and discussion;

° serving as an apprentice or trainee manager for as many events as it takes to feel confident with the phenomena embodied and style required. People differ in this, but intuitively both apprentices and managers know from the beginning whether a person is 'a natural' for the job.

These two simultaneous directions can be handled within the apprenticeship system as is usual in other fields and the rationale for doing both is as for other fields of learning. Routine practice without conceptual understanding becomes rigid and dangerous, especially when dealing with people who are unpredictable at the best of times, but even more so when they are working creatively with new problems in changing circumstances. The workshop must stress that it is only for people to get a feel for the SC and be able to discriminate it from other methods.

The actual plan for one of the introductory workshops depends on the time available, number of participants and any special needs they have. Sometimes the participants are from the one organization and have a need to integrate their abstract learnings with its presenting circumstances and problems.

Other groups may be disparate which necessitates the creation of a purpose for the experiential components in order to make it meaningful for all. This demands quick thinking and flexibility from the workshop manager as it would be demanded through a SC itself.

A fairly comprehensive overview of concepts and practice is possible in about seven hours. If time is short, various components are run together demanding good understanding of the priorities attached to certain concepts and strict time management. The following description of the workshop's process and content is in chronological order.

First Phase

This is always, except when time is extremely short, a briefing and 'introduction and expectations' session. Small groups compile their expectations of the workshop which avoids these surfacing at inappropriate times and alerts the manager to any special needs or perspectives they may need to address throughout the time. At the end, it is useful to take 10 minutes for a collective appraisal of whether these have been met and fulfil any that haven't.

Second Phase

This is the first presentation of the theoretical framework and its concepts (40-60 minutes, depending on questions).

Content

1. Strategic Planning as Product of Both System and Environment

I speak to the following overheads (Figs 3-5), explaining how strategic planning differs from short-term planning. Strategic planning depends on the core concept of directive correlation (Sommerhoff, 1969) as both system and environment acting on each other to produce a new outcome and state of affairs. As these change, so must our forms of planning.

This leads naturally to the concept of open system, all of whose elements must be addressed in effective future-oriented methods. The L in figure 5 refers to the fact that both system and environment are governed by lawful processes and that there are lawful and 'able to be known' transactive relations between them. The system is represented by 1, the environment by 2. Therefore, L11 means the internal dynamics of the system, L22 the internal dynamics of the environment, L21 expresses

Fig. 3. Planning

A **commitment** to bring into being a state of affairs that does not presently exist and is not expected to occur naturally within the desired time.

Strategic Planning is distinguished by:

> long time frames
> necessity for guidelines, philosophy.

Remember, strategy is a term taken from the art of war. Today, in this context, strategic means the art and science of manoeuvring, being a good general. Only in two types of environment does strategic planning have any meaning at all.

There are two basic interpretations of strategic planning, one from each of these two environments: **optimizing** (assumes linearity) and **active, adaptive** (assumes the possibility of discontinuities)

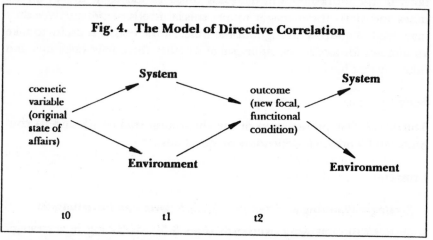

Fig. 4. The Model of Directive Correlation

the effects of the environment on the system, and L12 expresses the effects of the system on the environment. Each element must be contained within the work of the Search Conference if it is to be comprehensive and result in effective planning. Constraints and opportunities will translate into different questions for each custom designed event, but will be present in some form.

The Search Conference is unique as a planning method in that it addresses the L22, the broad environment, its internal dynamic of interdependence and change. Without knowledge of this component of the Open System it is possible to make plans which look beautiful but have not change of implementation. The L22 is a ground of value shifts and

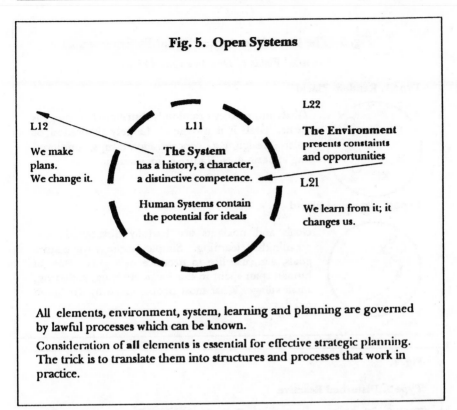

Fig. 5. Open Systems

L22

L12

The Environment
presents constaints
and opportunities

L11

We make
plans.
We change it.

The System
has a history, a character,
a distinctive competence.

L21

We learn from it; it
changes us.

Human Systems contain
the potential for ideals

All elements, environment, system, learning and planning are governed
by lawful processes which can be known.

Consideration of all elements is essential for effective strategic planning.
The trick is to translate them into structures and processes that work in
practice.

sometimes sharp discontinuities—a mine field for planners who follow
linear logic and/or concentrate on the L11 and L12.

A quick run through the Types 3 and 4, at least, of environmental
causal texturing (Emery and Trist, 1965) (Figs 6 and 7) provides needed
context for an understanding of the environment as a key player in any
form of effective future-oriented work. It alerts participants to features
they will find when they explore their own environment and partly ex-
plains the reasons for its methodology.

I sum it up with a table (Fig.8) adapted from Emery, F (1977) which
reinforces the message that the environment demands appropriate
choices of learning and planning. It also introduces the concept of ideals,
their role and practical importance for a successful SC.

2. Forms of Strategic Planning

This set of overheads (Figs 9-11) summarizes the choice of methods
available, outlines their advantages and disadvantages and highlights the
distinctive features of the SC as active adaptive planning. If time permits,

Fig. 6. The Causal Texture of Social Environments

Extended Fields of Directive Correlations

Type 1. Random Placid

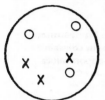

Goals and noxiants randomly distributed. Strategy is tactic. 'Grab it if it's there'. Largely theoretical or micro, design, e.g., concentration camps, conditioning experiments. Nature is not random.

Type 2. Clustered Placid

Goals and noxiants are lawfully distributed —— meaningful learning. Simple strategy—maximize goals, e.g., use fire to produce new grass. Most of human span spent in this form. Hunting, gathering, small village. What most people mean by the 'good old days'.

Fig. 7.

Type 3. Disturbed Reactive

Type 2 with two or more systems of one kind *competing* for same resources. Operational planning emerges to out-manoeuvre the competition. Re-

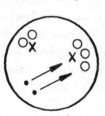

quires extra knowledge of both Ss and E. E is stable so start with set of givens and concentrate on problem solving for win-lose game. Need to create instruments that are variety-reducing (foolproof)—elements must be standardized and interchangeable. Birth of bureaucratic structures where people are redundant parts. Concentrate power at the top—strategy becomes a power game.

Type 4. Turbulent

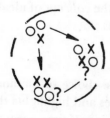

Dynamic, not placid/stable. Planned change in type 3 triggers off unexpected social processes. Dynamism arises from the field itself, creating unpredictability and increasing *relevant uncertainty* and *its continuities*. Linear planning impossible, e.g., whaling disrupted reproduction, people react to being treated as parts of machine. Birth of open systems thinking, ecology and catastrophe theory.

*Where O = goals (goodies) and X = noxiants (baddies)

Fig. 8.

Environ-ment	Elements to Know	Ideals	Forms of Learning	Forms of Planning
Random	system	1	conditioning	tactics
Clustered	system, action	2	meaningful	tactics/ strategies
Distrubed, Reactive	system, action, learning	3	problem solving	tactics/ operations/ strategies
Turbulent	system, action, learning, environment	4	puzzle solving	active adaptive planning

The four ideals in order are:

1. Homonomy – sense of belonging
2. Nurturance – caring for
3. Humanity – in broadest sense
4. Beauty – includes fitting together naturally

Fig. 9. Strategic Planning for Types 3 and 4 Environments

Type 3	Type 4
Aim: feasibility, extrinsic excellence	probability, extrinsic and intrinsic value
Expert fragmented knowledge (facts) not context	Context plus facts ⟶ understanding, purposefulness
Problem solving	Puzzle solving
Concentrates on means, ends are assumed	Concentrates on ends, choice of paths follows
'Rational' decision making two-dimensional, probable efficiency, relative value of outcome.	'Irrational' decision making three-dimensional, includes also probability of choice (intrinsic value of course of action)
Product: the plan	The planning community
Creates fear of change and resistance, self-defeating	Why resist your own desired change?
Narrow definition of cost-effective	Broad definition of cost-effective

Fig. 10. Type 3 Strategic Planning Example: Delphi

1. Concentrates on figure not ground—assumes no change in ground/context

2. Specific future outcomes already decided

3. Items reduced to discrete technical issues—ignores value trends

4. One issue at a time—denies interdependence

5. Individual judgement—fails to counteract weight of status and orthodoxy, fails to generate collective or even individual commitment

Fig. 11. Committees and Their Workings

Characteristics	And their Consequences
- negotiation from positions of different interest	* striving for individual advantages
limited delegated authority,	* constant looking over the shoulder to source of delegation
- either to committee, or to the individual members	
- rigid detailed structuring to contain conflicts of interest	* the structrue itself becomes a major focus of committee work
- search for simple structure of its business to facilitate negotiation and resolution	* painstaking attempts to re-assert the differences by splitting of hairs and nit-picking
- competition for allies and committee time to strengthen one's negotiating position	* (a) concern with gaining psychological dominance (b) to 'fix the race' beforehand

I discuss the Delphi (favoured by technocrats) and committees by bureaucrats as examples of what a SC is not. I also mention the current fad, in Australia at least, for a thinly disguised form of budgeting or competitive resource allocation which is passed off as strategic planning.

At this stage we take a quick break and resume to home-in on the SC (see Fig. 12).

Figure 12 spells out the relation of the various phases to the open systems model, the points at which ideals come into operation, the need for continuity of organizational or community 'personality' and the reasons for leaving constraints towards the end, etc., etc. If I have time, I will

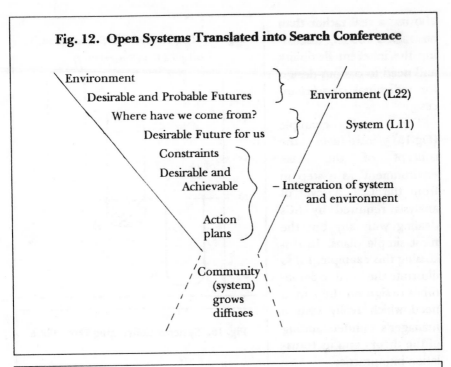

Fig. 12. Open Systems Translated into Search Conference

Environment
- Desirable and Probable Futures
- Where have we come from?
- Desirable Future for us
- Constraints
- Desirable and Achievable
- Action plans

Environment (L22)

System (L11)

– Integration of system and environment

Community (system) grows diffuses

Fig. 13. Strategic Planning at Local Industrial Level

The Future of the Canning Peach Industry in the MIA (NSW)

- Global environment (Extended Social Field) — L22
- History of the MIA — L11
- Essential characteristics of canning fruit industry
- Desirable and undesirable industry characteristics
- Desirable future industry
- Industry constraints
- What can be done?
- Who should do it?
- Immediate action

Task Environment

Planning community continues

Diffusion to other similar or local industries

also use a real rather than abstracted model, discussing the inherent flexibility and need to custom-design for individual circumstances.

This real example (Fig.13) introduces the concept of the 'task environment' as a step in from the L22, a level of analysis required by SCs dealing with any but the most simple plans. In discussing this example, I also illustrate the need to sometimes design on the run, a need which really tests a manager's understanding of the theory and its translation into practice.

We then zero in and ask, 'Well, how do we get to know our environment?' I run through this body of theory, concentrating particularly on the first diagram and adding in the others with examples, depending on time.

I explain the first diagram (Fig. 14.) as simp-

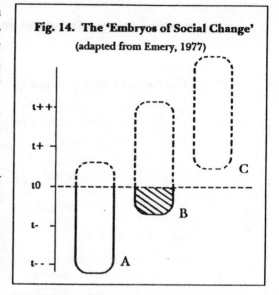

Fig. 14. The 'Embryos of Social Change'
(adapted from Emery, 1977)

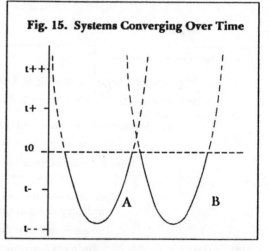

Fig. 15. Systems Converging Over Time

ly being systems (A, B and C) moving through time. The longer a system has been around (A), the greater the probability that we can predict its future. System C, which does not yet exist, must remain unpredictable. In analysing the extended social field or L22, we are looking at particularly the B systems, those which are new or emerging and which may be the forerunners of major social trends or movements. System B from recent past to present (hatched) constitutes the social embryo. It is these emergent systems or 'embryos of social change' that the instructions for the data collection session elicits.

Fig. 16. Search Conferences

Assumptions:

People are purposeful and can be ideal-seeking;
People want to learn and create their own future.

Purposes:

1. Participative Planning and Policy Making   *vs Planning org.*
2. Effective Implementation—Active and Adaptive — *in rel. to turbulent*
3. Learning *environment facilities 4*
4. Participative Democracy *redeals*
   p. 237

   Puzzle Learning in Non-Dominant Structures (Design Principle 2)

Concepts:

Open Systems Thinking
Design Principles
Theory of Learning—Ecological or Direct Perception
Influential (effective) Communication
Bion's Group Dynamics
Diffusion
Rationalization of Conflict

Obviously, systems moving through time can fragment, merge with other systems or simply fade away. Converging is illustrated in the second diagram (Fig. 15). These phenomena form the basis of the analysis and synthesis of the environmental data collected.

I then conclude the session by looking explicitly at the assumptions and purposes of the SC and alert them to other concepts that will be introduced after some experience (Fig.16).

The Experience with Integrated Concepts

At this point I brief them to engage as a SC community. The steps of preparation and planning which precede the actual event of a Search Conference are discussed and their importance stressed. Selection of participants so that they cover all aspects of the puzzle to be solved is inevitably a crucial factor in a successful outcome. We return to this below in a debriefing.

If participants are a coherent group they become, for example, a task force making policy for the future of adult education in Australia. If they are diverse, they become the first national Australian government selected by lot, rather than as elected representatives. This allows me to tie more strongly the SC into the concept of participative (design principle 2) rather than representative (design principle 1) government as a necessary tool for such a venture, where of course there would be no formal opposition and methods for large-large group decision making and the rationalization of conflict (SC) would need to be used.

To get Australia back on the track, for example, they will need to know the environmental forces acting upon the country as well as the history and character of their own people. So the scene is set and participants then receive a standard briefing for the first phase of the Search which is data collection of changes taking place in the extended social field or environment (Fig.14), leading to the preparation of desirable and probable future scenarios. The rationale has been explained and the rules for the conduct of this phase are given as 'All perceptions are valid; no argument is allowed at this stage. That comes later, when you have to make sense of all the data you have perceived.' I add the second ground rule: you may add to the list at any stage during the Search, but only when you inform the community that you are doing so. This is crucial when building a 'learning planning community'.

In the workshop I also explain the second level of meaning this entails which is the democratic levelling achieved by the ground rules and their

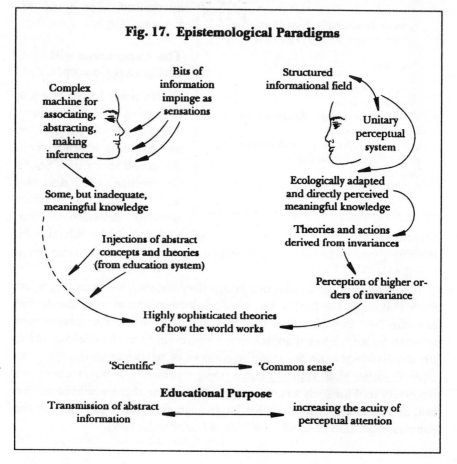

Fig. 17. Epistemological Paradigms

Complex machine for associating, abstracting, making inferences

Bits of information impinge as sensations

Structured informational field

Unitary perceptual system

Some, but inadequate, meaningful knowledge

Ecologically adapted and directly perceived meaningful knowledge

Injections of abstract concepts and theories (from education system)

Theories and actions derived from invariances

Perception of higher orders of invariance

Highly sophisticated theories of how the world works

'Scientific' ⟷ 'Common sense'

Educational Purpose

Transmission of abstract information ⟷ increasing the acuity of perceptual attention role in ensuring practice in effective communication. Participants begin to get a feel for the job of manager and the care which must be taken in regard to the subtleties of human communication.

All of this is done in the total group for the good reason that we are building communities—not small 'in' or 'out' groups, but big 'many hat wearing' groups who have to collaborate and have the ability to diffuse through many networks.

When the data about changes in the extended social field is collected, we stop and examine the overhead (Fig. 17, previous page).

This illustrates the difference between the theory of learning which guides the design and operation of our formal education system with its emphasis on *teaching* and the Search Conference which takes as its basic unit 'people *learning* in environment'. A quick note is made that the second paradigm is the educational foundations of Design Principle 2 and that the Search Conference integrates through its process and structure all the elements necessary for a full-scale learning experience of democracy. ('Educational Paradigms' is found in Part I and the explication of the 'design principles' in Part II.)

They reflect on the fact that it is this second paradigm which they have just used to explore the environment. Contrary to traditional beliefs about discrete bits of sensory information impinging on the central nervous system and requiring integration before meaningful knowledge is available, the perceptual system acts as a unit absorbing meaningful knowledge directly from the informational structure of the environment. In the first session of the Search they have drawn on their perceptions of the extended social field and will then continue to synthesize these into scenarios illustrating the collective pulling of invariants into sophisticated but realistic theories on their own. They are gaining confidence in their abilities to self-manage and see the true value of their perceptions and experience.

We then return to the experience where they must now analyse and synthesize the data they have collected about the environment, again using their own resources and values. I split them into heterogeneous groups, four if numbers permit, but there must be a minimum of four in a group. If there are only enough for three groups, it is desirable to have one group working on desirable futures and two on probable futures as this area is usually more conflicted and it is important to be able to see the extent of commonalities and differences between the groups. This also provides for a practice with a simple way of 'rationalizing' conflict (Fig.22 explained below).

After the groups report these scenarios, they are discussed and negotiated to the point where each is accepted as the property of the total conference. This is essential, as they become the benchmarks for measuring progress during the rest of the conference. This point in the process can generate a lot of learning. Many people are challenged, as they have to explain the values and reasoning which lie behind a particular decision and nobody can hide behind position, authority or status, as all participants attend just as people with something to contribute to the puzzle solution.

Negotiating skills are also learnt here. As is dealt with in more detail below, one of these involves learning the difference between the faddish concept of 'consensus' and the much more realistic and durable concept of 'rationalization of conflict'—agreeing to differ about some things, while working together on those matters which form the common ground.

When all this is achieved and explained, I present the following overheads:

The first, **The Dynamics of Conference Design** (Fig. 18, below), introduces the concepts of the design principles, the dynamics of groups and their relation to learning.

Design Principles

These two basic principles, **1. redundancy of parts** and **2. redundancy of functions** (as in Part II) underlie both organizational and conference design (as a conference is only a temporary organization) and determine its structure. A decision at this level will have profound implications for the outcome of the conference, the amount of learning it generates and its diffusive potential which is a flow-on from the emotional tone of the conference and its energy level.

In Figure 18(a) (see following page) we see that Design Principle 1 conferences mainly produce the Basic Group Assumption of *dependency*, the negative affects of humiliation and contempt, low energy and low or negative affect. Negative learning is included here to represent propaganda for which these conferences are traditionally acknowledged.

Figure 18(b) shows the 'mixed mode' and its predominant group assumption of fight/flight (see Fig.19). Correlated with this is some negative affect and some low (opportunistic) co-operation, medium levels of learning and energy. Figure 18(c) shows that the Search Conference, so far the most internally consistent method designed on the second principle. Affect is generally positive, mainly seen as excitement and joy, and with these come high energy and high learning.

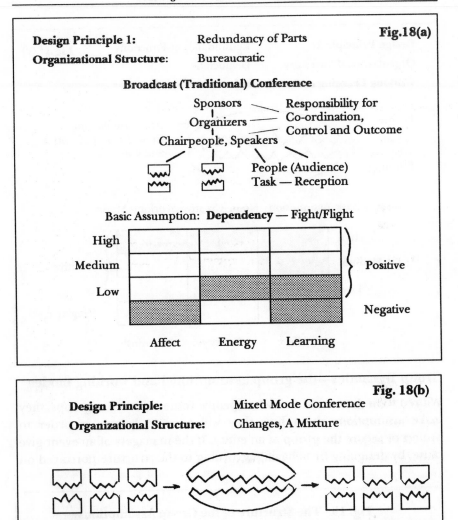

Design Principle 1: Redundancy of Parts
Organizational Structure: Bureaucratic

Broadcast (Traditional) Conference

Sponsors
Organizers — Responsibility for Co-ordination, Control and Outcome
Chairpeople, Speakers

People (Audience)
Task — Reception

Basic Assumption: **Dependency** — Fight/Flight

Fig.18(a)

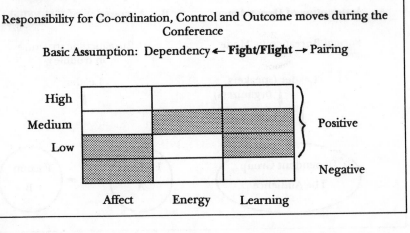

Fig. 18(b)

Design Principle: Mixed Mode Conference
Organizational Structure: Changes, A Mixture

Responsibility for Co-ordination, Control and Outcome moves during the Conference

Basic Assumption: Dependency ← **Fight/Flight** → Pairing

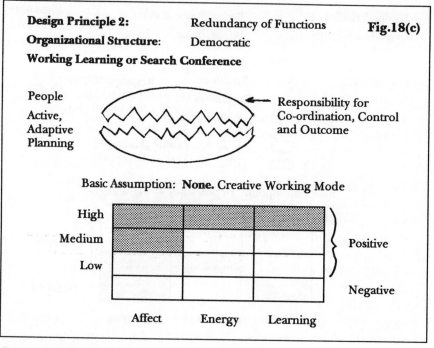

Design Principle 2:   Redundancy of Functions   **Fig.18(c)**

Organizational Structure: Democratic

Working Learning or Search Conference

People — Active, Adaptive Planning ← Responsibility for Co-ordination, Control and Outcome

Basic Assumption: **None.** Creative Working Mode

	Affect	Energy	Learning	
High				} Positive
Medium				
Low				
				Negative

Group Dynamics—the group assumptional and working modes

Wilfred Bion discovered that when people come together in groups, they make assumptions about how they will need to behave in order to protect or secure the group as an entity. If the managers of an event give cause, by designing or behaving according to the structure portrayed on

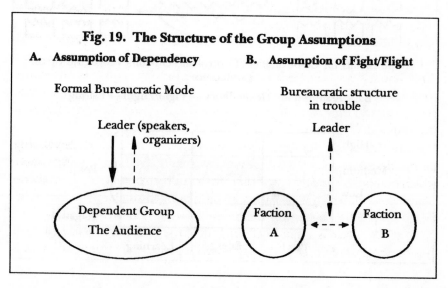

Fig. 19. The Structure of the Group Assumptions

A. Assumption of Dependency   **B. Assumption of Fight/Flight**

Formal Bureaucratic Mode   Bureaucratic structure in trouble

Leader (speakers, organizers)   Leader

Dependent Group — The Audience   Faction A ←--→ Faction B the left, the group will enter a state of **dependency**. They assume the management is prepared to be a great and powerful leader who will take responsibility for their behaviour and this absolves them from any responsibility to learn. Therefore, very little learning takes place in this mode (Fig.18a).

The assumption that there is a leader or force which aims to destroy the group results in **fight/flight** which may be expressed either as fighting behaviour or as passive resistance. This is most likely to occur in the mixed mode but these days is also sometimes seen in pure cases of design principle 1. Since Bion's times we have witnessed a growing awareness of the right to participate and an outright denial of this right, as often occurs in conferences with a packed program of speakers and little time for discussion, which can spark dramatic episodes of fight/flight. More learning is achieved in this mode than in dependency, as there is at least an active orientation, but the task to which the group addresses itself is that of removing the threat, not that around which it cohered (Fig.18b).

There are still conflicting views about the nature and meaning of **Pairing**, the third of Bion's assumptional modes. It can be a prelude to the **Creative Working Mode**, but it can also serve as a diversion to the task whereby the group shifts its attention to a subgroup or pair (Fig.18b).

The **Creative Working Mode** is most likely to occur when a group is carrying full responsibility for the control and co-ordination of their work towards their agreed purposes (Fig.18c). In fact, once this mode has been established, it is very difficult to stop it and managers who feel the need to decelerate or reverse it can find themselves in a great deal of trouble.

Figure 19 spells out dependency and fight/flight in greater detail which is often useful for those who are struggling within the confines of a loose or tight bureaucratic structure.

A Search Conference manager will have designed the process to avoid outbreaks of the group assumptions and should be trained to recognize them should they occur. S/he also needs the practical skills to redirect the conference back into the working mode before the assumptions become entrenched. If they do arise in the workshop, they should be debriefed at the end of that session.

From this point, the experience is continued or curtailed, depending on the time available. If it is available, it is useful to move into the phase which embodies the L11, the other aspect of the context for the creative planning work which is the ultimate task, and which illustrates and reinforces some other features of the method and its underlying theory.

This L11 phase is usually referred to as the **History** session as a brief run-down of the history of the organization, industry, community or X is

Fig. 20. The Properties of Influential (Effective) Communication

Theoretical	Design and Management
1. Opennness For exploration and checking of opinions and perceptions	Pre-briefing on content and process. Minimize threat to participation. Clarify roles and values. All recording is public (butcher's paper), visual, verbal, vernacular.
2. Mutually Shared Objective Field 'We all live in the same world'. It is commonly perceived as backgound to joint action, taking into account the interdependencies.	Scan the external social field using ground rule 'all perceptions are valid'. This is analysed and used throughout as a benchmark.
3. Basic Psychological Similarity 'We are all human with the same human concerns. Each is an action centre, can talk as equals and learn from each other.	Provide opportunities to see common ground—desirable futures based on ideals and use these as basis for co-operative work and the rationalization of conflict.
4. Trust: The Emergence of Individuals as Open Systems Will initiate communication which builds self-confidence, therefore vicious circle which generates energy and leads to action and diffusion.	No status difference between participants and managers. No management interference in the content, manages only the environment and process for all the above.

Note: assumption that indi. can read/perceive meaning/surrounding w[ith]out intermediary

$$4 = 1 + 2 + 3$$

Trust ⟶ (Collaborative Action + Diffusive Learning)

necessary to ensure that all participants share perceptions of the past as well as the future. Participants often have little knowledge of where X has come from and there is often intense disagreement about critical turning points. The significance of the history session accrues from the need to build into the future those continuities that have been appreciated and mark the character of X. Without them, there is little chance of implementation. These continuities define what people recognize and feel they belong to and their absence in the bureaucratic standard plan heralds its demise in an outburst of either active or passive resistance (fight/flight).

It is, however, for logistic reasons in a diverse group, better just described than attempted. For example, most participants will have a working (book) knowledge of Australian history so that it makes more sense to move on to the session where they must decide what to retain from amongst their continuities, what to discard and what they feel they should create. This is a critical preparatory step for the task of deciding what a desirable Australia should be.

By this stage the group should be in full creative working mode and it is a good idea, if time permits, to take reports from the small groups considering the 'keep', 'discard' and 'create' lists, negotiate these so that again the commonalities become conference property, and move straight on to the desirable future of X. This not only confers a partial sense of completion but also allows for a demonstration of another interesting little aspect of human working—the dynamics of deciding on priorities (more below).

At whatever point the experiential component is left, the remaining time is used to outline the rest of the process as it would probably happen, deal with the many questions which will be certainly raised by participants and highlight other concepts employed. To all extents possible, it is better to discuss novel concepts in the context of questions asked and to get participants to reflect back on how they actually went about the work they did.

One such which must be included concerns the nature of the conditions pertaining to effective communication, perhaps one of the most misunderstood of all human phenomena.

The set of guidelines (Fig.20) for the practice of Searching is a modified version of Solomon Asch's (1952) original learnings in this area. They document the four necessary conditions for effective communication and the ways in which they have been designed into the Search Conference structure and process. Any behaviour, particularly by managers, which disturbs these conditions can spell trouble for a Search Conference and managers must also ensure that other participants observe the principles.

For example, we are often asked why individual note-taking for reports is discouraged and butcher's paper is so important. Basically, this technology sets the scene by reassuring everybody that things are what they appear to be and there will be no manipulation of the content or process. In this dimension, as in all others, there must be a high level of consistency.

In the process of discussing these principles and participants' experience so far, much understanding is generated as bits of the theory and practice become integrated verbally and conceptually. For example, having meaningful knowledge directly available from perceptions applies as much to our knowing of those around us as it does to our physical environment, as Bion's work shows. Because of our traditional Western theories, we may not have learnt to be aware of our awareness of this knowledge, but the process of the Search Conference itself shows that it is there. The speed with which a group assumption appears in the total group leaves no doubt that all are aware of what is going on. In any social setting we can see people going through elaborate although subtle rituals to learn as much as possible about—and communicate adaptively with—others.

If it is possible, as it is in the two-day version, it is useful to have a practice with constraints and final action plans. These often induce quite different emotional reactions, sometimes quite depressive, as the group contemplates what a big job it has in front of it. This is, of course, why constraints are left to the end when a collective direction and positive working mode is established. The trick here is to convert this into more effective action plans. For this reason, I never say 'List the constraints'. I always say 'Bring back the most serious obstacles, together with a way of dealing with them'. A manager must constantly use and reinforce the power of the work culture, the positive affects (emotions) and build them into the process. In the creative working mode, jokes and asides flow fast from the participants and add to the sense of community. *Serious learning is fun!*

The Strategy of the Indirect Approach

I give a briefing on this strategy (Fig.21) before the group attempts constraints, strategies and action plans. Because there is so little conscious appreciation of it in our culture, groups tend to rush in with a heavy direct approach, neglecting the long term.

The Search Conference is, of course, an operationalization of this approach, as it progressively secures common ground and zeros-in on the issue. Basically, the Indirect Approach, also called the Broad Front Approach, attempts to maximize gains and minimize losses. There is little point in storming the barricades or putting all your eggs in the one basket. You could lose entirely the first time around. The strategy is played as a board game, known as W'ei chi (Chinese) or Goh (Japanese).

It is better to encircle the enemy. In Participative Design workshops (for democratizing organizational structures) this strategy is essential to avoid the demonstration or 'guinea pig' group. In the SC, it is critical

Fig. 21. Strategy of the Indirect Approach

Purpose: To control maximum territory with a minimum of resistance

Means:

1. 'Concentration as product of diversity'
   . broad-front approach
   . not putting all your eggs in the one basket

2. Effort directed towards points of least resistance and most future potential (multiplier effect). Capture the weakest link.

3. When attached, pull out.Learning doesn't disappear (good ideas stay in people's heads).

4. Go around or encapsulate sources of resistance.

    ○ ○ ○ ○
    ○ ● ● ○
    ○ ● ● ○
    ○ ○ ○ ○

5. Encircle from within.

    ○ ○ ○ ○
    ● ○ ● ●
    ○ ○ ○ ●
    ○ ● ● ● ○

6. Victory and defeat are relative, depending on context. Needs constant re-evaluation of the field while moving within it.May have to shift effort, or sacrifice some efforts, re-asses your priorities.

Fig. 22. Two systems in Conflict

Total Consensus   Rationalization of Conflict

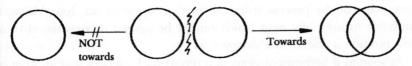

NOT towards   Towards

Two Systems as One   establishment of common ground, the area of which can be enlarged that participants are drawn from the total coverage of the issue and that as implementation continues, it involves wider and wider nets. This generates rather than uses resources. It is 'community development' at its best.

If there is time, it is also useful to discuss the relationship between the Search Conference and the Participative Design Workshop mentioned above, as there are many overlapping assumptions, processes and goals. Also, once the planning phase is complete, there is often a need to answer the question 'How do we organize ourselves to ensure that we meet our long-term goals?'

Other Concepts That Should be Fitted in

The complex realities of the world in which we live renders a simple dichotomy between conflict and consensus an impossible dream. Thus, the 'resolution' of conflict is really not a goal (Fig.22). Above all else, the Search Conference aims for realistic working relations and does *not* therefore aim for consensus, although it is a bonus if it can be temporarily achieved. It aims for the *rationalization of conflict* as it applies to achieving the purposes of all parties in the venture, not only in the short, but also in the long term, as they will need to continue on working, negotiating terms long after the event of the Search is past.

Some level of common ground can almost always be validly achieved through exploration of areas which lie outside or on the periphery of the conflicted issue, and the first level of agreement is sought in basic ideals. Once this ground is secured, it may be possible to find ways in which the parties can work to enlarge its sphere. It should always be remembered that there will be limits to this, as some parties must—by definition—play adversiarial roles. They can and do, however, often co-operate on significant matters of legitimate interest to both or all. The Search works by seeking indirect strategies for negotiated agreements, broadening the sphere of concern surrounding the conflict and then enlarging the area of agreement.

In practical terms the rationalization of conflict proceeds as follows: at each stage of the process from the first group work on desirable and probable futures, any item which cannot be agreed or negotiated to a new position is placed on a *'disagreed list'*.

As soon as it becomes obvious in a report-back plenary that an item is in conflict, an attempt is made to:

(a) Talk it through to clarify whether the 'issue' is semantic of substantive;

(b) if substantive, send off one or two of each of the conflicted parties to sort it out;

(c) if no new position is arrived at within a reasonable period, the item is placed on the disagreed list.

This procedure makes clear the boundary between, and the extent of, the agreements and disagreements. If some such clear-cut procedure is not instituted, there is a danger that one or two conflicted items (out of about ten-plus) will assume the priority for energy, totally distorting the balance between common ground and conflict. When it is perceived by all parties that the ratio of agreement to disagreement is about 85%:15%, the item in conflict is seen in its proper perspective, the energy for it dissipated. All parties can then get on with the job of working with (and hopefully enlarging) the larger extent of common ground.

It is our experience that the area of common concerns and agreement is always larger than either party or outsiders supposed. That it is often so much larger than the stereotypical view is itself a levelling one, and a significant learning experience leading to perceptual reconstruction.

Similarly, it is important to discuss spoken language and its role as 'social cement' (Ong, 1967). There is a faddish concern at the moment about 'verbal aggression', but it is preferable to have people yelling at each other than not talking at all. Wars start only after somebody decides to stop talking. Don't be dismayed if people express strong feelings: it means they care. Our worst nightmare should be facing a *dissociated society* (Fig.1).

Deciding on priorities is interesting. How do you get a group to do it? I sometimes do this little experiment in the workshop. Firstly, I ask participants as individuals to use a voting system, e.g., 'You have $100 to spend. Allocate it according to the importance you personally place on these issues'. The results are duly recorded. Then I put participants into small groups to choose five out of say ten issues for action *after* thinking about what criteria should be applied. We record the results. The results are often vastly different. What does this mean? Amongst other things it means:

○ the method the manager chooses has a significant influence on the outcome or product;

○ group working produces different outcomes to individual voting systems, particularly when thought has been given to criteria.

After this exercise, groups almost always prefer the group priorities to the individual. From their work on establishing the criteria against which priorities should be allocated, they see that such an important decision should not be made flippantly, but only after due consideration. Each manager and group must be aware of the consequences of their decision-making processes. Unfortunately, they often are not.

Diffusion

Whenever the experience is terminated, *Diffusion* must be mentioned, as this has been long misunderstood or its dynamics underestimated. Diffusion is much more a psychological process than a mechanical one of spreading information by various media, such as paper or spoken words. It is as much the communication of energy and enthusiasm, generated by the emotions of excitement and joy that drives diffusion as the importance of the content of the 'message'. When people are really 'working' towards their purposes, they generate high levels of excitement and joy

---

Fig. 23. Logistics-Ideal

Management. Designs and manages the environment, the structure and the process. Stays out of the content.

Venue. Social island for intensive work free of distractions, preferably residential to aid community building. Comfortable, plenty of wall space. Participants should not have to think about meals, etc. Flexible arrangements.

Timing. Start late afternoon, continue after dinner. Then full day and night, finish lunch or afternoon of next day. One and a half days is possible, but really only suitable for very simple situations.

Materials. Simple: butcher's paper, thick felt pens, masking tape. Computerized white boards and rapid word-processing and photocopying have advantages and disadvantages.

Numbers. Between 15 and 30, or go to multisearch to larger numbers.

---

and a successful Search Conference can immediately be identified by these characteristics. This energy is contagious and is also the driving mechanism for the implementation of the plans. This effect accounts for much of the diffusion of the concept of the Search Conference itself.

At the End

There are matters of logistics and practicality (Fig.23), e.g., the important

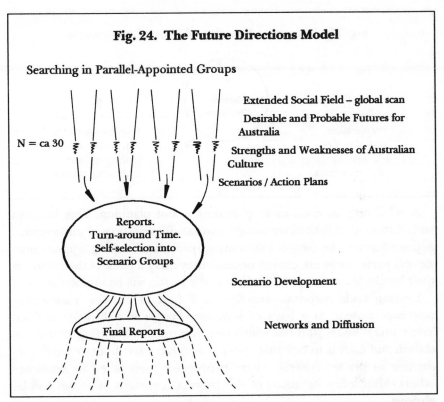

Fig. 24. The Future Directions Model

Searching in Parallel-Appointed Groups

Extended Social Field – global scan

Desirable and Probable Futures for Australia

N = ca 30

Strengths and Weaknesses of Australian Culture

Scenarios / Action Plans

Reports.
Turn-around Time.
Self-selection into
Scenario Groups

Scenario Development

Final Reports

Networks and Diffusion

of 'Zeigarnik' effects for the timing of the phases of the process, the nature of venues, reporting and a host of other matters. While describing the best, reassure them that often we have to make do with what we can get. All these matters are, however, fully discussed in *Searching* (Emery, M. 1982), along with more background material and detail of the conceptual framework as above. Numbers often demand special attention. What do you do when the number of necessary participants exceeds the roughly 35-person limit for a SC? The answer is the Multisearch or 'Future Directions Model' (Fig.24).

This model represents SCs in parallel until the point where all the groundwork has been done and self-selecting task forces are sufficiently well informed and trusted to do work on behalf of the total Search community. The critical element in a Multisearch is the co-ordination and good functioning of the managerial group.

The Role of the SC in the Total Process

Having dealt with the nature of the SC itself, it is necessary to reiterate its place in the bigger scheme of things (Fig.25).

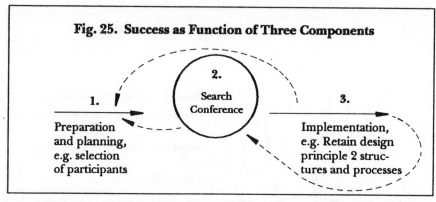

Fig. 25. Success as Function of Three Components

A SC is only as good as its preparation and planning. This includes such factors as collaborative design and careful selection of participants. Active adaptive planning is a continuous process of making a jigsaw puzzle and participants are chosen because they carry a piece of the puzzle in their heads. If a major piece is missing, the puzzle will be impossible.

Leaving aside corporate searches, it is best to use the 'community reference system' as a basis of selection. People in a broadly defined 'community' know who has which bits. A number of starting points are chosen and each is to nominate people who can contribute to the SC according to pre-set criteria. These people are then asked to nominate others. After a few iterations of this process, a pattern of names will be obvious.

Other forms of preparation will be required, depending on the purpose of the SC.

The Process of Implementation

It is important to maintain the nature of the process of the Search. So many (once the event has finished) return to the time-honoured formalities of appointing or electing a chair, rules of debate, etc., —design principle 1, only to find that there is a wholesale return to the territorial bickering, refusal to address the primary issues and, therefore, a waste of the gains made during the Search Conference. All of this latter is totally unnecessary, but its avoidance lies in the understanding of the dynamics discussed above. The more that can be consciously learnt of this during the SC, the better for implementation.

The dotted lines in the figure express the fact that often we are not dealing with a simple linear process. There may be points at which it is realized that additional information needs to be generated or collected.

Similarly, there may be a need to re-convene the SC community to re-assess priorities and adjust strategies.

All of this emphasizes the point that the SC itself is not a stand- alone event, but only a period of intensive activity within a much longer process.

References

Asch, S E 1952 *Social Psychology*, Prentice Hall.

Bion, W R 1959 *Experiences in Groups*, Tavistock.

Boorman, S A 1971 *The Protracted Game*, OUP.

Emery, F E (ed) 1981 *Systems Thinking*, Penguin.

Emery, F E 1977 *Futures We Are In*, Martinus Nijhoff.

Emery, F E 1993 'Educational paradigms' (This Edition).

Emery, F E and Trist, E L 1965 'The causal texture of organizational environments', *Human Relations 18* 21-32.

Emery, M 1982 *Searching*, Centre for Continuing Education, The Australian National University, Canberra.

Emery, M 1992 'Training search conference managers', *in* Weisbord M R (ed) *Discovering Common Ground*, Berrett-Koehler Publishers Inc., San Francisco, pp 326-343.

Fambrough, M 1992 'Doing by learning, learning by doing', *in* Weisbord M R (ed) *Discovering Common Ground*, Berrett-Koehler Publishers Inc., San Francisco, pp 347-360.

Weisbord, M R (ed.)1992 *Discovering Common Ground*, Berrett-Koehler Publishers Inc., San Francisco, p.325.

An Alternative General Studies Curriculum

A description, results and evaluation

Alan Davies

(Extracted from the original in ACT Papers on Education 1977-78, (eds) Mulford W., Hughes, P. and Burkhardt, C., School of Teacher Education, Canberra College of Advanced Education [now University of Canberra])

EARLY IN 1977, I formed part of a panel that had been invited by the Assistant Principal Curriculum to talk with some of the staff of a Canberra Secondary College about ways in which a General Studies program could be provided to:

> Educate the total person for survival in an unpredictable, turbulent future; that facts, concepts, theories, intellectual skills, and well developed cognitive maps are not enough; that attitudes and values must be explored, group morale maintenance must be developed.

The discussion led me to conclude that the sorts of objectives under discussion could not be met within the existing school structure and instructional modes. The high value placed by school on the choice of subject created an inflexible timetable and lack of possible overlap between the timetables of students. The instructional modes were such that the students were never in a time-flexible-setting long enough with the same group of students to attain the sorts of objectives alluded to above.

We all know how easy it is to be critical of the existing system and how much more difficult to actually do something constructive about it. Aware of this, I offered to conduct a pilot course with a view to structuring in such a way that it would meet the above objectives. The starting conditions were that: the students who participated would be volunteers; they would be prepared to work outside the college timetable; they were prepared to work off the school premises; and, students who wished to participate in the planning and management of the course.

This course was then offered at an Assembly. The course met with twenty-five students and five adults for the first time on Thursday, 25 May 1977. Two teachers who coordinated the course covered the ACT Schools Authority requirement that a registered teacher be associated with all formal courses. Two of my colleagues from the Australian National University attended most of the sessions, initially as observers and subsequently as my reference and support group.

Description and results

Five sessions were held over the second term. A description of these sessions and their outcomes follows.

First Session

The purpose of this first session was to clarify the expectations and purposes that I had for the course as well as the expectations of the students and their reasons for choosing the course. The objective was that at the end of this session we would be in a position to make a contract to proceed or not to proceed thus opting out if they so desired. The reason for conducting such a session was to diminish the possibility of misunderstandings developing later on in the course from the pursuit of different objectives. It has been my experience that if this was not done student expectations would intrude into or cut across the conduct of this course leading to frustration and producing a reduced chance of meeting the course objectives.

The first ten minutes were spent outlining the course background and my expectations and objectives for the course (see Appendix 1), after which the students broke up into four groups and spent twenty minutes on the following tasks:

○ Introducing one another to the rest of the people associated with the course;

○ Spelling out their expectations and why they chose the course;

○ Any other details they wished to contribute.

They were asked to record the information on butchers paper to facilitate presentation to the full group and so that a record of the session could be easily kept.

During the report back there was a general discussion and clarification of expectations and objectives and it was agreed that those who still wished to stay with the course would meet for a four hour planning session on the following Monday at the College from 4.00-8.00 pm. Name tags were used.

In the negotiation over the next meeting time, some of the participants tried to avoid the responsibility for the collective decision by trying to negotiate with me for separate individual times or arguing for times within the school timetable when they were free. I pointed out again that one of the agreements that we had come to was to meet as a full course out of school time at a time negotiated by us all and that part of my requirements of the course that they had agreed to was a four hour planning session in which they planned their own course. In any event it was not possible to miss out the planning session and get my instructions subsequently. This was the first overt expression of dependency.

Second Session

The tasks established for the second session on May 30 were:

- For students to spell out their view of the nature of the future they were moving into;

- To establish the skills, knowledge and experience they would need to adequately equip themselves for that future;

- To select the most important in 2 that they were not currently receiving from either school, home, or community activities;

- Form self managing task groups to plan and carry out a program of work that would achieve their objectives.

The procedure was as follows. Students were asked to list on butchers paper those changes they had seen occurring which they considered would be important into the future. They then formed self selected groups on the basis of their optimism or pessimism about the future and asked to spell out the eight points that were most important in determining their optimism or pessimism. They spent forty minutes on the task and reported back (See Appendix 2). They were then set the task of identifying the sorts of things that this implied and that they should be learning about but which were not currently being covered by the college, family or community activities in which they were involved. Eleven options were thrown up. They were then asked to order the activities and to do this each student was given three votes of equal value which they cast against the list of eleven items.

Some selection of this nature was necessary as one of my requirements was that no student could pursue an individual project—they must pursue a group project—this was essential if the objective 'of learning how to cooperate with others' was to be achieved.

Of the eleven items, four received no votes. I then proceeded up from the item with the least votes until I arrived at one which was in fact the first choice of one of those who had voted for it. It was pointed out that they may wish to pursue more than one of the items during the course and a chance to evaluate progress and change of direction would occur at least twice throughout the course and more if we all decided it was warranted. The remaining five items were listed on separate sheets of butchers paper and posted around the room. The students were then asked to make their choice and form a group around the item of their choice. At this stage we also broke for a cup of coffee so that the selection manoeuvring and negotiating could proceed informally.

After the break I asked them to form around the item of their choice. Three groups formed and were roughly of equal size; viz, Communication, Survival Skills and Helping Others.

Each of these groups then met to further define their task and after half and hour reported back. This was followed by a brief input session by myself on group self management and the need for coordination, planning and control.

We listed the constraints operating on the course, for example resources, money, time, transport, self management, time tabling, effort required, working in groups, reflecting on learning and management, etc. Also, we discussed the concept of goal setting and feed back as being essential parts of learning and hence the necessity of coming back in a months time to check our direction and whether we had achieved our goals or were on course, or whether we wished to change course as a result of our findings and experiences within the first month. A role call was taken at this stage to see who had contracted into the course.

Third Session

The purpose of the third session on June 27 was to: check on progress; establish whether new directions had to be taken; see if any of the groups had completed its task; and, establish the basis for evaluation—both of the course and the students.

Firstly, each group reported on the progress to date (See Appendix 3). A thing of particular interest to me, outside of the content of the reports, was the extent to which the groups had become cohesive in themselves, displaying concern with their own task and thus little concern with the task of the other groups. The most open group at this stage was the **Communication group** and the overtly cohesive, 'groupish' and self interested group was the **Helping Others group**. The least 'groupish' was the **Survival Skills group.**

Secondly, each group discussed the difficulty they felt in explaining to others that they had learnt something in the process of setting up and exploring their tasks, for example, the Communications group which had found themselves some structured exercises to explore the dimensions of verbal, non verbal interpersonal communication, considered that it had been a most valuable activity; however, even though they had learnt a lot about communication they felt they could not convey it adequately to others. They felt unable to convince outsiders that they had not just been sitting around talking. Learning was traditionally associated with books and the objective not the self, subjective and experiential. Learning was usually thought of as being individually based, not group based. Contributions had to be separate so that we could order and attribute individual contribution.

The Helping Others group were despondent about the nineteen knock- backs they had received from twenty helping agencies they had approached. They considered the time they had spent in making phone calls and other means of contacting organizations as wasted. Learning had to be positive and successful. The implication was that learning could not come from negative events. In fact, my guess is that they learnt more about the nature of organizations, their control over their boundaries, the nature of industrial relations problems, the capacity for organizations to deflect unorthodox and unsettling initiatives from outside, and the extent to which they stay with their founding brief rather than accept that their reason for existence might be a changing thing. They also learnt that organizations become more concerned with their own internal organization than their purpose and how to make phone contacts with strange organizations, to explain a case and a situation to the outside world. In other words, they were learning valuable skills.

They had difficulty in the third session in accepting that the time spent in the above ways was learning time and could be and should be counted towards the forty eight hours of the project. There was a certain amount of cross questioning at this stage about what they were really getting out of their projects, and there was a certain amount of group defensiveness. They had been surprised about the extent to which they had started to hang around together at the College.

They then started to talk about the various sorts of evaluation: of the full course; of individuals; of groups; by self; by home groups; by other groups; and, by the outside resource people. They then spent half an hour in groups coming up with their preferred form of assessment. They also saw the difference between assessment based on judgments, written and verbal reports, and the nature of the activity they were undertaking.

At the end of that session I gave a too brief and unsatisfactory input about the measurement of learning satisfaction and self management. I handed out a sheet setting out criteria of measurement (Appendix 4) and asked them to assess their own group functioning before the next session. In addition, I also asked them to individually take another group of six students from one of the other classes they were taking and repeat the exercise. Firstly, I asked them to check to see if their teacher was happy with this procedure.

We then made a time for the next meeting in another month, a meeting which was to be of four hours' duration in which they would report back, redirect and focus on an understanding of groups, group behaviour and the management of organizations.

Fourth Session

Groups reported back on July 4 on their progress to date and their plans for future activities. All groups decided to stay intact and they were well on the way to chalking up their required number of hours (all groups had chalked up twenty to thirty five hours by this stage). There were various levels of satisfaction with their product to date.

They had also filled out job satisfaction charts but found some of the criteria difficult to interpret (most likely because of my poor explanation at the previous meeting). They had not been confident enough to try out the criteria on a group of students in relation to another of their courses, and so at that stage we lacked a comparative basis with other teaching/learning modes.

The results of their own surveys were used as an introduction to the section on studying group and organizational behaviour. I spelt out the purpose of this section which was to reflect on their learning to date, particularly as it related to the way they had organized themselves and the way they had operated as a group. I was determined that the total group become a self managing learning group around this task in the same way as the small groups had obviously become self managing learning groups around their chosen tasks.

They had taken responsibility for their own direction, control, planning and coordination. There was uncertainty at the role that I took. I wanted them to start by examining learning satisfaction. Long periods of silence indicated that they lacked direction.

When I clarified the task on one occasion I then asked one of the students to repeat the task; the reply was stated in very different terms, and more akin to the different objectives they had. Only the staff and a couple of the students heard what I had said as I had meant it to be heard. The statement seemed to be fairly explicit when we analyzed it. The group was reluctant to become self managing and vacillated between dependency, flight and on occasions pairing (the basic dynamics of immature or insecure groups).

I interpreted the group behaviour to the students at the end of the session as I had seen it and the session ended on an ambiguous note. We agreed that the next time we met it would be to make and evaluate the final reports and the course. It was suggested that the session be conducted after the end of term because of the difficulties in getting projects in by the end of term. They also agreed that they would like to meet off campus as they had found some of the other meetings off campus productive, constructive and enjoyable, given this mode of learning. So they decided to meet at the Centre for Continuing Education at the Australian National University for two hours on a date seven weeks hence.

I was somewhat dissatisfied with the session and analyzed it with my two colleagues for two hours after the completion of the session. We came to the conclusion that the major reason that the students would not take responsibility for the conduct of the session was that the task was an imposed one (and as a result not entirely understood). It was *my* task, therefore, it did not relate to their needs or their expectations or what they saw as the agreements entered into earlier. They were prepared to get stuck into and self manage quite difficult tasks in interpersonal relationships around the tasks which *they* had identified or participated in the setting. They were looking for leadership where the task was externally set. The leadership had to relate to the ownership of the task and I was the owner of that task and they were unwilling or unable (because of a lack of understanding of it) to take over the ownership. There was not deliberate avoidance, in fact, there was some frustration at not being able to get into the task.

Fifth Session

I was somewhat apprehensive about the likely response to the final session on August 23 and so was quite relieved when all three groups turned up ten minutes before the appointed time on the appointed day. The purpose of this last meeting was to test their performance and evaluate the course.

I started by spelling out my expectations of the day. The group was pretty apprehensive, but there seemed to be general agreement that the task could be broken conveniently into four parts:

○ For the groups to assess their own performance;

- Reporting back on what they had achieved and done (to be done in plenary);
- For them to assess the value of the course and attempt comparisons with main stream approaches to learning used at the College;
- To evaluate as a total group the value of the course.

The students went into their groups for half an hour to assess their own performance. In fact most groups in that half hour worked out what and how they were going to report and took the opportunity to get down on butchers paper their findings about the course, what they did, what they had learnt and what they had got out of it.

When they returned each reported in turn. Once the reporting had started, I was out of the role of leader of the course as it became a work group and was away and running. Towards the end of the session I had to cut in to make sure that we were going to get through all the work in the agreed time. The session went thirty minutes overtime. During the reporting back, there was an all round interest between the groups and an active, intelligent and interested questioning, group to group, and active and intense involvement in the whole session. An extremely good rapport developed within the whole group. Again, I believe this situation related back to the fact that the task was agreed, negotiated and understood, and owned by all of us.

There was little reporting back on their own evaluations of their work except for general statements that they and I were all very satisfied with their performance. They again expressed the view that apart from the content learning, the support groups that developed were probably the most positive and valuable outcome. They also valued the amount of mutual support and respect that they were able to achieve that the other structures within the College were unable to provide. This was not because of a lack of a will to do it but because the high value placed on choice and diversity (which dictates the structuring of time) meant that people could not get close enough to associate at the personal and supportive level.

The groups then reformed to evaluate their learning satisfaction and the results were recorded. They evaluated this activity against English, another subject they all do, the aim not being to evaluate the teacher but the teaching format and approach to learning. They all came from different classes and so, in a sense, there was an averaging out of teacher influence. Our activity was, in another sense, also teacher independent in that I had fourteen contact hours of the fifty three to fifty eight or more that the students spent on the activity.

Evaluation Results and Conclusions

The significant outcomes of the evaluation at the fifth session were as follows:

- That the 'elbow room' was too great in our course and too little in the 'normal' classroom situation. In discussion it became apparent that the group in which the elbow room was insufficient differentiated between the limitations arising from course structure and that arising from the outside organizations they were relating to. They were the Helping Others group that attempted to help other helping organizations and found all but one knocked them back. This group found that elbow room from the course was too great and were in agreement with the other groups in their evaluation of its extent.

- It was suggested that the next time round a tighter framework could apply without loss of the self managing character of the course and the desirable outcomes that flowed from that. This would probably mean more clearly defined and shared objectives as they relate to the learning about groups and organizations and clarifying expectations early on in relation to what is an acceptable product and what is not.

- It is my guess that elbow room would need to be positive. People need freedom to learn, they need elbow room and this implies some ambiguity and uncertainty. This might be one of the important aspects of learning—to self manage, take responsibility, and hence, the sorts of learning that is being looked for in the General Studies program.

- My guess is that because we are using an approach of which the students lack experience, uncertainty is built in. All the explanations in the world would not allow an accurate understanding of this unfamiliar approach. The problem cannot be solved, in a sense, until it is translated into a different framework and that requires having the previous frameworks challenged. This, in turn, creates ambiguity to the learner.

- On the dimension of *variety* the course fared better than 'English'. I see the difference arising from the approach not the subject. I believe it reflects the fact that the groups did genuinely self manage, and so were able to choose their own level of variety. The only exception is the Helping Others group which was externally limited in this respect. Again, they specifically referred to that in the evaluation session.

○ In fact, this group went out and created its own helping organization in the form of the 'Belconnen Disco' which is an ongoing activity. They created some of their own variety.

○ The most significant factor and the one which demonstrates that the course did achieve its major objective is the criteria of *mutual support and respect*. It scored across the board higher than the conventional class-room approach and on average by an order of magnitude.

○ To develop a situation where mutual support and respect starts to operate effectively, one needs to be able to associate together for periods of time about an agreed task with the same group of people.

The other factors in the evaluation show few consistent trends varying from group to group and individual to individual. In terms of a different *mode of learning and content*, the communication group probably show the most interesting difference in that they point more to their experiential learning where the others point more to content learning. It is interesting to note that four of the nine students dropped out of the Survival Skills group before its completion whereas none of a group of seven dropped out of Helping Others, and one of a group of six dropped out of Communications.

It is important to note with respect to the mode of learning that the number of hours spent in teacher contact was fourteen out of the forty eight formal and fifty three to probably seventy or more that was actually spent by some students. This alternative certainly has deep implications for the role of the teacher.

My general observation was that the students learnt to deal very adequately with interpersonal conflict and with all sorts of concerns and support outside the course itself. This was because the groups had a life beyond, and provided support to, the immediate task of General Studies.

It might well be that the implications of this alternative Curriculum option exercise for school organizations is that it would be desirable for each of the pupils in the school to be associated with one such group and/or the approach to be used in other subjects. It is my guess that the need for school counselling would fall away if this was taken up as it would create a much more healthy school community, where problems would be dealt with within the fabric of the school population. However, the students thought that a more broad application would mainly be limited by the fear of freedom from the school staff—their non-acceptance of students' self management and the feeling that the students were not responsible and therefore they would not be prepared to give them the elbow room to be responsible. This fear might also mean that some students would not wish to participate and thus the approach used may only apply to self selected students and self selected staff.

On the other hand, the most significant finding from the exercise was the unequivocal evidence that students of this age are very capable of managing their own learning. I and the other people from the Australian National University were greatly impressed by the responsibility, capacity, creativity and initiative of the students and I certainly believe that they learnt more conducting their own course than if it had been managed and conducted by any of us or any of the school staff.

Reference

Quote from a letter from the Assistant Principal (Curriculum) at the College in question

Appendix 1—Course Co-ordinator's Expectations

One semester—12 weeks—48 hour course

Some record of having spent 48 hours required and some assessment of student achievement required. How this was done was for the total group to decide.

The next session would be devoted to planning and would take about four hours. This meant we either met after College, at night or during the weekend.

They would plan and manage their own program. I would only provide the framework within which they worked.

We would devote two to four hours to conceptualize about organizations and their management arising from their experience of conducting this course.

I would provide only one input session—about group self management.

No student could work individually on a project.

Appendix 2—Second Session: Points Most Important in Determining Student Optimism or Pessimism about the Future

Optimists

Potential to manipulate future

Man's natural instinct to survive!

Future seemingly more of a challenge
rather than a threat

Man's striving to better himself

Greater awareness of self and
world → others

Greater tolerance of diversities

Pessimists

In moral standards (e.g., crime, drugs)

In pollution through industrialization and consumption

In probability of nuclear war through the number of
countrieswith nuclear capabilities

In social instability; e.g., strikes, drugs, dropouts

In natural resources through abuse

In influence of the media

In materialism and leisure time and the consequences of a
materialistic society; e g , unemployment—dropouts

Increase in population, urban sprawl

On the Fence

Media

Living standards

Materialism

War (in general)

Breakdown of family unit

Self awareness (awareness of others)

Sexual equality

Unemployment

Appendix 3—Third Session: Progress of the Three Groups

Helping Others Group

had done:

Contacted 20 helping organizations by phone or direct contact All bar one had knocked them back

Marymead had welcomed them and they had spent a day
relieving staff and working with the children

planned to do:

Follow up a couple of the other contacts

Take Marymead kids to 2CC

Investigate possibility of a Disco-dance for 15-17 year olds in Belconnen

concerns:

Difficult to arrange meetings

The knock-backs were demoralizing

Found a deal of conflict within the group

Survival Skills Group

had done:

Spent a day in the bush

planned to do:

Look after a household for a day

Do first aid course

Have lectures on how to fill out financial documents, income tax, Medibank, unemployment

Communications Group

had done:

Spent a session in which they explored interpersonal communication

Had contacted artists and poets to discuss the meaning of communication with them

planned to do:

Meet with various artists etc

Develop a theory of Communication

Appendix 4—*Criteria of Learning Satisfaction*, adapted from Emery and Emery, 'Participative Design', Occasional Paper No 4, Centre for Continuing Education, Australian National University (see Part II of this Volume).

Participation and Self Management in Course, Workshop and Conference Design:

Principles and methods

Alan Davies, 1989

THIS CHAPTER originally appeared as *Participation and Self Management in Course and Conference Design* published by the Centre for Continuing Education, Australian National University in 1979. Much of this methodology has now become well established and I have consequently edited down. [Ed]

At that time little distinction was made between courses and workshops on the one hand and conferences on the other. While some of the principles and methods are common to courses and conferences, more recent experience has led to a differentiation of the two based on purpose, timing and numbers.

In the conduct of non-credit courses, conferences and workshops for adults we commonly meet a great diversity of expectations, needs and relevant experience amongst those attending. Most of those responsible for managing the learning would regard it as part of their responsibility to take such variety into account and to try and use it to advantage. This chapter is intended to provide the reader with information on a systematic and well tested set of principles and methods where the benefits of recognizing and using people's experience outweighs any costs. The methods can be used by course managers in jointly planning, managing and conducting courses with participants and other resource people. They are aimed at maximizing the learning and the commitment of participants to mutually agreed course objectives.

The chapter concentrates on that planning and self management which takes place once the course has started, although there is some reference to the planning process as a whole and pre-course planning. Problems can and do arise where the learning needs of participants have been externally and inaccurately assessed. This particularly applies to those sent by employers to training courses because of some perceived lack of skill or knowledge or because of inappropriate attitudes. Problems in organizations can have at their root, inappropriate structure, poor management *or* lack of the requisite skill or knowledge on the part of employees. If structure and management are the problem, the training of employees is not the solution. Participative processes will however bring participants to better see the nature of the such problems, which can in fact exacerbate the problem unless management is prepared to act on itself and the structures.

The approach describes a planning module for courses of two to twelve hours duration which is placed at the start of a program and a course framework which allows for in-course evaluation, adjustment and self management. The planning process for courses and workshops is set out descriptively and diagrammatically to illustrate the logic and the relationship between the various elements.

This chapter is based on a view that adults can take responsibility for their own learning if the necessary time and resources are available to them. These and other assumptions of the author about the way adults learn are made explicit in Section 1. The organizational concepts inherent to the approach are elaborated in Section 4.

Both the objectives, methodologies and educational design features of each element of planning, design and management are discussed, including data collection, programming and evaluation. The range of situations to which the approach has been applied is also discussed. Courses range from four hours to three months in duration, in residential and non residential settings: in single blocks of time or in modules spread over a period as long as six months; in mono and multicultural groups; using multiple languages and in eight different countries. Some of the pitfalls to watch for when applying this methodology are then outlined.

There are basic differences between courses and conferences and Section 3 spells out the design features for conferences in general and participative conferences in particular, describing some of the tools that have been developed to administer complex conferences. A range of situations is again outlined to give the reader a better appreciation of possible scope and flexibility and again some of the pitfalls are mentioned, particularly those relating to design. The selection of appropriate teaching and/or learning methods is of course, critical to success.

The chapter concludes with some of the handouts and instruments which the author has found of value in the management of self planned events.

I would like to acknowledge the assistance of the Trade Union Training Authority, Hawker College (ACT), the Australian Department of Education, the Australian Association of Adult Education, the Tasmanian Education Department, the Asian-Pacific Bureau of Broadcasting Development, the Asian-South Pacific Bureau of Adult Education, the

NSW Office of Aged Services, the Oslo Work Research Institute and the Centre for Continuing Education for providing opportunities to test and develop this approach. In particular, I would like to single out the Trade Union Training Authority where most of the thinking and development about courses took place and Des Hanlon with whom it took place.

Underlying Assumptions

In this section I have set down my usage of some terms and concepts.

The Place of Learning in Organizational and Social Change.

Our tacit knowledge is highlighted when we see or hear stated simply and clearly what we have known, or perhaps, half known, yet never stated. Eric Trist articulated some assumptions in his address to the Einar Thorsrud Memorial Symposium, Oslo, 1987, that have long motivated me in my work on participation but for which I could not find the words.

> To bring into being such (social) changes raises the question of transformation being personal as well as organizational. No one can force change on anyone else. One has to experience its presence oneself. Unless we can invent ways which allow a paradigm shift to occur in very large numbers of people, our hopes for substantial change will remain a myth.

My interest in participative processes derives from a drive to make a 'better society'. I have moved from believing this could be achieved through the political process to through changing bureaucratic work structures to seeing the problem as one at the level of the individual, nested within the organizational and the political.

The sort of learning that Trist alludes to is not learnt in the formal education system. One needs to develop particular attitudes and values, confidence, courage, a level of self awareness, self criticism and self management, the capacity to manage ones own learning and to understand organizational, social and political processes.

We learn these attitudes, values, and skills by participating in the planning, control, management and conduct of the events that affect us. We gain a knowledge of them by reflecting on the processes through which we participate. This knowledge is largely in the form of commonsense concepts about learning, groups and organizations that help people make sense of their experience and act more purposefully in the future.

One of the beauties about this form of learning is that it largely occurs while one is doing other things. The 'cost' is the 10-20 per cent of the time that is needed for reflection and concept development. Our need

reference notes: realization needed
felt one learns distinctly
without intermediaries)

learning = becoming more
human

Participation and Self Management

for this sort of learning is so great that in my view we should take every opportunity to build it into our normal endeavours whether they be planning, working, managing, recreating or educating.

Action researchers have long understood that: 'one of the products of work (or any human endeavour—author's addition) is people.'

This captures the fact that 'taylorized' work organizations leave people diminished in their humanity whereas participative organizations develop their humanity. I believe that the same argument applies to course and conference organization. The use of participative processes can leave participants better able to manage their own learning in any setting in which they find themselves.

Systems and Futures Concepts

Much of the underpinning philosophy of participation is premised on an open systems approach to organizations and their planning. It helps people to better understand the benefits of participation. (See 'A Training Workshop on the Theory and Practice of Search Conferences' above.)

The basic unit is a system in its broad environment. The system itself has an integrity and independent identity given by the system's organizing principle. You cannot change one aspect of a system without there being some effect on the other parts of the system. The individual human being, the family, or organization are all examples of systems. Thus anything that happens to one member of the family impacts on the others. Family therapy is based on this approach. On the other hand, shoppers in a supermarket are an aggregation rather than a system because they are not closely interdependent.

The open systems approach is essential for effective implementation of change.

In a course or workshop one may only have a temporary system, a temporary organization and a long term aggregation. However, the ongoing systems of which we are a part all lie in and are critically dependent on the same social environment.

Futures Scan

All planning and education are carried out against assumptions about the future. If a group of people are planning collectively it aids communication if they are aware of each other's assumptions and the extent to which they are common. While in most educational activities people are not directly concerned with a common future, they are part of a temporary community. Having a view, a context, of 'where others are coming from' greatly assists communication and learning.

We all carry around a view of the future against which we make decisions and act. It needs to be known for our actions to be understood. A joint look at the future is a safe, fast, comprehensive and yet incisive way of making attitudes and values explicit as well as providing a common context from which to work.

An environmental scan operationalizes the open systems approach to the future, gives recognition to the view of all participants, allowing them to be shared, re-assessed and used as an objective field.

The Shift from Teaching to the Management of Learning

As we increasingly come to recognize that people bring knowledge, experience, wisdom and purposefulness to any educational event, then ways must be found to bring the new and the old into a new integration. A shift from teaching to teaching/learning has taken us in the right direction but still leaves the learner in an inferior position. The concept of managing learning gives scope to a redefinition of the role and relative value of the experience, knowledge and skills of all involved in the educational situation.

Managing learning is the process of managing an event or environment to afford the maximum learning that can occur consistent with the central purpose of the event. It flows from ecological learning which states that much of the learning we do is taken directly from the environment without the mediation of a teacher. The new role is known as *The Manager of the Learning Environment*.

Educational Assumptions.

Most of our learning has to be directly tied to broader social and environmental purposes if it is to have meaning, relevance and provide a basis from which to act. There is little practical learning that can be totally abstracted from the context to which it is to be applied. By practical learning I mean that which informs our decisions and behaviour.

Many educators believe that education is a genteel endeavour and wish it to remain so. They are often in positions of status, power and influence and have no wish to change this situation. Participation and learning are whole systems concepts and include emotions and power relations. For example, people learn by their mistakes. By severely punishing people for their mistakes we reduce their capacity to learn.

Groups are able to manage their own affairs so long as the following conditions apply:

○ that the task is understood and agreed by all the group,

○ that they have the necessary resources, information, skills, knowledge and time to carry out the task.

If these conditions do not apply and/or if there is imposed control, the group will be dependent.

Learning is behaviour, not simply cognition. To open oneself to learning often means exposing vulnerabilities, as perceived particularly within a hierarchical structure. It is, therefore, important to be able to create a safe climate for all involved. Here the stance and values of the educator or manager are critical. Learning occurs in direct relation to participation in and responsibility for the planning, control and management of the events of which they are a part.

All individuals generally have something they believe they can contribute to a course. Unless individuals have a chance to table their contributions they will intrude it at inappropriate times which will retard the constructive and connected work of the group. Generally individuals will accept the group's judgment as to whether and when their contribution is relevant to its purposes. Thus an issue is either amplified or attenuated by the group. It is important to identify and use as much as possible of the relevant skills, knowledge and experience that reside in the group as each is a potential educator. People can become enabled through contributing and to avoid dependency there is a need to take course co-ordinators out of the content-expert role.

Some things are better learnt by doing rather than by being taught. Others require articulation. There is often, however, an unwitting oppression by the verbally articulate and educationally qualified of those who are not. While it is impossible to predict all the needs, expectations and capacities of participants in advance of a course or conference, this diversity is an advantage when people self direct their learning.

Nobody has the right to an audience. In conferences in particular, I have found organizers give a grossly disproportionate weighting to the feelings or ego of the contributor over the interests of the participants. In turbulent times we all need to be actively adaptive which in turn requires a knowledge of our own learning and adaptation as well as that of organizations and the society as a whole.

Given the above assumptions I sometimes find that I am espousing a view or ideology of participation which is not shared by sponsors or participants. However, sponsors and participants will usually run with the approach to the extent that it contributes to the realization of their objectives. But there is almost inevitably a tension during the course whereby the social, organizational and individual objectives are potentially in conflict. This can usually be managed in a productive way for most of those involved as long as everyone is clear about the different objectives at each of the planning and negotiating phases.

The best safeguard is to be clear about the different objectives at each of the planning and negotiating phases.

Courses and Workshops

I find it useful to distinguish between the **planning** and **management** of a course or workshop.

The Planning Process

The overall objectives of the planning process are to optimize the cognitive and effective learning and attitudinal change of those participating in the course and to enable them to apply that learning where they judge it to be appropriate. Good planning leaves people better able to manage their own learning, enhance their learning environment and jointly manage their collective affairs. This can be achieved by: the development of a self managing learning community which in turn requires:

- building a shared base of information and experience;

- clarification of roles and expectations;

- joint planning;

- establishing procedures for the ongoing evaluation, adjustment and management of the program;

- the identification of needs, relevant and available resources;

- the placement of the course in a broader organizational and societal context;

- arrival at an agreed program.

The diagram on the following page suggests a four stage logic for the conduct of the planning process.

First the pre-course planning by the course organizers based on course objectives, educational design principles, past experience, the resources and time available and if possible, input from the participants.

The Planning Process

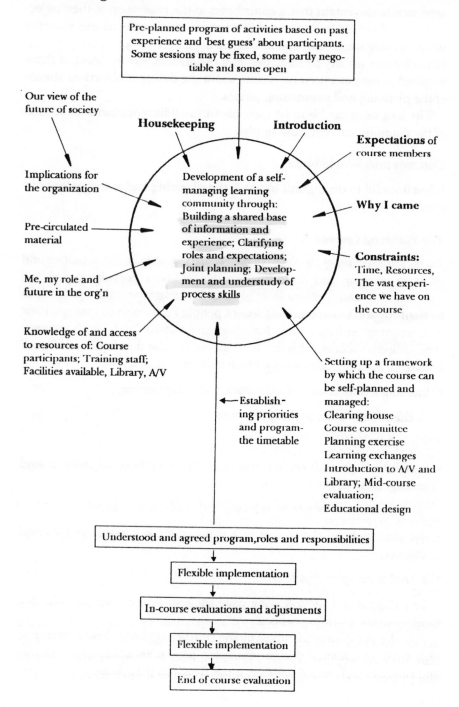

Pre-planned program of activities based on past experience and 'best guess' about participants. Some sessions may be fixed, some partly negotiable and some open

Our view of the future of society

Housekeeping

Introduction

Expectations of course members

Implications for the organization

Development of a self-managing learning community through: Building a shared base of information and experience; Clarifying roles and expectations; Joint planning; Development and understudy of process skills

Why I came

Pre-circulated material

Me, my role and future in the org'n

Constraints: Time, Resources, The vast experience we have on the course

Knowledge of and access to resources of: Course participants; Training staff; Facilities available, Library, A/V

Establishing priorities and program-the timetable

Setting up a framework by which the course can be self-planned and managed: Clearing house Course committee Planning exercise Learning exchanges Introduction to A/V and Library; Mid-course evaluation; Educational design

Understood and agreed program, roles and responsibilities

Flexible implementation

In-course evaluations and adjustments

Flexible implementation

End of course evaluation

Second the gathering and sharing of the information, concepts and experience necessary to participatively plan and manage the course.

Third giving priority to the information that has been generated in phase 2 and integrating it into the program devised in the pre-course planning.

Finally, establishing procedures for the ongoing evaluation, adjustment, control and management of the course.

Let us look at the first two stages in more detail. The third and fourth are covered under "Methodology".

Pre-course Planning

Prospective participants can be involved in defining or redefining objectives and in the detailed pre-course planning. The desirability, practicability, methodology and efficacy of pre-course participation will depend on a number of factors including:

○ the subject matter;

○ the way and the stage at which the participants are identified;

○ their organizational and geographical locations;

○ the organizer's previous experience of running the course;

○ cost;

○ the course objectives.

If the course is dealing with abstract subject matter the scope for pre-course participant planning may be limited. However, questions of motivation, previous experience, conflicting commitments, constraints, preparatory work, aptitude etc need to be taken into account in some way. In matters concerning management, leadership, problem solving, particularly where all the participants are from the one organization, there is great scope for participant involvement in pre-course planning. Such involvement may in fact lead to a different understanding of the underlying issues which led to the proposition of the course in the first place, and perhaps to abandoning the course in favour of an alternate course of action to solve the problem.

If participants are identified through a prospectus or an advertisement, come from many locations and for a variety of purposes, there is some, but limited, value in their being involved in pre-course planning. The basic assumptions cannot be re-negotiated. However, one can start the process of clarifying and negotiating expectations and one can allay apprehensions and, if there is an opportunity for face to face contact, create a climate of confidence, trust and hence risk taking. It also can extend dramatically the timescale over which one can rethink one's position. All learners and particularly adult learners also have a multitude of questions in their minds that can block them from thinking themselves into the course. Many of these questions can be answered prior to the course, particularly if participants can meet face to face.

Where people are from the one organization there is scope to achieve desirable outcomes beyond the primary purpose of the course. The chance of this is greatly enhanced by involving participants in the pre-course planning.

If one has run the course before for a clientele recruited in the same way, then one has some idea of the range of expectations, motivations and experience one will find amongst participants. Thus there is less need to involve the participants from the point of view of the subject matter, the starting level and the likelihood of any mismatch of expectations. However, there would still be the same advantage in allowing people to think their way into the activity over a longer period of time and to reduce any anxiety or defensiveness.

Pre-course planning is a costly activity as it takes the time of the organizers and the participants and one has to weigh up the advantage. In most cases the benefits outweigh the costs and if necessary, the length of the course can be reduced to make up the financial cost of pre-course planning. In the past I have had no difficulty in convincing clients that the cost to them of my time and travel to brief their employees about a course was well spent.

If the course objectives include such matters as team building, planning, job design and other organizational matters, then an in situ briefing in advance of the course can multiply its effectiveness. The participants can be doing all sorts of preparation, data collecting and negotiating not only amongst themselves, but with the broader group to which they will be returning. The latter will play a major role in the group's ability to implement any new learning they bring from the course or workshop.

Within the overall objectives, the extent to which participants are involved in pre-course planning can vary greatly from 100 per cent to virtually nil.

In-course Planning

At least 20 per cent of the program should always be dedicated to in-course planning and the adjustments and additions to the program that flow from that planning. This view is based on at least five assumptions. First, that in any course we meet a great diversity of expectations, needs and relevant experience among the participants. Second, that by involving participants in the planning, the resources available are maximized and the participants better understand and are more committed to the course objectives. Third, that the majority of courses can be modified with advantage after they are convened. Fourth, that a better knowledge of 'process' is of value to individuals in all the settings in which they find themselves, regardless of the extent of pre-course planning. Finally, any mismatch of objectives can be clarified and negotiated.

As most sponsors and organizers are unused to thinking of self management processes it is important to explicitly include them in the timetable from the outset If a participatory planning approach is to be used, the pre-planned framework must specifically allow time for in-course planning, course self management, in-course evaluation and adjustment, and the incorporation of new material arising from the planning process.

Gathering and Sharing Information

The data that needs to be collected and shared will vary and as the diagram suggests the order is not critical. However, experience suggests that a number of the tasks should be grouped together to avoid excessive variety and to allow the groups sufficient time to move through the process of group formation while still having adequate time for the task. A number of combinations have been tried and the most satisfactory found to date are as follows:

Session 1 starts in plenary with a full course briefing, including a rationale for the planning process. This is followed by exploring participants' expectations in small groups. This is followed by plenary reporting and negotiation of any discrepancy in expectations between the participants and the organizers. This can lead to changes in the program or in extreme cases some participants leaving the course or conference.

Session 2 begins with a *plenary* brainstorming of data about the changing and unchanging character of society. Small groups consider the implications of this for the topic of the conference or course. These are reported and collated.

Session 3 consists of small group discussion of each person's role and the future in the organization and a cataloguing of the skills, experience and knowledge of the participants.

Sessions following establish the in-course planning and management structures. In the process, participants learn where to find, and how to use, the training facilities. Establishment of the in-course planning, control and management structures.

A Briefing Session will have: provided a basis for understanding and judging the content and structure of the program as a whole; and enabled participants to become conscious of and knowledgeable about process.

Content will have included objectives, the negotiable aspects, the process and the role of manager to create and co-manage with participants, a climate for maximum learning.

Various matters may arise. Expectations at odds with the objectives must be dealt with immediately before their potential to reduce learning for all is realized.

Matters involving potential conflict of time can usually be accommodated in the planning when the program is redrawn. This often results in an arrangement that allows most people to fulfil outside commitments and retain the number of course hours intact. Usually people will start earlier, or work later to accommodate their various interests. However, the times need to be negotiated by the whole group. The outcome is usually an increased commitment to the meeting of the course objectives.

In some courses I have conducted people have left the course in some cases to return to work, in others to pursue their own interests for the remainder of the time of the course. I am often asked whether I report any absence to the participant's employer. The answer is no. Participative approaches are reliant on a level of trust between all those involved. If you are not prepared to respect confidentiality when people are being honest, then don't ask for that honesty. If you feel some obligation to your sponsors, negotiate that quite explicitly before you start and inform the participants of the results. But don't set up a situation of confidentiality and then misuse it.

The session on the **broader societal context and its future** assists participants to share some of their values and world views and hence allow them to act more purposefully as a community. It provides a collective view of what is going to be of importance in the next few years and some idea of the impact of that future on the topic of the workshop. It reduces the potential for misunderstanding and stereotyping, and establishes a climate of participation and risk taking.

I am often asked about the futures scan approach to planning. I now, therefore, whenever possible build the rationale of futures scans and open systems into the introduction.

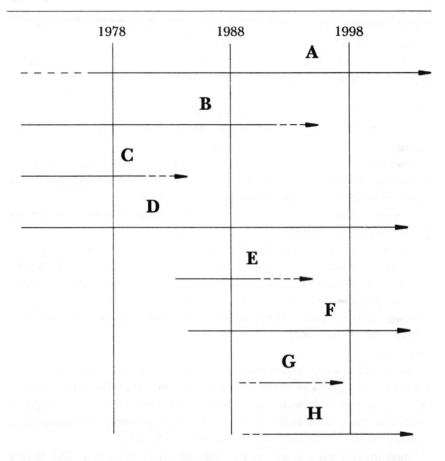

A, B, C and D are important ingredients of the 1978 environment
A, B, D, E and F are important contributing factors to the 1988 environment
A, D, F and H are important factors of the 1998 environment

Let us consider three points of time ten years apart, say 1978, 1988 (now) and 1998. We can plot the different types of events raised by these questions on this time chart and arrive at the attached diagram where:

A is something that became important prior to 1978 and will remain important through 1998; e.g., the commercial application of the microchip.

B is something that became important prior to 1978, is important in 1988 but fades in importance before 1998; e.g., the Australian Coal Industry.

C is something that became important prior to 1978 but fades in importance by 1988; e.g., student politics.

D is something that became important prior to 1978 and will remain important through 1998; e.g., human nature.

E is something that became important prior to 1988 but fades in importance by 1998; e.g., arms reduction negotiations.

F is something that became important prior to 1988 and will remain important through 1998; e.g., the resurgence of Islam.

G is something that will become important after 1988 but will fade in importance by 1998; e.g., the signing of a treaty between the Aboriginal people of Australia and the Australian Government.

H Is something that will become important after 1988 and will remain important through 1998; e.g., electronic mail.

You may disagree with the examples I have chosen, or in fact they may already have been disproved by the time you read this. Such differences of opinion will also arise in the 50-150 items that the participants proffer. The next stage allows the participants to argue such questions as they narrow them down to the eight or ten factors that they believe will be of most importance in the year you choose for the scenario.

The social context which determines what is or is not possible in a given period consists of the interaction between those that are of importance at the time. These ten factors then serve as a reference set against which the other work of the course or conference should be considered. Different methods for this task are included in Section 5.

Small groups then work on the data to order priorities. This forces people to argue and clarify their position and values using data that is understood and generated by all. Don't appoint a chairperson or rapporteur for the groups. If you do, the group becomes dependent on the appointed person or their shadow.

Allow 3/4 hour, and then check on the completion of the task. Give an extra 10-15 minutes if necessary, then ask for a report back on butchers paper. The facilitator should use the first report to synthesize the following reports as they are presented and hence highlight the extent of agreement between groups. If several diverse groups working independently arrive at similar results the validity of the outcome is reinforced and the fear of manipulation of the outcome reduced.

It is always important to spell out the ground rules to establish norms, prevent destructive conflict and avoid things that normally block people's participation and learning.

In plenary you ask the questions: 'What are the things that are likely to get in the way of your contribution or learning?'; 'Are there any special requirements that you have, or disabilities that require special facilities?' Start the process by giving some examples, such as smoking, hard of hearing or outside commitments.

Resources Available for the Course

Human Resources comprise the participants and training staff with a catalogue of their experience, skills and knowledge. Participants need also to be familiarized with the extent and operation of the training and other facilities. This acknowledges experience, reduces dependence on the course organizers and encourage self sufficiency and self worth. It allows the course community to make use of its own resources wherever possible and hence enhance learning and reduce cynicism. It also encourages participants to see that they can learn and make use of physical resources in unfamiliar settings.

It is often necessary to ask specific questions as people may not be prepared to push their skills, or even recognize their value, e.g. 'what relevant experience, skills, knowledge do you have that you are prepared to share on the course?' This list needs to be kept open, as later on people recognize the relevance of their experience and/or recognize that they are not taking too great a risk to offer it to the group. The early stages can be seen as the time to set the climate whereby this can happen.

This can be conveniently and logically dealt with at the same time as the exchange of experience about people is current role or it can be left to a later stage in the workshop when participants have a better idea of what aspects of their skill and experience might be of relevance. You can also list any other people around who may be of assistance and willing to contribute if suitable times can be arranged.

List any other people around who may be of assistance and willing to contribute if suitable times can be arranged.

Participants' Current or Future Role in the Organization

The objectives are to get people to focus critically on their current job, role or purpose, or the one they are moving to, with a view to identifying the needs that might be met by the course, and to give participants a detailed understanding of the way other organizations are structured. Clearly spell out the task.

- 'what do you do in your job or in the job you aspire to?'

- 'what is it possible to do in the job?' (you may have to spell out how the organization is structured to provide an adequate context)

- 'what additional skills, knowledge, experience do you need to better do the job?'

Strongly suggest that they break up the time so that each has an equal time to describe their job (10-15 minutes each), and ask groups to report on butchers paper about additional skills required. It is best done in groups of no more than five..

Constraints

The objectives of spelling out constraints are to ensure objectives ensure that planning is realistic and achievable given the time, resources and expectations of participants and organizers and to show that priorities need to be set and that all participants don't have to learn and experience the same things.

Establishing Priorities and Filling Out the Program

Once these segments have been completed a long list of learning needs should have been generated. These need to be categorized and prioritized.

- Go through the various lists and categorize all of the identified needs into one of three categories:

- those subjects that have been already timetabled and are adequately covered or where modifications can be made to cover the identified need;

- those items which fall outside the bounds of the course, or which could not be dealt with adequately on the course because of shortage of time, lack of adequate resources or because they are incongruous with the objectives of the course;

- those items which can be best served by devoting one or more of the undedicated sessions or learning exchanges.

List the learning exchange items along with resource needs and appropriate methodologies on a matrix with participants' names. Add to the list any opportunities the course affords for participants to gain experience at organizing, managing or presenting parts of the program.

Ask the participants to express their priorities up to the number of learning exchange spaces available. Indicate that as far as possible they will be programmed to avoid conducting participant's highest two or three preferences simultaneously.

Use the full matrix to program the learning exchanges. Check the program with the group as a whole to see if there are any anomalies or any scope for amalgamations.

Nominate a participant to design and co-ordinate each session, giving priority to those participants who have expressed a preference to gain organizational experience. They may need assistance to decide on the educational design of the session; i.e., to determine whether the session should involve information giving, information sharing, problem solving or resolving conflict etc and organize accordingly. Assistance may also be necessary to find adequate resources. You may need to provide a short session on educational design.

Hand out the program of exchanges along with a list of those items that are to be dealt with in other parts of the course or are not going to be dealt with at all (giving reasons). Attach to it the matrix of responses so that people can identify and chase up, outside the program, others interested in areas that don't have sufficient backing to be programmed.

Each day emphasize the learning exchanges in the clearinghouse and point out that people don't have to stick to their initial choices. It pays to point out that a session of two or three can be as valuable for those individuals who participate as one containing all the course participants. Sometimes a number of 'I want to hear about' topics can be picked up in one session by allotting five to ten minutes to a number of contributors. Such matters are best negotiated at the clearinghouse.

Control and Management

Increasing course self management enhances learning of subject matter through acceptance of responsibility by the participants for the content and quality of the program. It puts the responsibility for handling internal community issues onto the community, spreading the load and increasing the number of options available. It allows participants to gain experience in the conduct of courses and in leadership, to become conscious about group process, learning processes and organizational behaviour and thereby makes the course more manageable. It also builds up the self confidence of participants.

The planning process outlined above has provided participants with much of the information necessary to effectively control and co-ordinate the course or workshop. The key elements are the planning process, the morning clearinghouse, the learning exchanges and various groups the clearinghouse may wish to establish, educational, social, report, etc.

Establish the clearinghouse as the controlling body for the course and establish a program management group responsible to the clearinghouse for the implementation of the program. This should represent the sponsors, the participants, the administrative support staff (if any) and course managers. Give them a conceptual framework for the management of the course as a temporary organization.

In-course Evaluation and Adjustment

The Daily Briefing Session and Clearing House

The Objectives of these sessions are to:

° provide a forum and a controlling body for those matters for which the course as a whole is responsible and must make decisions;

° spell out the day's activities and allow for program adjustments;

° allow for any general announcements;

° provide a clearinghouse for any issues or misunderstandings;

° provide time for participants to meet about their own agendas;

° provide participants with opportunities to experience and practice leadership in small and large democratic groups.

At least 3/4 hour should be set aside for the purpose. If there is nothing to discuss the next activity can come forward.

One of the managers should chair the first clearinghouse to model the process. At this stage in the course no participant will have the knowledge to do the job without heavy reliance on the management. Subsequently the clearinghouse should be chaired according to a roster prepared by the participants. The one ground rule is that it moves each day to a new person until all have had a chance to act as chair or until the course comes to an end.

For short courses the clearinghouse should be held each day. However for longer courses (three weeks or more) it is my experience that the clearinghouse decides to reduce it to every second day or even twice a week. The time needed varies greatly. Three quarters of an hour is strictly an average and should not be rigidly adhered to. It should go to task completion whether that be three minutes or three hours, if there is an issue of some substance. If this happens there is usually great scope for learning about some basic issues as well as group process. In the latter case the management may wish to make some process observations to help the participants become conscious of these matters.

In-course Review

This period allows for adjustment or redirection of the course. It also gives participants experience of formative evaluation and emphasises its role in organizational adaptation. It may be conducted by a group selected by the clearinghouse. The course managers should list the matters they want evaluated so that they may be included in the overall process. These should include questions about content, balance, control, management and process. Participants answer individually and then come together and make group reports on separate forms. Both individual and group reports should be recorded and the differences discussed.

Applications, Modifications and Limitations

In-course planning as described here can be applied to a variety of courses, seminars, workshops and conferences. The time available for the program is obviously a limiting factor on what can be achieved, both in the way of participant planning and community self management. For programs spread over less than two days my experience suggests that self management of the course as a whole is of little value. It takes at least two days to establish the necessary information base, framework and roles. Much of the learning about self management arises from its practice over a period of days.

However, participation in the preparation and planning of the agenda is workable in an abridged form and I would claim necessary, in activities as short as two to three hours. The critical elements are the collection and sharing of participant's expectations and some agreement about the purposes. Even if it takes up to 50 per cent of the time any subsequent discussion is more informed, misunderstandings are avoided and much is learnt in the exchange and sharing of information.

For longer activities where it is important to develop a self managing learning community much more time must be spent in planning; I would say a minimum of six hours spread over four sessions for courses of five days or longer. One should also always allow small groups to self manage, no matter what the time available for reasons outlined herein. Similarly, the control of an exercise can rest with the group as a whole for any course of more than two to three days' duration.

Residential and non-residential courses differ in the possibilities and problems they present for participative planning. In residential courses more time needs to be devoted to the clearing house each day to deal with matters relating to interpersonal and community dynamics and housekeeping.

On the positive side it provides a range of real matters to be self planned and managed by the community. Non-residential courses require the course co-ordinator to take much more of the load and a much more visible and active role, particularly if the intervals between the sessions or days are of a week or longer.

A diversity of experience, knowledge, age, culture, institutional bases, skills, educational backgrounds and sometimes language is a characteristic of the participants in many programs. Participative planning and self management is one way of recognizing and constructively dealing with this diversity. Those with knowledge in areas that others lack can act as a resource. Project groups can be constituted to take advantage of the diversity as the community can be grouped in various ways according to their level of skill or knowledge. The matrix of interests and individuals provides participants with the information to get together in twos and threes around questions of common concern outside the formal course time.

One of the more difficult tasks in programming the learning exchanges and interest groups is to determine how much time to devote to each topic. Some tasks may warrant a workshop of several hours or days. In other cases where experience is being exchanged four of five topics might be dealt with in an hour long session. Where this uncertainty arises a learning exchange can be devoted to exploring the depth of the area, establishing the resources available and planning subsequent sessions or workshops.

Some Pitfalls for Course Managers

- Going through the motions of collecting the data and not taking account of it in a public way. This leads to cynicism and loss of commitment. Participants are content to have their expectations go unmet so long as they can see the reasons for it; e.g., not shared by others, no resources available to meet them or outside the scope of the course.

- Not providing direction and co-ordination where participants don't have the information, machinery, or the need to provide it themselves.

- Staying in the content-expert role when it could be readily taken up by one of the participants.

- Not recognizing or intervening when you realize a laissez-faire situation has developed because of your management or for other reasons.

- Not explaining the process and educational design questions as they are encountered.

- Delaying the production of a timetable incorporating the participant's planning and the information on which it is based.

- Failing to have a clearinghouse at the appropriate intervals and times even if it only involves asking the question about the need. For courses of two weeks or less this should be held each day, preferably first thing each morning and all participants should attend. If it is set up correctly it is in the interests of the participants to be there and peer pressure and self interest provide the motivation, not management coercion.

- Not modelling the underlying values of participation and self management. My experience is that this is the greatest barrier to the use of participative methodology. Participants can 'smell' hypocrisy and continually devise tests of consistency and authenticity. If you are not prepared to lose control of the course to the agreed controlling body, my advice is that you should not consider using participative processes in the first place as it will be seen to be manipulation and the course will become ineffective.

- Not clearly establishing the *extent* to which different aspects of the course are negotiable.

- Underestimating the capacity of the group to contribute to such tasks as priority setting, programming etc and to arrive at better solutions than those of the managers and organizers.

- Not clearly articulating, clarifying and if necessary negotiating groups tasks.

Conferences

Scope

To me the essential difference between a course and a conference is that in the former there is an expectation that those offering the course can assist participants to learn specified skills, knowledge, attitudes or behaviours. Those conducting the course contract to *supply* certain learning outcomes. It is in principle a one way transfer, an asymmetric relationship between the educator and the learner.

In the case of the conference, the organizers offer a forum where knowledge can be exchanged and/or developed; more of a market place. Those conducting the conference contract *to set up a forum or environment* within which this interchange or commerce in ideas can be most productive. The quality of the offerings depends on those who wish to use the forum for the presentation and clarification of their ideas. It is in principle a two way process, involving the interchange and development of knowledge. It is potentially an interchange amongst equals, a symmetrical relationship between contributors and participants. This aspect of a conference is clear in the way *The Shorter Oxford English Dictionary* defines a conference as 'a formal meeting for consultation or discussion'.

Arising from this essential difference are other secondary differences that apply to such factors as numbers, length, the use and distribution of materials and early knowledge of the numbers attending.

Here I focus on the way in which participative processes can be used in the planning, management, conduct and control of a conference. As some of the applications are very similar to those discussed in some detail above I will cross reference them.

Within the above definition of a conference there can be a great diversity of appropriate designs depending on purpose, the organizational connectedness of the participants, distribution of knowledge, the nature of the subject matter of the conferring or whether the emphasis is content or process.

I stress that the extent to which it is of value to build participation into conferences depends greatly on these factors. In a planning or search conference the content is almost entirely generated by the participants out of their knowledge and experience as the need arises, and all participants are involved. However, the conference organizers determine the process by which the subject matter is generated and dealt with. In an academic disciplinary conference the subject matter is determined by an individual or group in advance of the conference usually in the form of a paper. The process then allows for the presentation and or discussion of these papers, largely on an individual basis. Here there is minimal scope for participation. However, it is my view that there are few situations that do not benefit from participation and it should always be at least considered in the planning phases. My experience is that if participation is built in as an after thought it usually comes unstuck.

The Planning Process

Conferences usually have a wider range of interests involved in the planning process than courses and workshops. While those involved are not strictly representatives of the ultimate participants they are generally drawn from the range of interests and organizations that might be expected to attend. This generally makes the planning process more difficult than that for courses and workshops. All have a view of what a conference is and how this particular one might be designed and those views often differ greatly. As a result of this conferences are often an aggregation of unrelated parts with no overriding design principle. If, however, the planning committee can agree on some overriding design principle, then a diverse planning group is an asset.

While scope for participation in the pre event planning of a conference is greater than that for a course or a conference, the scope for in course planning is much less. The shortness of time, the large numbers and the diversity of expectations and purposes all dictate against it. However, there is some scope but it needs to be much more structured and normally needs to be done in sub-sections of the conference that have manageable numbers and some commonality of purpose.

Allowing the plenary session of a large conference to significantly change its direction may appear to be democratic, but in fact is not as most participants are not there as free agents. They came in response to an advertised program and there is not the time nor the forum to seriously consider alternatives. Unless the advertised program allowed for such discussion and redirection, the fact of using the conference time to debate such change is discriminatory and potentially antidemocratic.

Mechanisms for feedback should be built into the conference and the conference managers should have a responsibility to consider this in the context of their overall responsibility to participants. With large conferences one of the difficulties of building in flexibility and in conference planning is the communication of the information to the conference as a whole. My experience is that one has to introduce multiple mechanisms of communication which are integral to the planning process itself. Mechanisms for in conference planning, decision making and communication include the following.

Clearinghouse

A clearinghouse can be established at either the beginning or end of the day. Its purposes are multiple. These include announcements about program changes and new offerings, the debate of issues arising in sectors of the conference for which a conference wide discussion and decision is sought, and complaint.

My experience is that it is better to hold the clearinghouse at the end of the day so that organizers have a chance to respond to any feedback or can canvass issues through the next days newsletter. It should be chaired by one of the conference organizers or a representative of the sponsoring body.

Open Spaces in the program

These allow people to offer new workshops, discussion groups, or raise debates for example. It is important that there be administrative backup to allocate adequate room and equipment to new activities and to provide information about these new offerings in time for people to participate if they so desire.

Notice Board and Computer Systems for Programming

The notice boards need to be large and centrally placed as they become the hub of information exchange at a participative conference. Here people obtain the latest information about new offerings, sign up for various activities or make new offerings.

As the information rapidly multiplies, it is important to have some system to locate information, ordered either by time or purpose or both. There are now available computer packages that do this. I have experienced a number of problems with such systems. The first is the reluctance of people to use them.

This may change with time but I see it only as an adjunct to the notice board. The ability to scan the whole range of offerings, see how it is presented, who else is interested, discuss and clarify with others around is distinctive to the provision of the notice board.

Newsletter

A daily newsletter is essential in large participatory conferences. While announcements and notice boards complement the flow of information, there needs to be some permanent record of any changes that people can pick up at any time and take with them. It should be available in all the residences and at the conference venue prior to breakfast. The day's program should be on the front page. It can also be used as a place to publish letters and views and particularly any resolutions to be put to the day's clearing house. This often requires people to work into the night and early morning.

Breakfast Announcements

While it might sound like overkill, I have also found it helpful, where possible, to give announcements at breakfast. As we know that people are there for a variety of purposes which take them in and out of the formal proceedings of the conference, then it is our responsibility to provide communications that as far as possible recognize this fact.

Conference Office

A centrally located conference office is also an important part of the communications process. The conference office is ideally in two parts, a shopfront and a back room. The back room should have a place for planning and co-ordination meetings and for people to pursue urgent administrative tasks unhassled by participants.

Ideally the conference office should be fully equipped including telephones and fax connections with the outside world and a paging ability within the conference venue for conference managers and administrators. The radio telephone overcomes the problems of changing telephone numbers and the need to rely on Telecom connections.

Speakers' Corner

There are often ideas and opinions abroad in a conference that the organizers were not abreast of and so did not plan for. It is difficult to build these into the formal program late in the piece, but a speakers' corner can do the job. In a Speakers' Corner several participants may speak for say three to ten minutes on the subject of their choice. Providing a room, a program and a Chairperson so as to ensure all have a fair go, is all that is necessary.

Design

Given the above it is important to get early agreement amongst the conference planning team about the overall design features that are to be followed and applied to all decisions.

The following are the ones I have found useful to keep in mind when designing conferences. Not all apply to all conferences but they should be considered. To make changes at the last minute such as adding discussion groups can often be a waste of time or even destructive to the conference.

Diversity

Allow for diversity in the following:

○ Participants' reasons for attending (information, network building, knowledge, skills, rest and recreation, making new contacts and renewing old ones, outside business, social support);

○ Preferred learning and meeting styles;

○ Contexts from which participants come and the expectations they bring with them;

○ The subject matter people believe to be important or to which they are willing to contribute;

○ Expectations of what a conference is;

○ Meeting formats as dictated by the purposes, spread of expertise, size of the groups and the amount of time available.

Non-negotiable overall structure

The overall structure should be non-negotiable. However, within that overall structure one can design a great deal of choice both between predetermined options and for people to do their own thing.

I am of the view that the overall structure, with the exception of the clearing house and the opening session, should allow for competing activities and formats. One of these options should be the ability to meet in informal groups over a drink. Thus, except where the overall conference purposes are being served, 'nobody has the right to an audience'. Also, the venue should include a coffee and drinks facility where informal work can be done.

Flexible substructure

Subconference conveners and workshop leaders should be given a free hand in the design and management of their own section but the timing should be a matter of negotiation. The conference managers should see that competing offerings as far as possible, are attracting distinct audiences and offer alternatives in format. It should also be in a position to assist contributors in the educational design of their activities if so requested. It is useful to have a capacity to video sessions where people have to make choices between sessions that are all of high priority to them.

Information

The more complex the conference, the greater the amount and variety of information needed by participants about the overall structure, design features, choices and opportunities it offers. The majority of participants will not seriously inform themselves about the choices until they actually arrive, no matter how much information is sent out in advance. In part this is because people don't have the context within which to make good judgments. The degree of choice should increase during the conference.

Community Building

This is one of the most important aspects of a conference. Both the environment and the program contribute to community building. Facilities for informal meetings and structured conference activities encourage networking.

The personal computer and integrated database, spreadsheet and word processing packages can now greatly assist in the administration of large, complex conferences.

Evaluation

One can evaluate the content of a conference and/or the conference structures and processes. The latter is the most important because that is what the organizers can improve the next time around. However, as each conference is a very different animal it is important to try and tease out the basic design features. Participants tend to think in terms of the content rather than the process even when they are satisfied or dissatisfied with the latter and also we tend to lose our memory of the details of process and management more quickly than the subject matter. As a result where I have evaluated a conference I have done so at the end of the conference and have focussed on the design.

The most satisfactory method has been to put up sheets of butcher's paper with questions that can be answered with a tick or a yes or no and where comments can be added if so wished. I also add additional sheets for questions the participants may wish to add. This public evaluation allows for some development of ideas that the individual questionnaire misses.

Status of any Decisions, Recommendations or Reports

The status of any decisions made by a conference or workshop is often a vexed question. Even if it is explicitly mentioned in the conference publicity that it has no decision making status and will not be structured to facilitate the making of decisions, there will often be pressures on the conference organizers to change this. On other occasions it may suit the conference organizers to find out the strength of support for particular recommendations.

I have found that voting on reports can be very helpful in clarifying issues and in indicating where the weight of opinion lies. Often people are surprised at the results. They often presume that the more articulate and outspoken have broad support, or that silence means consent. Voting shows that this is often not the case. One needs to clarify the status of the decisions very carefully if one is to acquiesce to the pressure.

At the least one can say that any vote taken has the authority of the individual citizens who chose to participate in it, particularly if the numbers are alluded to in any subsequent report of the decision. It cannot have the authority of the conference organizers or of the owners of the venue unless authorized by those bodies. Some people become conflicted because they are representing organizations and are unsure of their authority to vote as individuals. Certainly they cannot vote for their organizations unless they have the authority to do so.

It is never easy to manage these situations and in fact your authority to manage is likely to be the first thing to be debated. The procedures I have found to work on most occasions are as follows:

○ Where it is your intention to ask participants to vote on recommendations, indicate this in the pre-conference papers.

○ Never include working party reports in a conference proceedings without indicating their status. If such reports are seen as coming from the whole conference then time must be given for the full conference to discuss, amend and vote on their adoption.

○ Clearly establish the procedures you are going to follow and ask the conference to appoint a chair.

○ Pay close attention to time and clearly establish the division of time before you start.

○ When recommendations are requested, brief the task groups, impressing on them the need to be specific.

○ Vote on these recommendations in the normal way.

○ With discursive reports, it becomes very messy and time consuming to amend wording. It is better to vote on the inclusion or exclusion of the report from the proceedings and whether it should be a report of the group that authored it or of the conference as a whole.

Concepts

In using participative approaches to course and conference planning, design and management, there is a need for participants to be able to call on concepts that assist them to reflect and learn from that experience in such a way that they can apply it to their own practice. Many of the concepts I have found useful are dealt with in earlier parts of this book.

Learning, Education and Teaching

The following 'learning map' helps people identify the different types of learning that are appropriate to different categories of education and gives recognition and value to the learning that occurs outside of educational institutions and courses.

Map of Learning

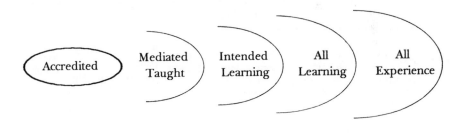

The outer ellipse includes all of our experience, only part of which we have learnt from; that is, guides our thought and behaviour. The second ellipse includes all of the learning that we do, planned and unplanned, whether it occurs at work, at home or in the classroom. The next concentric circle encloses all of that learning that is intended. Some people define this learning as being education, but others confine the word education to those learning activities conducted by educational institutions such as schools, colleges and universities. The penultimate ellipse includes our learning which is mediated by a teacher or educator and is usually, though not always, the province of educational institutions. Finally there is a part of mediated learning which can be and is objectified and credentialed by the State or other institutions.

Types of Learning and Appropriate Methods

The most fundamental distinction is between *Environmental Learning* on the one hand and *Abstract and Skills Learning* on the other. This distinction is covered more thoroughly earlier in this book under Educational Paradigms. I give participants a brief overview of these paradigms.

Before people begin designing their own learning exchanges and workshops they need to know which methods and design features are most effective in producing learning of various materials and processes.

The table below summarizes our experience with the major categories. While each method will always produce some learning in any area, the asterisks indicate the strengths and weaknesses of the teaching/learning methods and practical alternatives.

Skills covers a wide range from simple and routine to complex but there is an implicit 'know how' component. Reading or teaching abstractions is obviously not going to be particularly effective.

	Methods								
	Lecture	Seminar	Apprenticeship	Projects	Reading	Group Discs'n	Participative Design	Other Ltd Self Mgt	Search Confs
Required									
Skills			*	*			*	*	
Information	*	*	*	*	*	*	*	*	*
Perceptual Reconstruction		*		*	*	*	*	*	*
Attitudes & values			*			*	*	*	*
Organizational							*		
Design and Redesign									
Planning and Policy Making									*

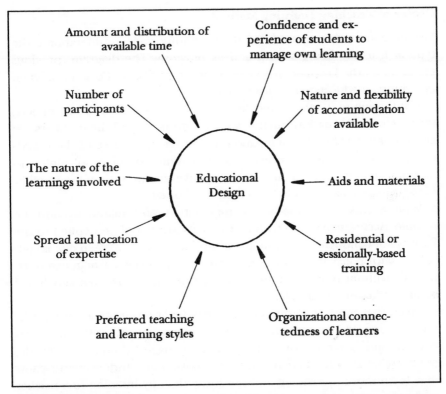

Acquiring information is an everyday function and never stops in fact. If the required information is of the abstract, disciplinary type, reading and some teaching, explanation or discussion are needed. This can happen as well in an apprentice or research trainee situation as in a formal seminar or lecture.

Perceptual reconstruction covers new understandings, changing attitudes and values and resulting shifts in directions and strategies. Participative methods shine here as Lewin demonstrated during the Second World War. However, the process of reconstruction can begin in an apprenticeship or hands on role.

Perceptual reconstruction is essentially a process of putting the building blocks or pieces of the individual jigsaw of meaning together in a different way. It is only possible in situations when people are simultaneously able to use their experience and evaluate it in the light of others' experience when these others are trusted peers. receiving information from an expert who is neither trusted nor an equal will have little power to achieve this most powerful form of human learning.

Choice of Teaching/Learning Methods

When we are choosing methods, the most important consideration is the type of learning being sought and its purpose. The diagram (previous page) shows the factors that I believe should be taken into account when designing an educational activity for adults.

If information is sought and the knowledge all rests with one expert, then lecture or broadcast methods are appropriate and the numbers are limited only by the accommodation or the reception area of the broadcast. If however, one is concerned with planning, problem solving or attitudinal change which demand participative methods, then the number of participants may need to be limited to 30 or even 10.

With a mix of methods, accommodation and materials must be flexible. Accommodation in which the seats are tiered and bolted to the floor is not conducive to learning and problem solving. When one is concerned with policy development, planning or problem solving, extended periods without distraction are important and hence residentially based accommodation is desirable.

Given that more than one method may be appropriate for the teaching, learning or management of a given subject, for example lecture/discussion and project work, the teacher/manager should choose the method that they are best suited to. Likewise some students/participants may learn more by reading and self study than by listening to a teacher and vice versa. The student/learner should, where possible, choose the method that is most effective for them. Methods that allow the learner maximum control, flexibility and self direction should always be an aim.

If a group of learners are able to take responsibility for their own learning, and have the confidence to teach each other, they will learn faster and more effectively. These competences can be developed quickly in a well designed and managed learning environment.

Modes such as problem solving, self directed learning and group discussion require sessions of a minimal length of half a day. Concept development sessions should be one hour at the most. If participants are organisationally independent most methods are open to be used. If, however, the participants are addressing a planning or organizational task, then it is important to choose methods that ensure that all can contribute according to their role and experience, develop a shared understanding of the environment and the history and desirable future of the organization. Thus brainstorming, nominal group and discussion methods become essential.

If participants are not or do not aim to be organizationally connected then methods which set the activities in a planning or problem solving environment are less effective.

If the intention is to enable participants to learn from the process of the workshop as well as the content, it is important to have some concepts which they can use as a framework for reflecting on that experience. The course, conference or workshop is in fact a temporary organization which is an instrument enabling us to achieve our collective objectives. At the same time it is a laboratory in which to get hands on experience of the management of an organization.

The issues relating to *planning* are exhaustively canvassed above and in the section on Searching. Control is discussed in Part II.

Until the course commences the control is with the sponsoring institution or entity. Once the conference is underway aspects of control can shift to a body which is based on the course participants as a whole. What those delegations are and how the interests of the controlling institution are carried into the control of the course need to be clearly defined. Usually the course manager is representing the controlling body and has a veto power on matters of central concern to it.

Control is best vested in a daily *clearing house* composed of participants and conveners and chaired after the first meeting or two by one of the participants. It has been argued that the participants do not have the knowledge to take responsibility. It is my experience that through this process they rapidly pick up that knowledge and that in practice the clearing house becomes a very important activity in responding to changing needs and in retaining the commitment and understanding of the need for these changes.

While the conveners have a veto power, if, as members of the clearing house they cannot convince a group of the importance of the particular activity, they are unlikely, via the veto, to get the participants' commitment to changes decided unilaterally by the convener. Such commitment is necessary if one is to maximize the learning.

Any non-negotiable aspects of the program should be clearly identified prior to the commencement of the workshop. These may be changed by the workshop clearing house only by unanimous decision. A participant has a right to expect what has been advertised even though its relevance may seem to most to have disappeared as the course develops.

The time necessary for the clearinghouse and can take upwards of an hour. In cultures where participative decision making is traditional they usually take longer, but the decisions are better understood and enacted.

I use 'management' in the sense of implementing the policies of an organization. All aspects of management do not have the same potential for learning and so I have found it of value to recognize the following areas of management; the educational and social programs; evaluation, administration and reporting. Each of these functions could be carried out by one manager or management team but if one is looking to provide participants with opportunities to practice and learn from the processes of management, segmentation provides increased opportunities.

Management teams can be formed for each of the above such that the educational management team should consist of a member of the organizing group plus three to four elected from amongst the participants. Membership can rotate but should be on a timescale that allows those involved to come to grips with the task and allows for continuity of management. The other management teams can be subgroups of either the educational management team or the clearinghouse. The differences between these organizational locations should be discussed in the debriefing.

Management of the core which is *educational design* cannot be handed over to participants immediately. Most participants do not have a comprehensive set of concepts and practices linking design and implementation. It takes at least two days of experience and discussion before this set is sufficiently developed for participants to take this responsibility.

The administration is concerned with bookings, registrations, finances, travel, liaison with the venue management and the preparation of information and materials. The transfer of responsibility for administration to the participants is even more time consuming and in my experience is rarely warranted in terms of the learning opportunities created. This contrasts sharply with permanent educational institutions such as Neighbourhood Centres where administration represents an important source of learning.

The following functions differ from the above in that they come into existence only after the workshop starts so that the question of transfer of responsibility does not arise.

Some participants will wish to gain experience in *evaluation and reporting*. Sponsors and managers will participate with them on the planning and content.

The social program is relevant only in residential activities where it may be critical to the development of a good self managing social climate. Often this group has a dispute handling as well as a planning and organizing role.

Political Concepts

Because the focus is on participative design and management, participants may request discussion of the relation between organizational and political uses of terms such as democracy, participation, autocracy, bureaucracy. These discussions should be broadened to include concepts of laissez- faire, anarchy and the difference between participative and representative democracy.

Tools and Handouts.

The following example is handed out at the start of or prior to the course.

Course Planning

As course participants you will be involved in the *planning, control* and *co-ordination* of parts of the program. There are several reasons why we have adopted this practice. Firstly, because each new set of students brings with them a unique set of needs, experience, skills, knowledge, attitudes, that cannot be adequately or efficiently determined beforehand. This process allows the program to be adjusted to incorporate these factors. Secondly, by being in-

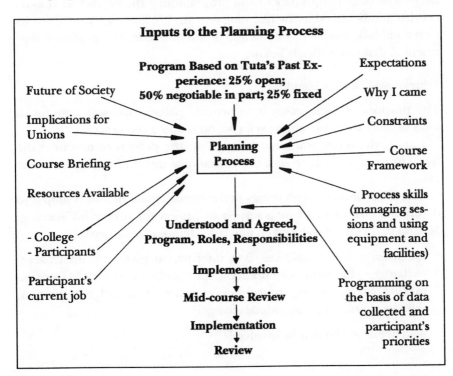

cluded in the planning you can better see the rationale, meaning and place-ment of each of the parts of the program and will be better equipped to par-ticipate in its management. Thirdly, our experience is that participation leads to enhanced opportunities to learn from one another, from contributors and from one's own involvement (learning by doing).

Of the program that you have been given, 25% is completely left open for you to plan (learning exchanges); 50% has been determined in broad outline but is open to some shift in emphasis. 25% is fixed as a result of commitments that had to be planned well in advance; e.g., guest speakers, which are an essential part of the overall management of the course (clearinghouse, planning session, mid-course review) or other which the sponsor has insisted upon. There are three aspects to the plan-ning process.

First, the collection and exchange of information about participants and trainers expectations of the course and reasons for participating, the broader shifts that are going on in society, the resources available (in-cluding yours), our role in the organization; and the constraints operat-ing on the course. **Second**, conducting the planning process in such a way that participants and staff are assisted in working together produc-tively. **Third**, giving priority to and programming the needs and resour-ces that are identified in the planning session. We find each course has its own emphasis, unique resources and different needs. The process is rep-resented diagrammatically below:

Educational Design Handout

The purpose of these notes is to provide participants with conceptual tools to assist them to become self-conscious about the process.

I apply the term 'educational design' to the process of matching the social or group structure with the educational task and available resour-ces.

One of the most difficult things in the management of a workshop is to determine how to structure a session or project for maximum learning. Several factors need to be taken into consideration including:

o the nature of the task; i.e., is it information giving or information exchange? Problem identification or problem solving? Decision making, agenda setting, concept development, knowledge acquisition, skill development or attitudinal change?

o who needs to know or be involved?

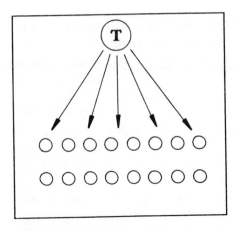

- how many people are involved?

- what are the resources (knowledge, skills, experience) that the group need to achieve its goals?

- what is the appropriate basis for division into small groups?

I find it of value to distinguish the following social structures:

Broadcast—One To Many

Application: When: Giving information, briefing, clearinghouse, enumerating ideas and conceptual frame-works.

When: The necessary information and skills resides in one person.

When: Everybody in the community needs and has a responsibility to know, so they can participate in the planning and management of the community.

This structure is the most time efficient for the above tasks. These sessions can be video recorded which allows for multiple usage and replay.

The *physical setting* is not critical and can be in rows or circular. It may help to have tables if participants need to take notes. There is no limit on

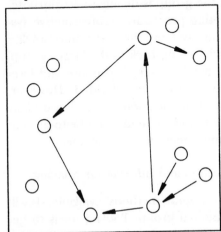

numbers as it is a broadcast. Direct feedback is desirable but not always possible and not essential.

Community Discussion

Application: When taking community wide decisions. The groundwork may previously have been done in smaller groups or in the large group. If the basic discussion (decision making) has been in smaller groups there needs to be an opportunity for each group to report to the whole community. If each group is discussing the same subject then it is most manageable to hear all groups before allowingeneral discussion (clarification questions only after the individual reports). If each group is discussing a different subject, then have the discussion on each groups report immediately after it has been given. Before starting, clarify the time available and divide equitably and adhere to it unless the *whole* community decides otherwise.

It is also appropriate when discussing issues of community wide concern at the clearinghouse. Some issues have to be dealt with at the community level if they are to be resolved, dissolved or agreed, to the community's satisfaction. Otherwise they will continue to fester and be in the way of the work of the community.

It is also applicable for problem solving, clarifying and developing concepts. This is a more creative mode but harder to achieve with large numbers. Its achievement will depend on the nature of the subject, the clarity of the task and the trust within the group. Trust in this instance depends on individuals allowing others to contribute in their stead. It is contributing by silence so that a connected discussion can be sustained.

In terms of *physical setting*, each member of the community needs eye contact with all others for this to work effectively. The physical setting places a desirable upper limit of 40 or 50 people. It is possible for larger numbers to be accommodated. However, the larger the numbers, the more fragile the fabric of understanding and trust. The more these factors diminish, the more easily the meetings can be sabotaged by one single minded individual or subgroup who don't see their interests being met by the process.

One can resort to other devices if the group is unable to act purposefully as a whole; e.g., the use of meeting procedure, representative systems, voting systems, breaking into smaller groups and feeding back to the larger group. The latter are necessary if win-lose and lose-lose questions are being decided. However, the quality of the decision or solution is likely to be inferior and there may not be total community commitment to the outcome.

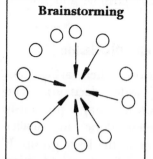

Brainstorming

Data Collection and Information Sharing

There are several methods available. I will mention two—brainstorming and nominal group. Pooling ideas to get the maximum number of possibilities—a creative activity. Don't allow discussion of ideas, only clarification. Discussion of ideas creates circumstances where the person has to justify their contribution and this immediately stops the less articulate and less confident from contributing, stifles the flow of ideas and so only the confident, articulate and the incensed contribute. Data collection is also a practice which heightens participation and gives value to participation.

The best *physical setting* is one where all participants are in eye contact but it is not essential. The product needs to be recorded so that all can see their contribution, preferably on butchers paper (flipcharts) so that the record can remain on view.

However, a black or white board will suffice if the record can be immediately recorded and circulated to participants. The recorder should not act as a censor or gatekeeper.

If the range of ideas is the primary objective, there is no real limit on numbers except your capacity to record the contributions. Three or four people can be recording the ideas at the one time.

If participation is important, the upper limit is 30 or 40 unless the conference breaks into subgroups for the task.

Nominal Group

The physical setting is as for brainstorming. The upper limit for numbers is 20-25 as each person usually takes two to three minutes over the course of the activity to present their three points.

Sharing Information, Expectations, Experience and Purposes

Purposes: Whenever a group of people come together to form a learning community there is a need to develop a pool of shared data as early and efficiently as possible. If the number exceeds six or seven this is best done by breaking into groups of four to five people for the following reasons:

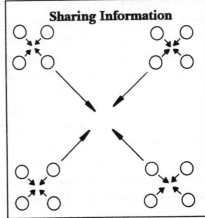

Sharing Information

More than one person can be talking at once and for longer given a fixed time for the exercise. Take as an example 30 participants in a 90 minute session. If each described their experience in plenary session each participant would have three minutes. If the full session broke into six groups of five, the group reporting would take 5 minutes x 6 groups=30 minutes, leaving 60 minutes for each group and hence

12 minutes per individual. That is four times the amount of information exchanged and sorted.

There is a limit to the number of successive contributions (seven to ten for me) one can hold in one's mind and later recall.

It takes time to sift our expectations, relevant experience and purposes, particularly as they often require an elaboration of context or environment if they are to be meaningful.

If four or five others have some detailed knowledge of your experience and/or situation, then there is four to five times the chance it will be called on subsequently at the appropriate time. Additionally, you don't have to advocate or push your own contribution, the other four to five will do it if they believe it appropriate. As well as amplifying the chance of relevant experience being subsequently built into the discussions, it also has the effect of suppressing or attenuating ideas that participants raise but which are not relevant or important to the work of the course or conference. This cuts out a lot of the noise and blind alleys that distract from the central purpose.

Each group can sift, summarize and prioritize its experience without going into the detailed story of every individual. If the summary is cumulative and on butchers paper, it rarely takes more than five minutes.

In a group of five, strangers are more likely to feel at ease and talk about their experiences, and take risks, than they are in a group of 20 or 30. Each person thus gets to know four to five others in some depth as well as an overall impression of the full membership.

If the rapporteur pushes their views inappropriately this soon becomes apparent and the group usually punishes the behaviour.

For the *physical setting*, you need either sufficiently flexible furniture to allow groups to form, or space outside the room for them to meet. Lobbies, corridors or bedrooms will all serve the purpose, particularly if butchers paper is used for recording.

Up to 50 participants in ten groups of five can exchange information while staying within an individual's concentration span and capacity to absorb information. Beyond those numbers, one needs to split the group into sub conferences and the compiled information from these circulated or posted. It is unrealistic to expect each participant to be able to develop and maintain shared world views with more than 30-40 others in the space of a week. Sometimes there are major parts of the world view that are given and unquestioned such as in a religious or political meeting and in these cases, numbers may go higher.

Small Group Discussion

Small groups should be used whenever:

- the large group (community discussion) is unable to deal with the job at hand in a connected and constructive way;

- it is more time efficient (a number of different tasks can be tackled at the one time);

- the larger group is searching for direction;

- there is a need to set priorities or sift a large quantity of material (e.g., following data collection);

- there are a large number of divergent opinions to be accommodated or worked through. Sometimes there is pressure to stay in the larger group. Possible reasons are needing the broader group to put all necessary views up, wanting to be in on all the gossip, inadequate trust or the overall or small group tasks are not understood or agreed;

- the relevant information is spread amongst the group.

Whenever small groups are used, there is be a need to report back to the full community.

Division of Labour

Some division of labour is necessary to deal with the workshop task efficiently and effectively. At some stage sufficient trust will develop in the conference or workshop for the task to be divided between different groups. This is the stage at which individual members are prepared to trust others to do parts of the task on their behalf. If trust is low, there is a danger that group emotional assumptions, particularly dependence, will prevent a group from breaking into smaller groups. To avoid this the group needs to become a democratic work group and as such have an agreed purpose, a clear task, sufficient time and the resources, including experience, to do the task. The first prerequisite is that the total community agrees on the way the task is to be divided. The second is that the manager clearly spells out the sub-tasks and the third is that the products return to the total community for modification, discussion, adoption or rejection.

Catering for Diverse Interests

In most conferences, workshops or course, there will be some information and issues that will be of interest or high priority to only some participants. Participant's priorities can be determined by making a matrix listing the topics on one dimension and the participant's names on the other and then asking participants to order their preferences up to the number of sessions to be devoted to these subjects. The workshops can then be programmed so that the majority can participate in their top priorities. In some instances several parallel sessions may be run, in others only the one, depending on the priorities. The procedure places the onus of priority onto the participants and guards against the provision being pushed in the direction of the interests of the articulate. It also allows the participants time in which to decide and negotiate their interests. I usually stress that attendance at such sessions is voluntary.

Timing

When a small group is given a task that involves decision making, problem solving or conceptualization, it helps to allocate them sufficient time to the work free of constraints such as fixed meal times or overnight break; i.e., they need autonomous working time. This allows people to have second thoughts, check things with group members in private or with others outside the group or sleep on the matters. If such a break is not allowed, people can doubt the validity of their work. They feel it could have been channelled or limited in some way.

Other Points

When a discussion is focussed on details that are of concern to only two or three in the group, the interested parties should be asked to get together after the session.

Matters of concern to the whole group and about which there is agreement in principle should be dealt with by a subgroup.

The drafting of detailed statements should be left to a small group which submits its product to large group scrutiny and approval.

When a meeting breaks spontaneously into a number of conversations, relevant to the task at hand, it may be a sign of loss of direction, a task too difficult for the whole group to handle, too much available information or the emergence of a new direction. Once identified, it is best managed by obtaining agreement in the large group about the nature of the impasse and then breaking into a number of small groups of three to four people for 10-20 minutes to devise ways to break the impasse. Then the plenary re-convenes and the groups report on a cumulative basis-only reporting on things not mentioned by previous reports until an agreed course of action emerges. When it does emerge it will be seen immediately and spontaneously and the community can continue on its task in plenary.

Butchers' Paper Handout

Why Use Butchers' Paper?

- It is a public record of meeting which cannot be manipulated without the acceptance of the whole group. It, therefore, meets the criteria of openness.
- Allows for clear, economical reports that can easily be amalgamated and kept.
- Cheap, now available in cut sheets at most stationers.
- Readily accessible to all present.
- Can use anywhere so long as you have a felt tip pen and masking tape, or are within cooee of a newsagent.
- Acts as a memory aid once you have passed onto other questions. One glance can remind you of the content or drift without unduly distracting you from the content of the discussion at the time. The record can be added to at any time.
- It turns the room into a home papered with shared artifacts.
- Learning Exchange Form

Example of Instructions for filling out learning exchange form

- Place numbers 1 to 7 in order of preference against the learning exchanges listed on the back of this page— 1 means first preference; 7 means seventh preference.
- Place a cross against sessions you are prepared to lead or areas where you have experience/skills/knowledge to contribute.
- Tick the relevant columns if you want practice at running a session or chairing a guest speaker.
- Please return by 5.00 pm Monday.

The Learning Exchange Form with its changes becomes a central tool for flexible, participative management and maximization of learning.

INDEX

A

Abstract learning/abstraction 19, 29, 38, 46-7, 55-64, 66-71, 78, 81, 88, 90, 233, 240, 242, 275, 300-301

Action research 12, 14, 22, 35, 176, 274

Adaptation, adaptive 3, 9, 14, 101, 121, 141, 185-199, 215, 219, 235

Adult/continuing education (ACE) 26, 79-80, 180, 197-8, 214, 217-9, 223, 226, 241, 264

Apathy 9, 188, 200, 227

Association(s) 39, 44, 46-7, 53, 57, 73-4, 242

Attitude(s) 218-9, 258, 273, 292, 300
 change 24, 136, 277, 301-2, 306

Autocracy, Autocratic 8, 10-12, 21, 35-6, 163, 166, 172-7, 185, 305

Autonomy 184, 312
 different levels of 21, 97, 106
 as elbow room 100, 113, 266

B

Basic Group Assumptions 83, 177-9, 245-7, 250, 264, 311
 dependency 22, 183, 192, 227, 232, 244, 260, 276
 fight/flight 134, 179, 194, 248
 pairing 245, 247

Broadbanding 95-8, 115

Bureaucracy(ies)/bureaucratic 2, 4, 11-12, 16, 18, 20, 22, 24, 68, 77, 98, 100-110, 123, 129, 133-5, 138, 148, 150, 154, 156-7, 162-5, 174, 179, 188, 194, 214, 226-7, 236, 245-7, 305

Bureaucratized society 65, 69, 178

C

Causal relations/causality 44-5, 50, 55, 92-3, 175

Commitment(s) 12, 35, 88, 92-5, 111, 130, 134-5, 141, 147, 154, 160, 166, 214, 271, 279, 285, 290, 303

Commonsense 29, 37, 60, 273

Communicate/communication 18, 38-9, 45, 52, 55, 64, 88, 105, 123, 130, 132-34, 140, 148, 1 50, 154, 167, 188, 196, 215-6, 227, 229, 243, 248-9, 262, 274-5, 293-5

Competence(ies) 65, 99, 215-7

Computers/computer systems 73, 79-80, 168, 294, 297

Conflict(s) 9-10, 23, 109, 165, 267, 282
 rationalization of 124, 251, 243-4, 248, 241-3

Continuing education/Learning See Adult/continuing education

Control 3, 16, 33, 38, 125, 130-1, 133, 136, 141, 143, 146, 158, 162-3, 166-7, 185-7, 226, 287, 303, 305
 responsibility for 17, 87-8, 101-110, 116, 138-9, 148, 178, 245-67, 263

Co-operation 12, 131, 134, 139, 168-171, 186-7, 198, 211, 217-220

Co-ordination 3, 16, 91, 125, 130-1, 133, 136, 161-3, 166-7, 185, 191, 255, 287, 291, 305
 responsibility for 17, 87-8, 101-110, 116, 138-9, 141, 143, 148, 178, 245-67, 263

Creative, Creativity 12, 34, 148, 153, 268
 working mode 244-7, 249-50, 308

Cynicism 95, 133, 146, 196, 285, 290

D

Deep slice 19, 116-7, 130
Design 1, 12, 86-140, 229, 295-6, 299-300
    principles 1 and 2 2-6, 20, 28, 32-9, 86-8, 100-122, 123, 128-9, 141-6, 148-9, 166, 180, 214, 217, 220, 223-4, 226, 228-9, 230, 241, 244-7, 256, 293
    features 272, 295-9
    educational 272, 277-8, 306, 287, 291, 301, 304
Deskilling 9, 89, 92, 131
Development of Human Resources Workshop (DHR) 14, 17, 79, 123-4, 223
Diffusion, Diffusive potential 2, 3, 23, 32, 111, 125, 143, 145, 147, 214, 239, 248, 254-5
Dignity 25, 29, 134, 136
Dissociation 9, 22, 39, 146, 253
Dynamics/relations 100, 106, 187, 231, 233
    group 30, 132, 168, 244
    in group - out group 138, 243
    interpersonal 60, 290

E

Ecological/direct perception/learning 10, 19, 26, 28-9, 60, 79, 87, 167, 242, 275, 300
Education/system 6, 8-9, 19-20, 26, 63-5, 81, 89, 214-221, 273, 299
Environment(s) 9, 137, 147, 157-8, 164, 167, 189
    dynamic/changing 25, 219, 234-5, 239-241, 248, 282- 5
    for learning 9, 63, 180, 243-7, 277, 292, 297, 301
    informational structure of 28, 50, 52, 73, 81, 242- 3
    social 54, 283-4
Environmental interdependencies 21, 234-8
Environmental scan 226, 230, 275
Equal employment opportunity (EEO) 135-140
Equifinality 4
Extract, Extraction 54-8, 60, 74, 81

F

Figure - ground 28, 54, 81, 238
Future(s) 138, 268-9, 274-5, 282-3
    desirable 101, 113, 115, 239, 242-3, 248-9, 255
    probable 239, 242-3, 255

G

Generic concepts 29, 56, 58-60
Genotype(s)/genotypical 11, 123, 130, 141, 147, 288
Group/social climate(s) 11, 18, 21, 100, 125, 170, 172-5, 176-9, 304

H

Hierarchy(ies) 18-9, 61, 128, 131, 150, 165, 192-3, 203, 210
    dominant 4, 20, 33, 37, 117-8
    non-dominant 10, 38
Human nature 132
Human relations 2, 24, 93, 152

I

Ideals, Ideal seeking 25, 29, 36-7, 139,

195, 235-7, 241, 248
Inference/inferred 44-6, 51-3, 60-3, 67, 69-70, 242
Intelligence/IQ 47-9, 61-2, 67-8
Invariance(s)/invariants/invariant order 28, 50, 52-3, 56-8, 61, 66, 69, 70, 75, 81, 242

J

Job enrichment/enlargement 2, 24, 93-4, 101, 104-5, 122, 169
Jury system 180-1, 192, 201-13

K

Kondratiev (50-year) cycles 31, 35

L

Laissez-faire 5, 11-12, 20, 88, 108, 172-5, 177, 222, 228, 291
Leadership 11-12, 109-110, 121, 135, 159-160, 176, 287
Learning(s) 1, 18, 22, 48, 86-7, 100-117, 123-140, 152, 176, 179, 185, 197-9, 206, 214-20, 222-5, 231-7, 244, 260-9, 271-4, 299
    as conditioning 63, 237
    continuing 3, 14, 26, 88, 101, 148, 169
    environment(s) events 1, 9, 38, 83, 111, 121, 123, 137, 180, 277, 292, 301
    exchange(s) 286-8, 290, 300, 306, 313
    from experience 29, 72, 299
    needs 226, 271, 286
    organization 2, 148, 151
    process 21, 69, 110, 217, 223

    puzzle 19, 237
    to learn 78-9
    unlearning 70, 78, 138
Literacy 48, 58, 67, 73

M

Management 5, 87, 94, 100-110, 116, 119-120, 133, 143, 151, 153-166, 185, 188-199
    middle 17, 87, 98, 117, 128, 186
    top 128-9, 135
Managerial 171
    prerogatives 96-7, 104
Manager(s) 2, 89, 130, 149, 172
    of learning environment 19, 21, 216, 220, 224, 226-57, 271, 275
Meaning/meaningfulness 101, 113, 170
Mechanical world, see Newtonian
Memory/memorization 47, 57-60, 72-3, 167, 313
Mirror group(s) 17, 117, 121, 123-4
Mixed modes 228-9, 244-5
Motivation 7, 69, 76, 86, 89, 98, 100, 111, 115, 144, 221, 279-80
Multiskilled/multiskilling 1, 26, 94-7, 107-9, 115, 119, 161, 166, 168-171, 191, 197

N

Newtonian/Euclidian universe/world 10, 19, 40, 43-4, 49, 81

O

Object constancy 44, 49-50
Open systems 2-3, 18, 29-30, 66, 155, 167, 214, 232-4, 248, 274, 283

P

Pedagogy/pedagogue 45, 68, 83
Personality(ies)/character 138, 238
Planning 11, 88, 116, 153, 157, 169,
  256, 277-9, 293-4, 302-3, 305- 6
    incourse 272, 280-2, 289
    precourse 279-280
    strategic 18, 229, 233- 48
Power 7, 24, 138
    as energy 31
    social 139-140, 186- 8
    organizational 104-5, 187, 191
Production/productivity 1-2, 34, 68,
  88-91, 93-5, 97, 100-110, 141, 145-7,
  152, 173-5, 185, 218, 227
    agreements 96-7, 116, 131
    increased 4, 12, 90-1, 118, 148
Purposeful systems 2, 16, 220, 241

Q

Quality 182
    of products and services 89, 92-5,
  97, 101, 141, 168, 170
    of working life (QWL) 4, 17, 24

R

Radiant light 28, 49-50, 57
Reflected light 28, 49-51
Representative structure(s) 10, 100,
  146-7, 200-13
    forms of 16
    system(s)/democracy 20, 26, 37-9,
  94, 181, 182-4, 186-199, 241, 308
    Westminster 185, 187, 194, 207,
  210
Resistance(s) 6, 21, 36, 99, 120, 214-6,
  219, 251
    as paradoxical inhibition 13, 17

Respect 148
    with mutual support 21-2, 101,
  113, 267
Restructuring/reconstruction 72, 78,
  89, 91, 95-8, 157
    perceptual 224, 300-1

S

Schools/schooling 45, 61-63, 76-8, 83,
  216, 299
Scientific management 12, 102, 120
Search Conference(s) 1, 4, 10-11, 15,
  18, 37-8, 79, 124, 130, 194, 198,
  211, 219-20, 223-4, 226-57, 292, 300
Searching 66, 194
    the principle of reafference 192
    multisearch(es) 1, 254-5
Self government/governing 182-4,
  195-9
Self manage 16, 107, 151, 192, 195,
  261-7, 271-313
Self managing group(s) 3, 7, 20-1, 68,
  90, 97, 102-110, 118-9, 121, 129,
  130, 149-50, 156, 161-5, 168-171,
  178-9, 188, 260-3
Serial genetic concepts 28, 58-61
Similarity 44, 57, 61
Skill formation 89-92, 98
Socio-technical analysis/systems 2, 4,
  13-14, 87, 141-2, 155, 166
Speech/spoken language 18, 38-9, 48,
  55, 64, 130, 253
    learning of 41, 74-7
Strategy(ies) 17, 110, 130, 140, 230,
  236, 301
    of the indirect approach 17, 219,
  250-2
Stress management 22, 140
STS 5, 6, 87, 141-7
Supervise 159, 161-2, 168, 171-2

Supervisor(s) 21, 91, 98, 102-122, 141,
    145, 151, 159
    as TLC 6, 87, 143-4, 148-152
System principle(s) 34-5, 83, 98, 124

T

Tabula rasa 44, 52
Teacher(s) 29, 42-3, 70, 81-2, 265-7
    teacher-pupil/student relation 43,
    62, 69, 83, 224
Teaching 19, 48, 67, 69, 73, 80, 82,
    197-8, 217, 243, 272, 275, 299, 301-2
Technology(ies) 16, 35, 121-2, 185-6,
    228
    determinism 16
    new/high 13, 89-91, 96
Text, see Written language
Think/thinking 65-68, 71, 78-80
Trainer(s)/training 63, 78, 89-90, 92,
    106, 115, 119, 140, 143-152, 176,
    189, 215-8, 226-7, 271-2, 285

Trust 14, 108, 201, 248-9, 280, 282,
    301
Trusteeship 189

U

University(ies) 30, 36, 61, 119, 180,
    214-220, 223, 259, 299
Unionist(s)/unions 2, 89, 90, 118, 120,
    122, 131, 133, 204

V

Values/value system 22, 26, 36, 125,
    139, 195, 218, 220, 230, 258, 273,
    276, 282, 300-1
Variety 101, 113, 130, 266

W

World hypotheses 37
    contextualism 31, 37
Written language 38, 55, 58, 61, 64,
    74-7

Name Index

Abrahms M H, 83, 84

Ackoff R L, 78, 84, 222, 225

Aristotle, 32, 34, 56-7

Arnheim R, 82, 84

Asch S E, 39, 54, 73, 76, 84, 229, 249, 257

Bamforth K W, 12, 27, 141, 147

Beer S, 193, 199

Berkeley, 43-45, 49, 51

Bion W R, 83, 84, 134, 140,177, 179, 241, 247, 250, 257

Blake, William 40, 42, 65

Bloom R D, 69

Bloomstein M J, 211

Bohm D, 56, 84

Boorman S A, 17, 27, 257

Born M, 64

Brady R A, 192, 199, 200, 206

Brunswik E, 51

Carmichael L, 215, 220-1

Cassirer E, 58-9, 60, 84

Chandler A D, 157, 161

Chambers J H, 41, 84

Chein I, 62, 67-8, 81, 84

Chomsky N, 41

Collier G, 209

Darwin, Charles 45

Davies A T, 215-8, 220-1

Davies L, 142

Dawkins J S, 214, 221

de Bono E, 65-7, 70-1, 77-9, 84

De Nitish, 180, 199

Dewey, John 43, 65

Dickens, Charles 82

Doman G, 73, 76-7, 84

Drucker P F, 162-3, 166

Duke C, 199

Einstein A, 43, 49

Emery F E, 2, 4, 6, 10, 11, 13, 14, 16, 27, 30, 39, 40, 54, 63, 66, 70, 78, 84, 100, 102, 105, 111, 122, 125, 140, 141, 147, 175, 180, 185, 186, 187, 188, 189, 190, 199, 214, 219, 221, 222, 225, 232, 235, 240, 257, 270

Emery M, 1, 6, 11, 18, 27, 40, 54, 84, 105, 122, 123, 130, 140, 145, 147, 177, 179, 186, 188, 199, 219, 224, 225, 255, 257, 270

Engels F, 35

Euclid, 45, 49, 51-2

Fambrough M, 229-30, 247

Fanshel D, 55, 85

Fiorelli, 172, 175

Frayn M, 153

Freire, Paulo 41, 79

Frye, Northrop 40-41, 84

Geschwind, 74, 84

Gibran, 82

Gibson E, 69, 72-4, 76, 84

Gibson J J, 28, 41, 51-6, 63-4, 66, 73, 84

Gloster M, 40-41

Goldmeier E, 57, 84

Greco M C, 18, 27

Habermas, 2

Harrelson W, 36, 39

Hart L, 17, 27

Heider F, 28, 41, 49-51, 54-6, 59-60, 63-4, 66, 73, 84,

Helmholtz H, 43, 49, 53, 59, 85

Herbart, 43, 45, 82

Herbst D P, 148, 152, 191, 199

Herzberg F, 93

Hill P, 189, 199

Howell R A, 166

Hughes F, 73, 76-8, 85

Hume, D 43-45

Hull C, 45

Illich, Ivan 41

Jackson R G, 193-5, 199, 200-6

Jakobson R, 74-5, 85

Johansson G, 52, 85

Johnson-Laird P N, 85

Jones A W, 183

Jones M R, 55, 85

Julesz B, 54, 85

Kant E, 45, 50, 59

Katona, 73

Kingdon D R, 165, 166

Kondratiev, 31

Kuhn T, 64, 85

Labov W, 55, 85

Land E H, 53, 85

Levin H, 73, 76

Levinson H, 162, 166

Lewin K, 30, 35, 39, 43,

Lewin (contd) 59, 65, 88, 172-3, 301
Lindblom C E, 183-4
Lippit R, 11, 27, 173
Lobachevski, 49
Locke, John 40, 43-46, 49, 51-2, 82
Luneberg R K, 49
Marrou H, 85
Marx, Karl 31
Mayo E, 93
McGregor D, 100, 122
McInnis H, 40
McLuhan M, 40, 63, 85
McPhee I, 91
McWhinney W, 189, 191, 199
Miller G A, 85
Montessori, 43, 65
Muller J, 43, 53
Naschold F, 2, 6
Nash K, 1, 6
Neill, 43, 65
Neumann J, 98
Newton, 40, 43-45, 49, 65
Nietzsche, 32
Oeser, 70
Ong W G, 18, 27, 253
Olson D R, 47, 48, 58,

Olson (contd) 67, 85
Orbison, 57
O'Toole J, 24, 27
Pavlov, 45
Pepper S C, 37, 39
Piaget J, 41, 82, 85
Pierce C S, 37, 38, 39
Pittinger J, 81, 85
Plato, 32, 34, 45
Polanyi, 41
Pratt D, 44, 85
Pribram K H, 57, 85
Pritchard R M, 85
Reimann, 49
Rice A K, 199
Robertson J, 138, 140
Rock I, 73, 76, 85
Taylor F, 92
Thomson P, 1, 6
Thorndike, 43, 45
Thorsrud E, 13, 16, 27, 100, 111, 122, 185, 187, 189-190, 199, 273
Toynbee A, 32
Treyvaud E R, 215-7, 221
Trist E L, 11, 12, 27, 141, 147, 235, 273
Turvey M T, 85
Sawyer W W, 72

Shaw R, 81, 85
Sherwin D S, 166
Skinner B F, 45
Sommerhoff G, 199, 233
Spain J W, 210
Spengler, 32
Stavrianos L S, 32, 39
Stern C, 70, 72-3, 77-8, 85
Stern M, 72, 85
Studdert-Kennedy M, 74-5, 85
van Beinum H, 24, 27
van Creveldt M, 159, 161
van Eijnatten F, 4, 5, 6
von Bertalanffy, 4, 6
Walls G, 51, 85
Weber M, 35, 77
Weimar, 57, 85
Weisbord M R, 5, 25, 27, 228-9, 257
Werner H, 75, 85
White R K, 11, 27, 173
Whitehead A N, 49, 85
Williams T, 78, 85, 111, 122, 185, 199
Wilson A T M, 161
Yeats W B, 82